HE
5611
Z83
1991

Zuckermann, Wolfgang,
1922-

End of the road.

END OF THE ROAD

END OF THE ROAD

The World Car Crisis and
How We Can Solve It

Wolfgang Zuckermann

The Lutterworth Press
Cambridge

Chelsea Green Publishing Company
Post Mills, Vermont

Illustration Credits: *9, 60,* Fabian Sabates, Paris; *9, 81, 273,* EcoPlan, from various sources; *21, 33, 75,* U.S. Motor Vehicle Manufacturing Association; *18,* Mercedes Benz in Aller Welt; *20,* World Population Data Sheet, Population Reference Bureau, Washington, D.C.; *26, 97,* World Meteorological Organization and United Nations Environment Program, Executive Summary, 1990; *30, 31,* Neftel and Keeling, cited in Worldwatch Paper no. 91, Worldwatch Institute, October 1989; *37,* Energy Statistics Yearbook, United Nations, 1987 and Statistical Abstract, United States, 1990; *42,* illustration by Eva M'Barki; *76, 226,* RATP, Paris; *79,* Schimmelpennik (designer of the system); *89, 260,* illustrations by Patricia Clauss; *90,* sticker widely distributed in France; *105,* Department of Transport, United Kingdom; *106, 107, 109, 110,* Norway Institute for Regional Research, Oslo 1979; *123, 132* illustrations by Bettina Geraudel; *137,* illustration by Philippe Labits; *139,* World Almanac, 1991; *150,* Peugeot, Paris; *166,* Conservatoire des Arts et Metiers, Paris; *180, 210,* Lawrence Berkeley Laboratory, Berkeley, CA.; *186,* Jean Robert, Transport Museum, Paris; *194,* U.S. Dept of Transportation booklet "Transportation Innovations in Five European Cities," 1980; *207,* British Petroleum, Annual World Energy Statistics; *212,* John Whitelegg, "Traffic Congestion"; *216,* Worldwatch Paper no. 100, Dec 1990; *224,* U.S. Dept of Commerce, Housing Statistics, and Construction Reports.

Library of Congress Cataloging-in-Publication Data

Zuckermann, Wolfgang 1922–
    End of the road: the world car crisis and how we can solve it /
Wolfgang Zuckermann.
        p. cm.
    Includes bibliographical references and index.
    ISBN 0-930031-46-6 : $21.95
    1. Transportation, Automotive. 2. Automobile—Environmental aspects. I. Title.
HE5611.Z83 1991
303.48'32—dc20   91–31904
                                                                             CIP

British Library Cataloguing-in-Publication Data

Zuckermann, Wolfgang
End of the Road: the World Car Crisis and
How We Can Solve It.
I. Title
388.3

ISBN 0-7188-2832-1

ACKNOWLEDGMENTS

The ideas and reflections expressed in this book are based on a wide body of work drawn from writers and sources representing many disciplines, countries, and points of view. In particular, I would like to single out for mention the following to whom I have a special debt:

- Many of the materials which gave this book its shape and overall direction were gathered over 1989 and 1990 for the preparation of a "reader," a compilation of excerpts from important works in the field of transportation that was produced by EcoPlan under the title *Cars, Transport & Amenity in Urban Places.* For many of the ideas included in this collection, I relied most especially on contributions by John Whitelegg, Peter Newman, Jeffrey Kenworthy, Stephen Plowden, Jane Jacobs, John Roberts, William II. Whyte, John G. Adams, Michael Renner, Kenneth Orski, Francis E. K. Britton, Brian Richards, Marcia Lowe, and Frederic Vester.

- The considerable body of articles, papers, extracts, and private communications which are cited in the endnotes to this book.

- The sources given in the partial bibliography following the endnotes.

I am also grateful to the many friends and colleagues who gave their valuable time and ideas to this project. Among them are the following reviewers of the manuscript who offered many valuable suggestions: Donald Brackenbush, Los Angeles; Peter Ekenger, Göteborg; Paul Hainsworth, London; Dorothea Hass, Boston; Ann-Louise Martin, Melbourne; Mikel Murga, Bilbao; Robert Panero, Bogota and New York; Serge Raffet, New York; Jerry Ravetz, London; Michael Renner, Washington; Brian Richards, London; Jim Schley, Vermont; Emin Tengström, Göteborg; and John Whitelegg, Lancaster. I would also like to thank the artists who made some of the drawings included in the book: Eva M'Barki, Philippe Labits, Bettina Geraudel, Patricia Clauss;

my research assistant, Ilse Obermayr; and finally, the publisher of the American edition, Ian Baldwin.

It would not have been possible to gather the materials on which the book is based without the support of Volvo AB, the South Australian Department of Transportation, the Sutter Bay Corporation, the Ahmanson Land Company, and Home Savings of America all of whom have been directly concerned at a policy and investment level with many of the issues to which this book is addressed, and who contributed funding, critical ideas, and useful reactions to EcoPlan's ACCESS program in its early and most difficult moments.

Finally, I would like to express my special thanks to my friend and colleague Eric Britton, without whose untiring energy, knowledge in many areas, and unflagging support this book could never have been written.

NOTE ON THE USAGE
OF AUTOMOTIVE TERMS

Because the edition for the two countries has been combined, there may be a number of terms unfamiliar to readers on either side of the Atlantic. In general, I have followed the practice of using American terms when talking about American practices, British terms for British practices, and continental terms and measurements when writing about continental Europe. However, in a general discussion it has sometimes been necessary to put in a double term like gasoline/petrol. When discussing costs and finances, the sums given are usually expressed in dollar terms, as this is international practice; but in some cases they are given in local currencies, like Francs and Deutschmarks.

Below are some oft-used terms with their British and American equivalents:

British	American
articulated lorry	tractor trailer
car park	parking lot
carriageway	roadbed
lift	elevator
lorry	mass transit
motorcar, car	automobile, car
motorway, dual carriageway	freeway, expressway
pavement	sidewalk
petrol	gasoline, gas
public transport	mass transit

Weights and measures: 1 pound = .45 kilograms; 1 mile = 1.6 kilometers; 1 inch = 25 mm; 1 square mile (630 acres) = 259 hectares; 1 acre = .4 hectare; 1 British ton = 1.01 metric tons; 1 foot = .3 meters; 1 yard = .9 meters; 1 U.S. gallon = 4.1 liters.

CONTENTS

INTRODUCTION

Insight, it has been said, is not so much a matter of finding the right answers as asking the right questions. This is nowhere more true than when it comes to how we as a society interact with our environment. If we are to reverse the pattern of environmental degradation that has become one of the hallmarks of the past century we need to start asking ourselves some different questions. Instead of thinking in terms of parts, we need to look at the whole; instead of focusing economic development on how to maximize the next year's GNP, we need to explore how we can satisfy our current needs without jeopardizing the ability of our children to meet theirs.

As in all changes of perspective, things look different once one takes this position. The effect is similar to taking a step back from an impressionist painting. What appear up close to be autonomous and unrelated patches of color emerge from a few steps back as part of a clearly recognizable whole.

When we look at our environment, this recognition of what has been right in front of our eyes all along can be particulary dramatic. Taking a step back from the fray of the mid-70s energy policy debate, Amory Lovins made an arrestingly simple observation that would open up an entirely new dimension to the debate. Energy is not an end, he argued in his book *Soft Energy Paths*, but a means: "People do not want electricity or oil . . . but rather comfortable rooms, light, vehicular motion, food, tables, and other real things."

In *End of the Road*, Wolfgang Zuckermann brings a similarly simple but penetrating light to the long benighted realm of transportation. For the vast majority of people, transportation—like energy—is a means to an end. Generally speaking, people do not want to spend hours driving on highways; they want quick and convenient access to where they work, play, eat, and live.

Over the years, however, the car has become such a commonplace fixture of our world that we have lost sight of this. Instead of moving peole around, transportation policy all too frequently becomes a matter of moving cars.

Even worse, this familiarity has not bred contempt, but a strange kind of acceptance, if not affection. Because of its ubiquity and some extremely effective advertising, the car is thought to be a necessary corollary to modernity, and we either ignore its negative consequences or rationalize them away as one of the prices we must pay for our quality of life. To the extent they are acknowledged at all, the shortcomings are generally thought to be relatively minor flaws capable of resolution within the system: build a few more highways, make existing ones a little wider, and make the cars a little smarter, and our problems will be over.

This is not the case. The problems with our transportation system are not cosmetic, but systemic. No amount of minor readjustment will return it to working order; the system needs an overhaul.

With *End of the Road* we now have a clear, comprehensive, and eminently readable manual for that overhaul. To some, the metaphor of a manual may seem mundane, but I don't think Wolfgang Zuckermann would be displeased. He is interested not in disembodied analysis or reflection, but teaching people how to fix something that is broken. His focus—quite literally—is where the rubber hits the road, and the success of this project will be determined largely by the extent to which people take the lessons from *End of the Road* out into the world.

The organization of the book reflects this mission. He begins in part one by demonstrating that our current transportation system is indeed broken at a fundamental level and in need of repair. There is a powerful case here and Zuckermann makes it well. Our current system comes up short on virtually every criterion by which we measure the health of a transportation system: safety, convenience, speed, cost-effectiveness, and environmental impact. One color at a time, Zuckermann assembles the dismaying portrait of what this system has done to our world, defiling the air, land, water, and—not least—our very character as a society.

Having lifted the veil from our ignorance of the problem, Zuckermann goes on in part two to show us how to fix it. Here the carrots are as numerous as the sticks, and again comprehensiveness comes at no cost to comprehensibility.

Like all manuals, however, *End of the Road* ultimately refers to us, because it is our individual decisions that make up the fine grain of what constitutes a "transportation system." At the very least, we should be actively making these decisions, instead of being stuck in place by the inertia of the past.

Like most environmental issues, the shape taken by these decisions is ultimately a matter of personal values. *End of the Road* clearly sets out the kind of paved and polluted world of sprawl and congestion we are currently headed toward. But, more importantly, it gives us a strong sense of where we ought to be headed. The rest is up to us.

Lester Brown
Washington, D.C.
17 June 1991

Afoot and light-hearted I take to the open road,
Healthy, free, the world before me.
Walt Whitman, *Song of the Open Road*

PROLOGUE

When someone, just about one hundred years ago, invented a carriage which could go all by itself, without animal or human power to pull it and without even a rail to run on, humanity seemed to have fulfilled an ancient dream: to have an easy, painless means to move about. No more trudging along hot and dusty roads; no more tramping along wet and muddy tracks; no more carrying of heavy packs and bundles. We had finally found a mechanical beast of burden to move us with dreamlike ease wherever our fancy would take us.

But in time we became so enamored of our new helpmate that all those who could get their hands on one did so. Some even had to have two or three. And then something unforeseen began to happen. Vast numbers suddenly started to fill the open roads Walt Whitman had sung about, obliging the dream wagons formerly so fleet and faithful to move ever more sluggishly.

And yet, in spite of this sluggish motion, most of us still love our cars. Even those who recognize the problem and those who think we have quite literally come to the end of the road, continue to have a great deal of affection for this means of transport. At the heart of the issue lurks a fundamental problem of perception. Most of us still think of cars as they *once* were, not as they are today.

What this formerly innocent conveyance was meant to do was not only to move us painlessly, but to get us to wherever we were going—and to do so promptly and with ease. When it started to fall down on that job, people in different parts of the world who think about such things began to worry. One group of such people was EcoPlan, a small policy research collaborative that was started in Paris two decades ago. Its aim was to study the impact of technology on people in their daily lives and to try to do something about it. In 1989, after having completed a lengthy survey and contact program of concerned people and institutions around the world, this group launched a technical transportation project called ACCESS.[1]

ACCESS looked at ways in which we could arrange our transportation (and our lives) so that people could obtain better access to the places they live and work. The project eventually led to a search for ideas, suggestions, and possible solutions from people and places around the world.

Right at the outset the project revealed a dilemma: The very cars which were formerly providing such easy access were now responsible for making this access more and more difficult. It seemed as if most of our present problems were someone else's old solutions.

So we found ourselves in a situation where governments and industries which promoted the production of automobiles were being caught in a vicious cycle: The greater the number of cars produced, the harder it would be for these cars to move around— road space being limited. And the more difficult it became to move around in those cars, the less eager people would be to buy them.

Perhaps this is a different way of thinking about cars. All of us know about congestion, pollution, and danger, but we think modern science will fix all that. And we go on liking—even loving—our cars. Just think how beautiful they were! Take the Stutz Bearcat of 1912, the Marmon Speedster 74 of 1925, the Model 733 Packard roadster with rumble seat of 1930 (which went for $2425), and the French cream-colored Hispano-Suiza K6 of 1936. Those were wonderful cars. Think of the joy and pleasure it was to own and drive one of those beauties on an open road through unspoiled countryside, with a picnic lunch in a straw basket and a bottle of champagne. . . . All right, perhaps cars are less beautiful today, and, yes, crowded roads and accidents have diminished the joy of driving.

But still, a motorist might say, I love my car. I can use it to pick up my invalid mother-in-law from the other end of town, I can take the girls to their ballet lesson, I can lug home my five big shopping bags from the supermarket. It's true that there is congestion, but that's just because there aren't enough roads. It's true that it takes me over an hour to get to work, but someday they'll fix that with automatic guidance systems. It's true that they tell us to use car pools to cut down the number of vehicles, but frankly I don't like sharing my car. This is the only time I have away from work and family so I enjoy sitting all alone and listening to my favorite programs.

So we reason. We think of our cars fondly and accept them without questions. At least in this impersonal world they are something that belongs to us. We choose our cars to suit (and express) our personalities, and put personal touches in their interiors.

Transportation itself is an abstract concept; the very word is apt to make one's eyes glaze over. If we have to get from point A to point B, let's make it quick and efficient. And if we can have our own personal steeds like the horsemen of old, so much the better.

But transportation also enables us to make voyages of discovery, and unlikely as it may seem, my research on this project called ACCESS sent me on such a voyage of discovery. And a funny kind of trip it turned out to be—a voyage in reverse. A journey not to somewhere but away from somewhere. This voyage, on which I would now like to take you as others have taken me, may start out as something of a rough ride for those who love their cars and will have nothing said against them. That is so because the first part of this book looks at the ways the world has changed—mostly, it seems, for the worse—since the invention of the automobile about a hundred years ago. But if you can hold on and stay with me through those first unpleasant bits (which I'll try to make as short as possible), we will get to the more hopeful area of solutions for the problems connected with cars, and finally to the proper use of motor vehicles.

Before we go any further, I must be honest and tell you that I am a driver and car owner, and at one time in my life was the proud possessor of a vintage Mercedes convertible and later a Morgan sports car with a belt around its English bonnet. I'm neither a wild-eyed radical nor a Luddite. Like many of us, I too am torn between the pleasure of using a car and the knowledge of what that use implies. So let us start off together to see if we can't solve this dilemma. This is one journey, though, in which we will leave behind our Mercedes, Morgans, and Toyotas.

Instead, we will travel on a sort of magic carpet—a quilt I have stitched together from the hundreds of articles and papers by academics, transport writers, and specialists whose work I have sifted through and assembled into a kind of patchwork. To this varied collection of information and ideas I have added the thoughts of poets and novelists in an attempt to broaden the scope of our journey together. Because it turns out that when you touch the way people move about, you quickly get into issues which go much beyond mere transportation.

Transportation is not only about getting from point A to point B, but about time, space, and movement, and these somewhat abstract concepts are now not exactly what they were before technology intervened. All three of them have acquired different meanings. Villages which used to be an hour's distance from each other are now only five minutes apart. "Distances are only the link between space and time and change with it," was the way Marcel Proust put it. "A village which seemed to be another in a different world becomes its neighbor in a landscape whose dimensions have changed."

To come to grips with the world car crisis therefore, we will look not only at the environmental impact of five hundred million motor vehicles and the effect that impact has had on sustainability—the idea of handing the planet on to our children in a condition not worse than that in which we received it from our parents—but we will also have to go a little beyond these obvious considerations and look at ideas which may be unfamiliar to many readers.

We will have to ask questions about values which are generally taken for granted, and consider whether we should perhaps look more critically at modern ideals such as frequent and fast movement, shrinkage of vast distances by quick and easy transport, and the trend to replace most human exertions by mechanical means. And if we find answers to some of these questions, or solutions to some of our modern problems, we will have to ask ourselves if our solutions won't end up being someone else's future problems. Our task on this journey together will therefore be to look not only at the practical solutions to our traffic problems, but at some of the more theoretical issues behind those problems.

With all of that to think about, I have tried not to get bogged down in statistical detail at the risk of losing my way. In his own Italian journey, Goethe took a somewhat similar approach:

> There is much in this record, I know, which I could have described more accurately, amplified and improved, but I shall leave everything as it stands. . . . I console myself with the thought that, in our statistically minded times, all this has probably been printed in books which one can consult if need arise. . . .

Without getting enmeshed in numbers and without advocating pet theories and projects (as transport specialists are often wont to do), I have tried to retain a balanced perspective on the perplexing problem of the automobile's unchecked growth. Because it is a worldwide problem, we have to look at ideas, both good and bad, coming in from every corner of the earth. Most of the examples given here are from places where people have attempted to deal with the problem of cars in some way, even if they have failed.

Many of those people have tried to find a way out of the new type of prison we have built for ourselves, a prison which ironically owes its origin to our desire for freedom—freedom for unlimited movement. And a funny kind of prison it turns out to be, since we are at the same time jailers and jailed. But, as I hope to show, we possess the key for our release.

Paris
August 1991

Part One

THE WORLD CAR CRISIS

What's wrong with cars anyway? If there is a problem, however did we get to this point without being aware of it? And if some of us were aware of it, why have we done so little to correct the problem?

The first part of this book will try to answer these questions. It is given over to an introduction and reflection on the role automobiles have played in modifying every aspect of our world and our lives. We will therefore consider the impact of motorcars in four categories: what the car, in all of its complexity, is doing to the world; what it is doing to nature and our fragile environment; what it has done and is continuing to do to our poor battered cities and the countryside around them; and finally what it has done and is doing to each one of us, inside ourselves and in the ways we choose to live our lives.

It is perhaps this last issue which is going to pose the toughest task for most of us. Even if we recognize a problem with all these masses of cars on our roads, we will be tempted to look for solutions in the real world which surrounds us rather than in ourselves. Yet one important message of these pages is that the crux of the problem may reside right inside each of us.

If we are ever going to get the car back to its rightful place (which is definitely not the one it has in our lives today), it is very important to understand the complex nature of the car's impact on us, and the share of the problem which is our own responsibility.

Once we recognize this, there may be a great deal each one of us can do about the world car crisis. This is a message which perhaps will not be very popular with those who look elsewhere—to governments, to the automobile industry, or to technology—to do the job. But for those who have energy, a sense of self-reliance, and the courage to confront what may be an unpalatable truth, it is quite a cheering message.

Because it means there is something you can do—for yourself and for the rest of the world.

1

THE WORLD: BEFORE AND AFTER

The motor vehicles that we love so much have increased their numbers to such a degree that they have become an unchecked menace—yet another menace to threaten our hapless planet.

Some of the evidence for this threat is set out in these pages, but much more of it is all around us, in front of our eyes, ears, and noses. If we had been confronted with such evidence in Biblical times, we might have thought of it as one more of the plagues of Egypt, we might have said that the eleventh plague has been visited upon us.

That is not to say that if the eleventh plague were suddenly to vanish like its ten predecessors, we wouldn't have many regrets. Automobiles have served us well, giving us easy mobility. We all know a multitude of little tasks which without our cars would become tiring and trying. Many who read these pages, and many whose research is cited here, are themselves drivers and cannot really conceive of living without their vehicles.

The problem with this particular plague, though, is that its effects seem to have brought about an irreversible change in the world.

Our Lovable Companion

How much do we love our cars? If many of us wish to be honest about it, a whole lot. As a result anyone who attempts to point out character flaws in the automobile finds himself in the unenviable position of a dinner guest who criticizes the enormous dog belonging to his hosts. Even if that ferocious beast has been known to maul the occasional visitor or take a hefty bite out of the passing postman, our dinner guest has to make a feeble attempt to pet the animal while his hosts, amid great cries of "Down, Rover!" assure him that old Rover only wants to play and is the dearest and most harmless thing in the universe. Since the car has given such great pleasure to its owners, we'll start out on the right foot and make our timid attempt to pet it.

Today the otherwise revered motorcar is often blamed for three evils—congestion, danger, and noise—for which it alone

60 km/h

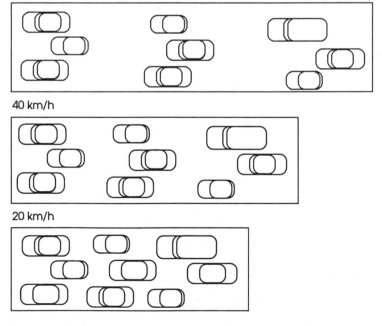

40 km/h

20 km/h

The faster its movement, the more space it needs to swallow.

cannot be held responsible. We tend to forget that all of these traffic-connected evils existed long before cars made their appearance.

When our ancestors abandoned their two feet (which take literally only a square foot of space) and surrounded themselves with a personal means of transport bound to be bigger and

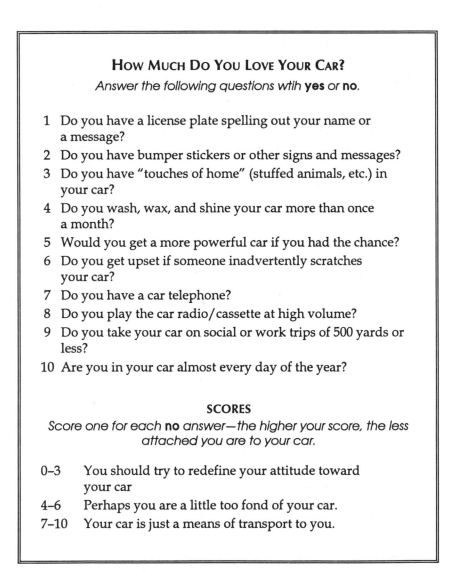

How Much Do You Love Your Car?

*Answer the following questions wtih **yes** or **no**.*

1 Do you have a license plate spelling out your name or a message?
2 Do you have bumper stickers or other signs and messages?
3 Do you have "touches of home" (stuffed animals, etc.) in your car?
4 Do you wash, wax, and shine your car more than once a month?
5 Would you get a more powerful car if you had the chance?
6 Do you get upset if someone inadvertently scratches your car?
7 Do you have a car telephone?
8 Do you play the car radio/cassette at high volume?
9 Do you take your car on social or work trips of 500 yards or less?
10 Are you in your car almost every day of the year?

SCORES
*Score one for each **no** answer—the higher your score, the less attached you are to your car.*

0–3   You should try to redefine your attitude toward your car
4–6   Perhaps you are a little too fond of your car.
7–10   Your car is just a means of transport to you.

faster—be it a Roman chariot, a horse, or an innocent bicycle—
the greater amount of road space required and the faster movement in that same road space inevitably led to trouble. The car is
not the only means of personal transport to share the drawbacks
associated with increased space and speed, it is only the latest. It
is a simple fact which has somehow escaped attention that the
greater the space occupied by a means of transport, the less it
leaves for other road users; and the faster its movement, the more
space it needs to swallow.

The private car, being bigger, faster, and more numerous than
other transport means, just eats more space.

B.C. and A.C.

It should come as no great surprise therefore that the world before the car was no paradise. Ancient cities, too, had many
"modern" traffic problems.

Serious traffic congestion existed in the Roman Empire. Julius
Caesar was moved to prohibit the movement of carts in Rome
during daylight hours, leading to many complaints of nighttime
noise nuisances; his ban was later extended by Claudius to the
other municipalities of Italy and by Marcus Aurelius finally to
every city in the empire.

The emperor Hadrian could have been talking about Broad-
way or the Edgware Road when he said that "this luxury of
speed destroys its own aim; a pedestrian makes more headway
than a hundred conveyances jammed end to end along the twists
and turns of the Sacred Way."[1]

In 1520 civic planners in Paris warned that "in a few years we
will be paralyzed"; and the 18th century *Tableau de Paris* describes
the "threatening wheels of the overbearing rich (who) drive as
rapidly as ever over streets stained with the blood of their victims."[2] A century later and on the other side of the Channel,
Thomas Carlyle considered London the "noisiest Babylon that
ever raged and fumed on the face of the earth."

Those who look back with romantic longing to the days of the

7

horse would do well to ponder an eyewitness account from the end of the 19th century:

> The whole of London's crowded wheeled traffic—which in parts of the city was dense beyond movement—was dependent on the horse. The characteristic aroma was that of stables . . . whose middens kept the chandeliers in middle-class reception rooms . . . encrusted with dead flies, and in the late summer veiled with living clouds of them.
>
> A more assertive mark of ze 'orse was the mud that . . . flooded the street with churnings of pea soup that . . . covered the road surface as with axle grease or bran-laden dust. The swift-moving hansom or gig would fling sheets of such soup— where not intercepted by trousers or skirts—completely across the pavement, so that the frontages of the Strand had an eighteen inch plinth of mud parge thus imposed upon it. And after the mud the noise, which, again endowed by the horse, surged like a mighty heart-beat in the central districts of London's life. It was a thing beyond all imaginings. . . . It was not any such paltry thing as noise. It was an immensity of sound. . . .[3]

Not only the horse, but even the bicycle could cause problems. At the same time that the horse was making a hell of London, the American scorcher (a name applied to bicycle speeders in 1897) darted in and out of traffic, head down, rump up in the air, and feet flashing in the pedal stirrups, scattering pedestrians at street crossings in larger cities. An officer's order to halt was usually answered by a mocking laugh and the derisive command to "chalk it down, old man!" as the cyclist sped off down the street.[4]

Even the deteriorating countryside often blamed on cars was a problem well before automobiles. Fifty years before their invention, at a time when most towns and villages were still connected by unpaved country lanes, Charlotte Brontë wrote that "steam, trade, and machinery had long banished from it [a town in the English countryside] all romance and seclusion . . . " and "a dense, permanent vapor brooded over this locality . . . "[5]

For centuries, the world has had examples of traffic and accompanying blight, manifestations of man's carelessness and nature-unfriendly handiwork. The special contribution of the mo-

We still think of cars as they *once* were . . .

THE WORLD CAR CRISIS:
PROBLEMS & CONSEQUENCES

1 Five hundred million vehicles on the road
2 Mounting traffic congestion
3 Air, noise, and aesthetic pollution
4 Total dependence on dirty, imported fossil fuels
5 Highly wasteful usage
6 More than two hundred fifty thousand traffic deaths each year
7 Negative impacts on cities and land use
8 Fifty million new vehicles added each year (one hundred each minute)
9 Emerging limits in the "carrying capacity" of the planet
10 Climate modification with serious consequences

. . . not as they are today.

torcar—and here we must unfortunately abandon our feeble attempt to pet that faithful companion—has been to multiply by a millionfold this traffic and accompanying blight, and export it to the four corners of the earth.

Those four corners have survived cataclysms, natural catastrophes, reigns of terror, tidal waves, invading armies, nuclear explosions, and ecological disasters. But the automobile has left what appears to be a permanent imprint on the planet.

Look out of the window and what do you see? One, two, or scores of shiny flitting metal objects which have trouble integrating well into natural settings. If cars weren't such part and parcel of our everyday life, we could be excused for believing them the vanguard of some invading army from outer space. And the soldiers of that invading army in their outer space bubbles are everywhere. As the rural landscapes and wildernesses left to us become crisscrossed by roads and invaded by day trippers, as cities are torn up by gray freeways and faceless car parks, and as dreary suburbs stretch endlessly in all directions, we must hold the car responsible for having done its bit to change, probably forever, the *look* of the world.

That world truly is not what it was before cars. And the difference between B.C. and A.C. (before cars and after cars) is much greater than the difference between, say, pre- and post-Roman, or pre- and post-Victorian times. After previous eras the world, though changed, was recognizable.

Now, finally, we are changing it out of all recognition.

The Lost Connection

All of this happened in one century, a split second of geological time. In that period we have changed the face of the globe from that of a rosy-cheeked young boy to the shrivelled face depicted in the portrait of Dorian Gray. We have covered the earth with asphalt scars and wrinkles where once were beckoning earth lanes, grassy tracks, and color- and texture-rich paving stones.

What we lost in this process of change is what the American

forester and planner Benton MacKaye sixty years ago called "connectedness," our direct link to the earth and its landscapes, three of which—city, country, and wilderness—he considered to be essential for the maintenance of our psychic health and well-being.

Gradually, and without our ever being aware of it, the car has literally disconnected us from the ground we walk on by putting us in a closed metal container with four wheels. One might argue that the post chaise did the same; but, as so often in car-related issues, better is worse. The car encloses us more fully, drives us more smoothly, and speeds us faster through the landscape and in vastly greater numbers than the horse-drawn cart, making our isolation considerably more complete.

MacKaye wrote about the effect that making or breaking daily landscape connections has on the lives of large populations. He held that our lives are diminished whenever our connections with any one "elemental environment" are blurred or broken.

"Together," he wrote, the three environments we need "seem to form . . . a complete and rounded external world adapted to man's psychological needs. Depletion in any one of them means a corresponding depletion in man's life." MacKaye considered that the personality of a place evaporates when development covers an area with "structures whose individual hideousness and collective haphazardness present that unmistakable environment we call . . . the slum of commerce."[6] The car's contribution to such landscape deterioration is threefold: first, it is largely responsible for this "individual hideousness and collective haphazardness" that MacKaye talks about by allowing structures to be scattered about in no particular order with a sea of parked vehicles around them; secondly, and more surreptitiously, it isolates us and speeds us through these very same landscapes so that we lose our distaste for them and they bother us less; and finally, having created the nondescript landscape and having isolated us from it, the car then gives us the means to leave such an area behind and embark on a search for an unspoiled landscape eventually to be blighted in its turn.

Since MacKaye wrote about the three essential environments, they have experienced shifting trends and disturbances, mostly

11

car-engendered. People have fled city centers and countrysides alike with the aid of their cars in a search for jobs, affordable housing, and the rural peace MacKaye wrote about.

Many American city centers have become empty shells, and many rural areas have suffered from similar trends. The 1990 census in the United States has put into numbers what people in small towns around the country have been experiencing through so many sad farewells. The small town, which has long occupied a revered place in America's history, is little by little becoming a museum piece. Living out in the country or in the heart of the city, according to *Time* magazine, has become a lifestyle declaration for Americans only slightly less exotic than a commitment to vegetarianism or the Latin Mass.[7]

In the United Kingdom, the National Travel Survey reports that only 11% of the British population now lives in rural areas, with agricultural workers not even numerous enough to merit a mention within that percentage.

The worldwide trend, aided to a large degree by personal transport, has been to break up groups of people—such as cities, towns, and villages and disperse them, while putting their amenities—shops, workplaces, schools, and medical, entertainment, and cultural centers—together in clusters. If we were looking for the most efficient method to minimize social contact and maximize transport, then this would be the very way to do it.

The tendency in many countries is to close village schools, post offices, train stations, and small stores, and to concentrate such amenities in large, impersonal centers, from which the people themselves are excluded, forcing them to rely on personal transport to get there, or else to quit their local area for lack of jobs or lively neighborhoods.

By dispersing people in that way and relying on countless roads to bring them together again we have also lost the experience of beauty or adventure in the context of the natural world. You cannot easily explore a pristine countryside with a sense of adventure when just beyond it are yet more roads, yet more noisy, smoking, multicolored, metallic moving objects.

Motor vehicles are destroying forever the sensation of being remote and far away. Even if you hike a hundred miles through

WORLD MOTOR VEHICLE TRENDS

Registrations (millions)

the mountains, you are all too likely to encounter a skimobile, a speedboat, or a tourist bus somewhere along the way.

The same cars which thus destroy the healthy isolation of different physical landscapes contribute to our own unhealthy isolation from those same landscapes (or what is left of them) when we traverse them in our hermetically sealed, air- and heat-conditioned space bubble.

The Dog's Breakfast

If we have, in a sense, lost our roots and our innocence by this overdependence on the car, what have we gained? One of the less pleasant things we have gained is what is sometimes known as a dog's breakfast. MacKaye called the places in which many of us now live, work, and amuse themselves a "rootless, aimless, profoundly disharmonized environment."[8]

But MacKaye hadn't even seen the worst of it. He wrote these lines at a time when, say, Tysons Corner, Virginia—now the center of a vast urban sprawl—was still a green field with cows peacefully grazing upon it.

A few decades later, when the green grazing fields of the world's Tysons Corner had been replaced by gray parking fields, and the gently mooing cows by nervously honking cars, the former American statesman George Kennan had an even more somber impression of the newly created no-man's land when he returned home after his service abroad:

> Not a sign of actual life except, here and there, a moving car, its occupant likewise walled off against nature in his own tiny, lonely, air-conditioned world. Not a touch of community, not a touch of sociability. Only the endless whirring and roaring of the air-conditioners, the wild wasting of energy, the ubiquitous television set, the massive bundle of advertising pulp that masquerades under the name of a Sunday newspaper. All unnatural, all experience vicarious, all activity passive and uncreative. And this wasteland extending, like a desert, miles and miles in every direction. A fine end-of-the-world we have created in the American city.[9]

Mohammed and the Mountain

Some of the enlightened spirits of our age have accurately predicted the devastating effects of mindless mechanization: Aldous Huxley, Henry Miller, and Lewis Mumford come to mind. What they and others were trying to tell us was that mechanical objects do things for us which by all rights we should be doing for our-selves, and that this substitution could have unpredictable conse-quences.

This is a difficult argument to prove, but there seems to be a subtle though necessary relation between the size of the effort re-quired to do a given task and the result of that effort. If only a split-second touch of a button is needed to perform a task which would "normally" take two weeks of human effort, if it takes only three hours to cross an ocean which is "normally" crossed in three weeks, the technology-aided person's involvement in the effort is minimal and he therefore appears not to understand the full implications of the results so easily achieved.

If it takes only a few days and the movement of a few levers to bulldoze a small mountain, instead of a team of men shovel-ling dirt for a year or more, then the temptation to move that mountain and bring it to Mohammed's door is compelling, whether such a move is necessary or not. And more often than not, the easier the mechanical means to accomplish a given task, the less necessary that task is likely to be. Because so much can be done in so little time and with so little effort, accomplish it we will.

One day there is a green field. The next day teams of survey-ors appear, followed by regiments of bulldozers. Before you have time to reflect, a web of four-lane highways has been spun, soon to be filled with cruising vehicles, going who knows where. . . .

While we can, and perhaps should, argue endlessly over the philosophical implications of inventing mechanical means to ease our burdens, the practical consequences of such inventions are transforming our world; and while they make our life much eas-ier, the gift of a more comfortable life has a subtle price tag at-tached to it.

Technology gives us the means for a quick fix, but we have not yet learned to harmonize the speed of that fix with the pace of human labor and activity unassisted by mechanical means. Just as cities which once took weeks to get to can now be reached in hours, so the removal of Mohammed's mountain takes days instead of years. In spite of the time we have (or should have) gained by this quick fix, we are busier and more harried than

15

ever, suggesting that the human scale of doing things meshes uneasily with this new and so much quicker mechanical scale.

But such subtle considerations do not seem to bother the inventors or the promoters of our industrial age. The 20th century that we are about to leave behind us has devoted virtually all its energies to this business of bringing the mountain to Mohammed. We have perfected the mechanical means to do a given task and put them within reach of most people.

Humanity in this century has given itself over, without second thoughts, to what it considered progress. Each new invention brought in its wake astonishment, praise, and a vision of a glorious future. At the same time each new invention also carried within it the hidden danger of establishing itself as man's master and dictator instead of his obedient servant.

And no invention has established this diktat more emphatically than that of the automobile.

The Great Dictator

> Above all, it is the young who succumb to this magic. They experience the triumph of the motorcar with the full temperament of their impressionable hearts. It must be seen as a sign of the invigorating power of our people that they give themselves with such fanatic devotion to this invention, an invention which provides the basis and structure of our modern traffic.[10]

The sentiment expressed in this statement, made early on in the century, perhaps still holds true today and is surprising only in its source. The author of the statement had just laid the foundation for the largest automobile factory in the world. It was not Henry Ford. It was Adolf Hitler.

Because cars and America are so closely linked in people's minds, one tends to forget that another country shares in the dubious honor of having given birth to the automobile. The motor to power the self-moving vehicle (auto-mobile) was basically a German invention, having been developed almost simultane-

16

ously (though independently) by Gottfried Daimler and Karl Benz in 1885.

While Henry Ford was the first to mass-produce automobiles and to promise fulfillment of the dream "a car in every garage," it was Hitler who invented and built the first motorways, promising a *motorisierte Volksgemeinschaft* (motorized populace) where "every member of the German people" could become a car owner.

Propaganda films from the 1930s now in the Bundesarchiv of Koblenz and the Copenhagen film museum reveal what might be called the *Asphaltlyrik* of Nazi Germany. In addition to the autoroute poets and painters, there were the autoroute movies, which showed how the man who took the highway always got the prettiest girl. This was the girl who admired fast drivers and men who knew where they were going.[11]

As if to demonstrate the affinity between powerful men and powerful motors, a recent book, *Mercedes in Peace and War* by Bernard P. Bellon, reveals Hitler's intimate relationship with carmaker Jakob Werlin of Daimler-Benz. Werlin's ties to the Führer dated back to the 1923 Munich Putsch, and Hitler himself generally rode in Mercedes cars as did the rest of his entourage.

Neither Hitler, nor Ford, nor any other promoter of automobiles then or now gave any thought to what would happen to the world if there were truly a car (or two or three or four) in every garage. Left out of their thoughts and dreams were the implications of such a world—the immense amounts of space swallowed up by roads and car parks, the necessary redesign of our cities to accommodate them, the factories to produce them and the cemeteries finally to bury them, not to speak of the noxious products with which they would fill the air.

The spirit of the 1930s lives on in more recent political statements. "Paris must be adapted to the automobile, even if it means giving up a certain outmoded aestheticism" said French president Georges Pompidou in 1971. Ingvar Carlssen, the Swedish prime minister, recently expressed the opinion that "the ownership of a motorcar belongs to human rights." Peter Bottomley, U.K. transport minister in 1989, thought that "more roads

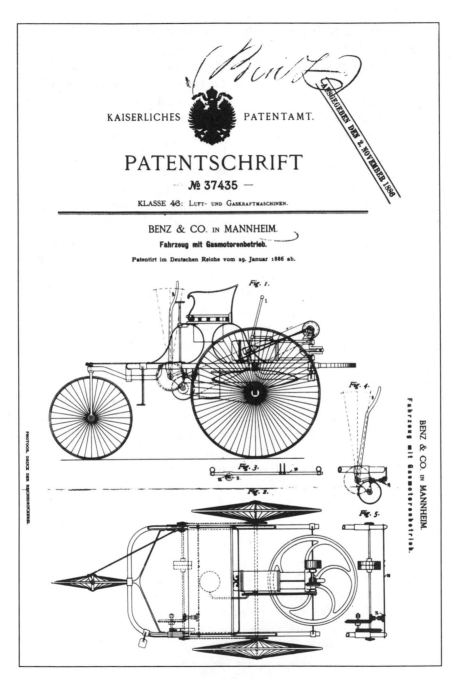

Patent office grant and drawing of first Benz car.

must be built for cars yet to be acquired by women, ethnic minorities, and council tenants who do not enjoy the benefit of personal transport at present."[12]

The British solution to the problem of the social inequality posed above was thus for those who already possess cars—in the words of the late politician Anthony Crosland—"not to pull the ladder up behind them" but to let everyone else climb up after them.[13] "Everyone else" in Britain means 60% of the people who today do not have regular use of a car. Even in America, almost half the population (according to 1985 figures) is carless. In Western Europe two out of three don't have one. In South Africa and Eastern Europe only one out of eleven people has a car. That number rises to one out of twenty-four for the Soviet Union, one out of sixty-five for Asia (excluding Japan, China, and India), one out of five hundred for India, and one out of two thousand for China.[14] So the vast majority of the world's people do not "enjoy the benefit of personal transport at present."

Those that do, generally the better off and more powerful members of the community, give their wholehearted support to what they call "the great car economy" (the words used by the British prime minister in March 1990) without any second thoughts, even though the results of such policies are plainly visible in all the world's major agglomerations.

Such support would perhaps be less forthcoming if these leaders considered calculations which show what would happen if the whole world were to achieve this desired growth:

> There would be a tenfold increase in the world's car population. Parking alone for such a vehicle fleet would require a motorway round the equator sixty lanes wide, not to speak of the energy and raw materials to make all these vehicles, the fuel to drive them, the roads for them to drive upon, the environmental sinks to absorb all their emissions and junked remains, the additional manufacturing to maintain such a fleet, and the rebuilding of the world's cities to make space for them.[15]

Even if such a goal were technically feasible, would it be desirable?

The argument for its desirability runs as follows: Statistics show that the world's population is increasing at an ever faster rate, and that, in addition, there are still many people (such as Peter Bottomley's women, ethnic minorities, and council tenants) who do not have personal transport. But more and more people will be acquiring cars in the near future, and we must prepare for this by building the roads for them to drive on. This will be good for the economy and for social justice. And while we are at it, better be on the safe side and provide a little more than needed.

Such reasoning falls under the heading of a self-fulfilling prophecy. We give them the roads, just in case; they see the roads beckoning. It is hard to think of a single political leader or official who doesn't think along these lines. The chief of the Paris police, in charge of a city with one of the best public transport systems in the world and obliged to deal with one hundred thousand illegal parkers each day, was able to say in April 1990 that "today the Parisian hasn't got two legs but four wheels. I don't want to

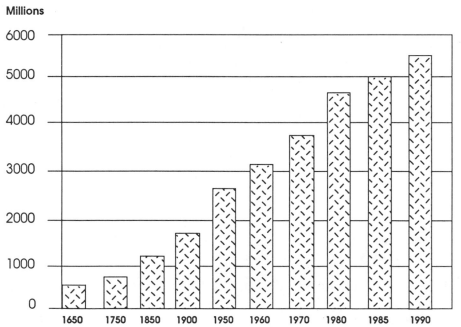

WORLD POPULATION GROWTH

throw a Chinese wall around Paris. A city barred to traffic is a city which dies. Traffic is life."[16]

In a city like Paris those one hundred thousand illegal parkers (a third of whom don't even bother to pay their parking tickets) constitute only a fraction of the city's population yet they effectively block the free circulation of much of the remainder who, even without illegal parkers, have been crowded into narrow sidewalks/pavements, shunted around barriers and chains at major intersections, and chased liked hunted animals at unprotected crossings by the legally circulating vehicles which in their rush manage to maim or kill ten Parisians each day.

But their chief of police updates Marie Antoinette with his counsel to "let them get wheels." Partly as a result of such counsel, according to a recent poll in the French monthly *The Globe*,[17] more than half of Parisians would live elsewhere if they could; among the reasons they gave were pollution, traffic, and noise.

Such a state of affairs, which exists in most of the world's cities, might be thought to contain the seeds of a new and worldwide French Revolution against the misuse of power by our motorized dictator. But there are two reasons why we are unlikely to have such a revolution. The first is that the nondriving majority doesn't think of itself as such; wherever they look there are cars which intimidate them by their size, number, and power. The second is that this incipient revolt has been co-opted by the classic formula of the American Dream: why fight them (the privileged minority) when you can join them and get a car yourself?

Success and Suicide

The almost indecent rush to acquire an ever bigger and more powerful motorcar has for the moment obscured sentiments like those of the microbiologist, cancer researcher, and social philosopher Frederic Vester, who warns us that:

> We have begun to act more and more like tumor cells, without being aware that we begin to destroy our host organism, the

21

biosphere. Teaching managers and politicians to be aware of this development is as difficult as teaching a tumor that what it thinks is its greatest success and achievement, namely exponential growth, is really suicide.[18]

World passenger car production rose from 8 million vehicles a year in 1950 to nearly 40 million a year in 1988; motor vehicles in use worldwide rose from 53 million in 1950 to 500 million today, an almost tenfold increase in forty years. Fifty million new vehicles are added to the existing car fleet each year. This means that one hundred vehicles join our already congested roads every minute, day after day, year in and year out.

Cars are heading for exponential growth, and our task therefore must be to convince their makers and promoters that what they think is their greatest success and achievement may really be the kind of suicide that Professor Vester warns us about.

WORLD PRODUCTION OF MOTOR VEHICLES

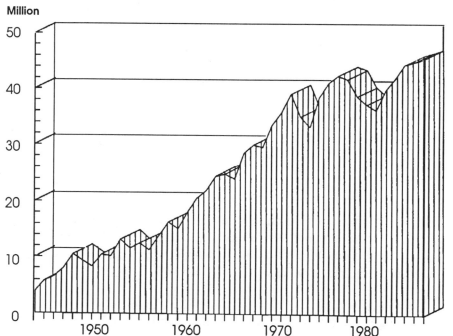

But before we can even begin to convince carmakers and promoters, we must first convince ourselves that life is possible without total reliance on cars. That's not an easy task since such thoughts rarely enter the minds of most "reasonable" people. But if we were to consider it, we might find that suddenly changing conditions such as strikes, emergencies, or wars, give us a foretaste of such a life. It seems that we can—if we absolutely must—modify our habits radically from one day to the next. The power blackout in New York in 1965 made private cars into public cars and showed people an entirely different way of life, engendering a spirit of camaraderie and brotherhood—if ever so briefly—they had not known before. The more recent oil blockade of Lithuania brought people in Vilnius out on their bicycles en masse.

A life with many fewer cars would mean that we could live and work and shop and travel in a different way. So different, in fact, that we cannot even imagine it. Or if we can imagine it, we do nothing about it because, as Oscar Wilde said, "I can resist everything except temptation." It's so tempting and comfortable to mount the trusty chariot sitting in front of the house; walking or waiting for the bus would be such an effort! In we go, without giving a thought to the costs of our little trip—costs to ourselves, to our neighbors, and to the world. Since we apparently cannot stop ourselves from using means which have destructive side effects, we have little choice but to restrict those means.

That is one reason why we ought to curb cars.

Coming Down to Earth

No doubt the ultimate solution to this problem should go further than mere car restraint. We ought profoundly to change our attitudes and the way we live. A powerful Mercedes flashing its lights to demand the seigneur's right of passage must not excite envy but revulsion or even pity.

We should be able, someday, to arrange our lives in such a way that we all but eliminate the need for cars, that a car trip is looked upon as a necessary evil, like a visit to the dentist. But for the moment such goals as phasing the car out of our lives seem unattainable or childishly naive or even conspiratorial. Nevertheless, the dominance of the motorized minority may come under attack before the end of the century. Needless to say, like all attacks by a suppressed majority upon a privileged and often arrogant minority, this one, too, must have justice on its side to succeed.

No one will easily renounce the goal of a car for everyone, unattainable and undesirable though it may be, unless everyone else does so as well and the burden (if it *is* a burden and not a boon) of doing nearly without is borne by all in an equitable fashion. We must therefore neither pull the ladder up (i.e., stopping everyone else from getting a car after we have one), nor let the rest climb up after us (which has a justice of its own), but simply climb back down. It is many steps down, it will take time to do it, and it can only be done as if that mythical ladder were a real one, that is to say step-by-step.

But climbing down that mythical ladder will eventually bring us back to the earth where we still feel more comfortable than anywhere else.

2

NATURE: THE OLD GRAY MARE

"The old gray mare, she ain't what she used to be"since cars made their appearance. The impact of cars on nature is at least fivefold: they are responsible for half of all air pollution and therefore have a serious effect on human, animal, and plant health; they make an important contribution to noise pollution; they swallow up ever larger chunks of land; they are responsible for the deterioration of the natural landscape and therefore can be accused of aesthetic pollution; and finally, they contribute to global warming.

But governments, automakers, and the general public still find themselves in the position of a smoker who has been told by his doctor to quit. The smoker defends himself by saying things like "All doctors say that—that's their job," or "I know of an eighty-eight-year-old lady who smokes like a chimney and who is still going strong. In any case, we all have to go sometime. I'll give up if I really have to, but please not now. Just let me enjoy myself for a little while longer, will you?"

The Wind Is for Washing

On a single bad day in Athens the smog, which is known there as the *nefos* (cloud) is blamed for the admission to the hospital of up to two hundred people. Doctors believe that it kills at least six people on such a day.[1] But we continue, quite literally, to keep our heads in the clouds when we should be taking T. S. Eliot's advice from *Murder in the Cathedral*: "Clear the air! clean the sky! wash the wind!"

The pollutants emitted by cars, buses, trucks, planes and the rest—carbon monoxide, nitrogen oxide, hydrocarbons, lead, fine particulate matter (aerosols) and fibers (asbestos), photochemical oxidants, acid deposition, and chlorofluorocarbons and carbon dioxide—have significant negative effects on human, animal, and plant health.

Such effects are caused directly by the pollutant itself before it undergoes chemical transformation (if any) in the atmosphere, and indirectly by a mixture of pollutants; and these latter can

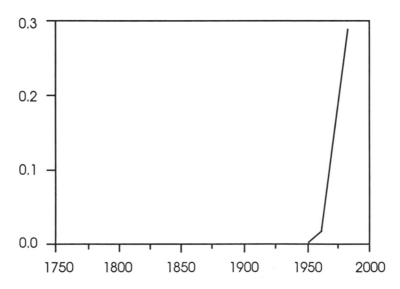

CHLOROFLUOROCARBON EMISSIONS WORLDWIDE

CFC11 Concentration (parts per billion)

often be found at sites very distant from pollution sources. The problem may therefore be greater than the sum of its individual parts, since the gases act together and on each other in complex and unpredictable ways.

Such a combination is held to be responsible for the death of the central European forests, a phenomenon still not completely understood. The extinction of the trees is now thought to be due to a poisonous cocktail of pollutants, including acid deposition, ozone, and heavy metals. This fallout makes forests susceptible to a range of natural stresses such as droughts, extremes of heat and cold, and blights. Some 50 million hectares were destroyed in Europe in 1988 alone. But all those acres and all those chemical names on a page make us fall asleep and when we wake up we have forgotten about it.

Automobiles play a role, perhaps even an important role, in the destruction of these forests, but political leaders and the general public are confused by the complexity of the interaction and the difficulty of digesting statistical information. To make the situation really clear to our decision makers, they should be obliged to take an eight-hour walking tour through a damaged forest.

Carbon monoxide, 65% to 80% of which comes from vehicles, is toxic. It causes respiratory tract irritation and coronary damage and combines with other pollutants. Oxides of nitrogen emissions react chemically with other pollutants to form ozone and other highly toxic pollutants. Hydrocarbons, still another category of pollutants, a third of which come from motor vehicle emissions, include benzene which is of substantial carcinogenic concern and can cause leukemia, while other hydrocarbons, though relatively nontoxic, cause side effects like eye irritation, coughing, sneezing, and drowsiness. Most hydrocarbons also react with nitrogen oxides in the presence of sunlight to produce the ozone of photochemical smog.

Tropospheric, or surface, ozone—not to be confused with the ozone at higher levels which protects us from the sun's damaging rays—is the most widespread air pollution problem in temperate zones. Exposure causes eye irritation, respiratory problems, headaches, and increased asthma. Although ozone in the lower atmosphere does not come directly from motor vehicles, they are the major source of the ozone precursors, hydrocarbons and nitrogen oxides. Automobiles are thus responsible for bad surface ozone and contribute at the same time to the depletion of good high-level ozone.

Even though the link between vehicle emissions and environmental damage is as clear as the link between cigarettes and cancer, we are still in the position of the reluctant quitter.

A Kinder, Gentler Generation

Many governments and even some environmentalists pin their hope for cleaner air on a new generation of vehicles equipped with the electronically controlled three-way catalytic converter, a gadget which is generally seen as the key to a better treatment of the environment. It is true that this helps to minimize the worst effects of some automobile emissions, but it is by no means the panacea most people think it is.

To begin with, at least a tenth of the catalyzer's own emissions are carcinogenic. Catalyzers are useless when it comes to carbon dioxide, and they do not even come close to dealing with emissions produced in the stop-and-go traffic of heavily congested areas. In addition, they do not work when engines are cold. And since most car trips are short, that is a serious disability. If conditions are right, the catalyzer succeeds in removing some of the pollutants, but at the cost of increased fuel consumption. And since it has been estimated that fully half of all the converters in the United States don't work efficiently, the clean air advantage is not evident in places like Los Angeles.[2]

The faith many people have in catalyzers would be shaken further by calculations which show that of the fifty million new vehicles added each year to the world car fleet, few are currently "state of the art" in either energy or environmental terms. But even if they were, it would take years for them to make an appreciable impact because they are only a small percentage of the existing half billion (almost all dirty) vehicles out on the road already. The moral of this calculation is that we must not rely on technology alone to fix the environment for us.

Diesel engines too are sometimes thought to be kinder to the environment because they are more economical in the consumption of energy. They are so only because governments have set the price of diesel fuel arbitrarily lower to please the haulage industry. This has led some private drivers to jump on the diesel bandwagon. Diesel engines emit thirty to seventy times more particulate matter than gasoline engines equipped with catalytic converters. The particles emitted by diesel engines are small enough to bypass the respiratory system's mucous filters and penetrate to the lungs where they may cause bronchitis. They may also be toxic and carcinogenic. The diesel engine's destructive power was demonstrated in Treblinka where it was used to asphyxiate the death camp inmates.

There is extensive evidence linking diesel emissions with lung and bladder cancer.[3] A recent Harvard University study shows that people regularly exposed to diesel exhausts may be 42% more likely to develop cancer.

To make matters worse, diesel engines are more difficult to start than gasoline/petrol engines, giving truck and bus drivers a handy excuse to let them idle for long periods of time and to increase still further the nefos which surrounds our heads.

Some Like It Hot

Although catalyzers do remove some pollutants, they have no effect whatsoever on carbon dioxide emissions. Transportation now emits about a quarter of the total man-made carbon dioxide (the principal greenhouse gas) and is its fastest growing source. For every 15-gallon fill-up at the service station, an incredible *300 pounds* of carbon dioxide is eventually released into the atmosphere.[4]

Simply put, the greenhouse effect means that some of the gases discharged as by-products from the production of energy

Carbon Emissions Worldwide

Carbon Concentration (parts per billion)

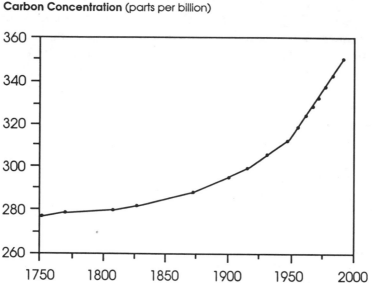

get trapped in our atmosphere the way heat gets trapped in a greenhouse. Carbon dioxide, one of the substances emitted by motorcars, accomplishes this by letting through the sun's rays while absorbing the infrared rays reemitted by the earth's surface. Thus carbon dioxide is responsible for keeping in our atmosphere a lot of heat which in the normal course of events would escape back into space.

Carbon dioxide is not a "pollutant" since it is a natural component of the atmosphere and indispensable to photosynthesis. Without it the earth would be cold and uninhabitable. But the five hundred million motor vehicles on the roads of the planet have helped to tip the natural balance. The double accumulation of carbon dioxide from both natural and man-made sources has steadily increased to the point where it is having an adverse effect on vegetation and ecosystems as well as on the climatic equilibrium of the planet.

Governments and ordinary people are still skeptical about the so-called greenhouse effect. "Look here," they are saying, "the

Carbon Emissions from Fossil Fuels

Carbon (millions of tons)

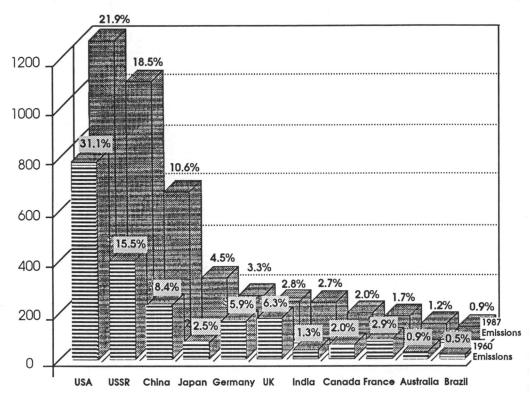

This table shows the growth of carbon emissions from countries around the world. While the United States is still the world's worst polluter, its world percentage has sunk from 31% in 1960 to about 22% in 1987. In other words, the rest of the world is catching up.

scientists themselves don't even agree. They can go totally wrong with their computer models. O.K., there have been a few hot summers in a row, but what does that prove? My aunt Emily from Canada told me that this winter was the coldest she can remember! And if it really does warm up, so much the better. I can stay in Vermont during the winter instead of moving to Florida."

The most compelling evidence for the relationship between carbon dioxide and global warming does not come from computer models but from tiny air bubbles in Antarctica. By analyzing these bubbles, scientists can infer what happened to the earth's climate during the last 160,000 years. During that period carbon dioxide and temperature have gone up and down in lockstep. The more carbon dioxide, the warmer; the less, the colder.

In past times, levels of carbon dioxide have fluctuated between 200 and 300 parts per million. Within that fluctuation we have had the last two ice ages and periods of the greatest warming. Now, however, even skeptics among scientists think that concentrations of carbon dioxide will be pushed to levels of 600 parts per million, thus doubling the presence of carbon dioxide in the brief period of the next forty years.[5]

One might say that carbon dioxide is "all dressed up with no place to go." The figure of 600 parts per million means that you can take your pick of doomsday predictions. Possibilities include melting ice caps with massive inundations (a one yard rise in sea level would flood an area the size of Massachusetts in the United States); diversion of the Gulf Stream; heat-related destruction of the plants which feed the world; mass migration to escape the effects of hard-hit environments; and the browning of the earth as the desert spreads beyond its historical boundaries.

For This We Thank Our Leader

The French ecologist René Dumont, who ran for the presidency of his country in 1974 in a bid to draw attention to the coming environmental disaster, is convinced that global warming has begun already. He cites as evidence the rise in concentrations of carbon dioxide from 316 to 346 parts per million between 1960 and 1985; the 30% drop in rainfall in the African Sahel region since 1968; and the appearance of the century's five hottest years and the great droughts of India, China, and the United States in the 1980s.[6]

Perhaps by pure coincidence the 1980s was also the decade in which environmental protection was willfully disregarded or overturned in a spree of deregulation and conspicuous consumption. Looking back to these years for the effect they might have had in bringing us closer to catastrophe, Americans (as well as Britons and a number of other nations) might well repeat the German slogan of the 1930s: "For this we thank our leader."

Partly because of the profligate use of energy and the habits formed during those years, the authors of the annual Worldwatch *State of the World* report now give us only ten years to reverse current trends. After that, they have concluded, the die is cast.[7]

It is only fair to report here that not everybody agrees with such gloomy predictions. Some scientists have lately found that there is somewhat less carbon dioxide in our atmosphere than called for by theoretical calculations, which leads them to suspect a mysterious source of carbon dioxide absorption not as yet identified. A German-Indian project in the Arabian Sea, for instance, found that carbon dioxide is partially absorbed by surface marine plankton, which eventually sink to the ocean bottom, taking carbon dioxide with them. The stormier the sea, the more plankton plus its carbon dioxide is "pumped" to the bottom.[8] Other scientists argue that trees, stimulated by increasing levels of carbon dioxide, are getting bigger and are thus able to absorb more carbon dioxide.

And some scientists have even thrown cold water on the entire idea of the "balance of nature," asserting that the only real constant in nature is turmoil.

Two climatologists at the University of East Anglia have made a thorough study of actual temperature readings, both in the air and in water, for the last three hundred years. The only thing they were able to conclude with certainty was that our planet has warmed half a degree Celsius in the past century.[9]

There are so many complex factors pulling in all directions that one can only make an intelligent guess with regard to global warming and its consequences. That guess has now been made by much of the world's scientific community.

Perhaps the same guess of the coming ecological disaster, forest destruction, and resulting inundations had already been made much much earlier by the unknown writer of this old nursery rhyme:

If all the seas were one sea, what a *great* sea that would be!
And if all the trees were one tree, what a *great* tree that would be!
And if all the axes were one axe, what a *great* axe that would be!
And if all the men were one man, what a *great* man he would be!
And if that *great* man took the *great* axe, and cut down the *great*
    tree, and let it fall into the *great* sea, what a splish-splash
That would be!

Tigers and Lions

Reducing greenhouse emissions means restraining, among other things, the tiger in our tanks. And while we are at it, we could also do something about the lion's roar.

It has been estimated that in the OECD countries (Organization for Economic Cooperation and Development, sometimes called the Rich Man's Club), more than 50% of the population is exposed to noise levels in excess of 55 decibels. Decibels can vary from 10 in the desert to a 120 for aircraft take-off. For some 130 million people living in those countries, noise levels are in excess of 65 decibels. This is approximately the outdoor noise level in the vicinity of a motorway or expressway. And the percentage of people living in the "gray" area of noise levels between 55 decibels and 65 decibels is steadily increasing.[10]

Noise generates stress. Quite apart from the permanent damage to hearing, it also has a considerable impact on how an individual functions in body and mind, both because of the effort necessary to adjust to noise, and because of the frustrations which result from a poorer quality of life and loss of sleep. It is therefore sobering to reflect that neither in the city, nor in the country, nor even in the wilderness is it easy to find fifteen consecutive minutes of silence not disturbed by evidence of the internal combustion engine. Characteristic of the violence this engine has inflicted upon the natural world is the way it works. The engine is driven by a continuing series of explosions. And these explosions are heard around the world.

We cannot get our fifteen minutes of silence in the city without being interrupted by the racing of a motorcycle engine, the failure of a car to start, the screaming of vehicle-mounted ambulance and police sirens, the honking of impatient drivers, the constant malfunctioning of car alarms, and the crunching of wheels on the pavement. The altered soundscape of our cities has been regarded as one of the reasons why modern popular music is often played at such a high level.[11]

In the countryside the problem is sometimes even worse because silence there is thought to be more natural; to the car sounds of the city are now added the noise of tractors, road building machinery, airplanes, and distant road traffic. And in the wilderness we are assaulted by fuel-powered saws, jet engines, snowmobiles, and motorboats. A single cross-country motorbike or a single chain saw has the enormous (and totally unjustified) power to pollute the peaceful silence for miles in every direction. Anyone complaining about the shattering of rural peace is apt to be put down as a crank.

We have therefore pretty much lost the experience of being away from it all which is so important and reposing for the human spirit, The world, in modern times, is truly "too much with us."

The Great Land Grab

In addition to its effects on human, animal, and plant health, and its contribution to the world's noise level, the motorcar is responsible for a third kind of pollution, not often considered as such. This is the tendency of the car and its infrastructure to consume large quantities of land. In the United States 60,000 square miles have already been paved over, amounting to 2% of the country's total surface and 10% of all arable land. In Britain each mile of motorway requires 25 acres of land and each year up to 4000 acres of rural lands are lost to roads. The size of the parking lot Britain would need to accommodate the expanded fleet of vehicles its Transport Department envisages for the future has been

35

calculated as being around 625,000 acres, twice the county of Berkshire; and additional Berkshires would be required for the roads on which these vehicles would move, ending forever any resemblance of such an England to that once "green and pleasant land."[12]

The consumption of arable land is the more serious, as such land is under simultaneous attack from other sources such as pesticides and topsoil erosion, and the likely expansion of deserts in the coming global warming will make the remaining arable lands even more important. Here again the car's contribution is twofold: it is responsible for swallowing up arable land with its infrastructure, while its emissions reduce such lands even further by pollution and global warming.

Some scientists and economists scoff at the idea that arable land is getting scarce, pointing to the fact that Malthus' gloomy predictions of such land running out have not come true. Yet 10% is not a negligible figure, and it must be set beside the fact that modern farming methods exhaust topsoil in the long run by such practices as removing hedges, using chemicals, and making no provision for letting the land lie fallow.

But it isn't only arable land which is threatened by the car. In a graphic demonstration of the space required for just one simple cloverleaf access to a superhighway, a German exhibition called *Alptraum Auto* (nightmare auto) showed a photomontage of such a cloverleaf superimposed on the city of Salzburg. According to that photo, a single four-ramp cloverleaf would destroy almost all of Mozart's birth city, including 4000 apartments, 920 houses, 430 companies, 16 churches, 13 schools, and a university, as well as marketplaces and narrow winding streets.[13]

Beauty and the Beast

In eradicating the old town of Salzburg, the automobile would not only attack space, but beauty. It would be doing so by destroying beautiful objects which get in its way and replacing them with ugly ones.

AVERAGE ANNUAL ENERGY CONSUMPTION

Kg. Coal Equivalent per Capita

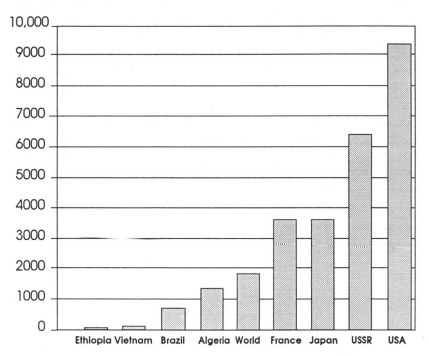

Average energy consumption of the world and selected countries in terms of coal equivalent per capita (1987).

Aesthetic pollution is, of course, difficult to measure and verify, because some people surely believe that cars and their by-products are themselves beautiful. But the fact that some objects are almost universally considered beautiful does mean that some standards exist. It can be said without much fear of contradiction that most people would give to Salzburg a higher beauty rating than they would say, Tysons Corner, the urban sprawl we discussed earlier.

Aesthetic pollution has the advantage over something like carbon dioxide of being at least "honest"—you don't have to be a student of chemistry or rely on statistics to be aware of it. It makes itself known in no uncertain terms. But that is perhaps the very reason why most people don't even notice it.

It would be hard to exempt even a single item associated with automobiles and their infrastructure from the charge of aesthetic pollution. Certainly no one can claim that a gasoline/petrol station or a car cemetery is a thing of beauty and a joy forever. Nor are oceans of parked cars soothing to the eye. Ever greater numbers of such silent seas surround buildings of indiscriminate shapes and angles, set down in willy-nilly fashion with no regard to order, aesthetic discipline, or overall integration into the landscape. Ever bigger and bolder signs and shapes go up to call a speeding driver's attention to a product or service, and to distinguish such from its competition. None of these signs and shapes are what one might call landscape-friendly.

Yet few people who have grown up in modern times are even conscious of such aesthetic pollution. And even if they were, does that mean that we must restrict all economic activity just to keep the landscape beautiful, pure, and nature-friendly?

Dr. Pangloss' Painless Path

Robert U. Ayres, a physicist and technology analyst at Carnegie-Mellon University, tries to give an answer to the conflict between ecology and economy which is implied in this question. He uses Dr. Pangloss' Painless Path as a catchphrase to characterize the way most political leaders think about our economy. According to Ayres, their view (supported by most mainstream economists) is that market forces left to themselves without intervention will operate in this best of all possible worlds to produce automatically the necessary technical responses to resource exhaustion and environmental degradation.[14] Such a view assumes that a world in which we rely chiefly on economic and technological growth will not only make sure that the market repairs the environment, but provide us with the mental calm and spiritual strength to control the genie we have freed from its bottle.

According to Professor Ayres, however, a painless pathway to an ecologically sustainable future may not exist. Prices for almost all economic goods (most certainly including transport) are too low and thus heat up the economy, because they do not reflect costly environmental damage and do not "tell the ecological truth."[15] Stimulated by these artificially low prices, most of us in the West eat too much, drive too much, use too much energy, and produce too much garbage (literally and figuratively). We hardly need the help from humorist Art Buchwald, who wants to get his hands around consumers' throats to make them buy twice as much as they need as a boost for the economy. Consumers are doing that already.

If our economy were arranged differently, if we calmed it the way we are now beginning to calm traffic, if we went along with John Whitelegg, a professor at Lancaster University (U.K.) and transport adviser to the German government who counsels us to give up the "fruitless search for the holy grail of mass consumption, unlimited movement, and economic growth," perhaps our consumer's psychic and physical health would be in better shape.[16]

But even if we don't give up that fruitless search, it would be safer to adopt a more cautious approach and consider every one of our actions in the light of a new perception that undisciplined use of technology and resources brings with it unfathomed dangers, and that we had better think very carefully about such use. That means we must think carefully before leaping into such activities as building new roads and keep in mind two near certainties: each new road generates new traffic; and each new road will extend further the automobile's infrastructure and the air, noise, and aesthetic pollution which go with it.

The Trout and "The Winter Journey"

Rachel Carson opens *Silent Spring*, her powerful lament on what man has done to nature, with a description of the world before our current merciless attack upon it. In that former world "towns lay in the midst of a checkerboard of prosperous farms . . . where, in spring, white clouds of bloom drifted above the green fields. Along the roads, laurel, viburnum, alder . . . and wildflowers delighted the traveler's eye. . . . People came to fish the streams, which flowed clear and cold out of the hills and contained shady pools where trout lay."[17]

In this world of shady pools Franz Schubert was able to write his charming song about the playful trout. But that world is now gone. The clear bubbling brook described with such joy and tenderness is murky or dry; the trout which moved as "quick as an arrow" is infected or extinct; the poet sitting at the water's edge "in sweet repose" cannot hear the murmur of the brook for the noise of modern life around him; and the forest in which he sits is dead or dying.

After some major key changes we have unwittingly slipped into a much more somber Schubert piece, this one called "The Winter Journey." In it, the hero wanders aimlessly through a barren landscape until he comes to a fork with a signpost pointing to the road from which no one has yet returned. The hero, like all of us, is fatally attracted to that particular direction, and the piece ends with a question, as does contemporary history.

Though it would be quite natural to react with anger or righteous indignation to what has happened to our planet, there still are some birds singing, there still are some fish even in polluted waters, and the sun is still up there, ozone holes or not.

We can look at the enormity of what we have wrought with a mixture of bittersweet nostalgia for what has been and panic for what is to be; or we can face up to the mess we have made of the world calmly, and with a glimmer of hope that what we have done, we can undo. To repair the environmental damage we have inflicted upon our world gives us another reason why we must curb cars.

3

THE CITY: NECROPOLIS OR ECOPOLIS?

If the automobile has done its bit to disfigure the world and to contaminate nature, it has gone one step further in cities—it has begun to destroy them altogether. Jane Jacobs, a social and architectural critic whose ground-breaking study of American cities has become something of a bible to city lovers, explains this process of destruction:

> Erosion of cities by automobiles entails so familiar a series of events that these hardly need describing. The erosion proceeds as a kind of nibbling, small nibbles at first, but eventually hefty bites. . . . A street is widened here, another is straightened there, a wide avenue is converted to one-way flow, a bridge is double-deckered as its capacity is reached, an expressway is cut through yonder, and finally whole webs of expressways, and more and more land goes into parking, to accommodate the ever-increasing number of vehicles while they are idle. No one step in this process is, in itself, crucial. But . . . it not only adds its own bit to the total change but accelerates the process. . . . it is something like the grip of a habit-forming addiction.[1]

The Captain's Leg

We might say that cars *eat* cities. And they do it—to use a particularly gruesome analogy—the way it was done in the recently popular novel *John Dollar* by Marianne Wiggins, the tale of a group of children and their paralyzed sea captain stranded on a desert island. The starving and by now savage children *ate* the paralyzed captain's legs piecemeal and by stealth. The hapless captain, like our equally hapless cities, seemed not to notice it.

Two Australian transport researchers, who studied the car-dependence of thirty-two world cities, divide these cities into five classes. Their categories range from those cities most dependent on cars, including Phoenix, Houston, Denver, Detroit, and Los Angeles, to those least dependent, including Munich, Paris, Sin-

Parked vehicles fill up every nook and cranny.

gapore, Hong Kong, and Tokyo.[2] For our purposes here we would like to suggest three categories, according to the amount of irreversible physical destruction which has taken place.

The most benign form of destruction (only because it isn't as yet permanent) can be seen in a city like Paris, where illegal parkers and their legal confreres take up crosswalks, block alleyways, place themselves unashamedly across sidewalks, leave not even squeeze-through space between parked vehicles, and fill up every nook, cranny, and square centimeter of the city.

A more debilitating form of car bulimia takes place in many American cities where the automobile has literally sucked city centers dry. In those cities all the commerce, culture, and entertainment, as well as many residences, have been shifted to strips of highway outside the city. Such strips then become a part of the famous U.S. of A., the Urban Sprawl of America, where people can park to their heart's content. In that kind of city the traffic problem has been "solved," because there is no further reason to go there. The old city has become an empty shell, a hollow memorial to the past, to be left to the odd group of tourists who can only discover what may still remain of architectural interest in the center by traversing miles of sleazy no-man's land surrounding it. And after they have recorded their impressions by clicking away on their cameras, they are unlikely to find a human establishment to serve them a decent lunch.

But even this category of city is not physically dead and may someday be revived by processes called gentrification and reurbanization. Gentrification involves a renovation or new construction of inner city buildings which drives up rents until only the rich can afford to live there. (The ten thousand new housing units which Toronto built in 1976 in the center city for relatively high income households without children demonstrate such a process. Along with these units, offices were constructed and a survey showed that 35% of residents walked to work in the summer and 29% did so in winter.) In the more positive reurbanization people are enticed back into the center by a more modest repair of the old buildings, often by the occupants themselves.

It is, however, when cities are crisscrossed by expressways that a form of city destruction occurs that will make later reurbanization extremely difficult if not impossible. Elevated high-ways often do little to alleviate the congestion in the streets below. What they do is to create traffic which didn't exist before, as they tempt the motorist into what he thinks will be a trouble-free car ride. Many who formerly took public transport, cycled, or walked, have now been lured onto the new expressways which quickly fill to capacity.

Thus a new north-south route through the inner city of Stock-holm, for example, which opened in 1984, led to an increase in car traffic of about 50% in three years.[3] Similarly, the Westway corridor around an inner-city motorway in London showed in-creases by a factor of 7 or 8 in travel demand due to the new road, in comparison with a control area. In London, the M25, Westway, A4, and M4 have all created a vast amount of new traffic.[4]

Aside from eventually leading to gridlock above as well as below, elevated highways create a dead space under them, a kind of continental divide. Pedestrians are loath to traverse such spaces because they are often dark, dangerous, and ugly.

Adding Up to Noplace

The city is thus cut into ribbons, destroying the intricate social web which had been spun through the ages since its origin. Traf-fic engineers and city planners who build such roads do so with the best intentions: theirs is an engineering solution which takes nothing into consideration except the movement of traffic. But fi-nally, by ignoring architectural, environmental, and social consid-erations, these engineers end up with inefficient traffic movement as well.

Marshall Berman calls this process of urban blight "urbicide." He describes this urbicide at work in the once proud neighbor-hood of his childhood:

> The South Bronx, where I spent my childhood and youth, is the site of one of the greatest recent ruins outside of Beirut. The physical and social destruction of the area began with the con-struction of the Cross Bronx Expressway in the late 1950s and

44

early 1960s, spreading gradually southward from the highway and northward from the emerging Bruckner Expressway in the late sixties. . . . Then in the early 1970s the disintegration began to spread at a spectacular pace, devouring house after house and block after block, displacing thousands of people like some inexorable plague. "The Bronx is burning" resonated all over the world. . . . [5]

The formerly lively streets of the South Bronx now became a kind of urban jungle with burnt-out and derelict apartment blocks, forcing anyone who was not at home there to retreat into his locked automobile and keep to the expressways which caused the disaster in the first place.

What happens to someone not native to that jungle who makes a wrong turn and finds himself under the expressway instead of above it is well documented in Tom Wolfe's *The Bonfire of the Vanities*. The protagonist's life in that novel was shattered by a single wrong turn. Had there been no expressway, this protagonist might either have been discouraged from taking his car or, having lost his way, would have driven through a lively and less dangerous neighborhood.

In the 1970s the mayor of Lyons invited the French Autoroute du Soleil (the Paris-Marseilles motorway) to traverse the center of his city because he thought it was a cheap way to build a fast route for local use through his city—the state was picking up the tab for its construction. Anyone who has been to Lyons since the motorway was built will know that Monsieur Pradel helped to give it a blow from which it has not yet recovered. He cut the city in two and caused, over his citizens' heads, some of the most momentous traffic jams in France.

Almost like the Swiss sculptor Jean Tinguely, who thirty years ago invented a machine to destroy museums, it seems we have invented a machine to destroy cities. Tinguely's tongue-in-cheek machine was three stories high and had a number of spindly arms which flailed away in reckless abandon at the museum next to which the machine was set, before finally destroying itself. The car has been a more efficient and less quixotic agent of destruction. Again we will let Jane Jacobs describe in her eloquent way how such destruction is accomplished:

Traffic arteries, along with parking lots and filling stations, are powerful and insistent instruments of city destruction. To accommodate them, city streets are broken down into loose sprawls, incoherent and vacuous for anyone afoot. Downtowns and other neighborhoods that were marvels of close-grained intricacy and compact mutual support are casually disembowelled. Landmarks are crumbled or are so sundered from their contexts in city life as to become irrelevant trivialities. City character is blurred until every place becomes more like every other place, all adding up to Noplace. . . . [6]

Cities as Endangered Species

Cars and their drivers (as well as the mayors who want those drivers' votes) are doing their bit towards making the city, along with the bald eagle, the blue whale, the sea turtle, and the long-tailed chinchilla, another endangered species. This is something of a paradox, because cities are growing ever bigger, and contain ever more of the world's people.

In 1900, for instance, an estimated 10% of the world's population was urban. By 1950 that percentage had risen to 30%. By 2010 fully half of the world's people are expected to live in urban areas. While in 1950 there were 10 metropolitan areas in the world with 5 million or more people, there were 33 such areas in 1990, 6 of them containing 15 million people or more.

So aren't cities thriving?

Over fifty years ago the farseeing social thinker and architectural critic Lewis Mumford predicted a rather gruesome end for the city, which he called "Necropolis." This was the sixth, and final, phase in the life of a city, with many of its residents living in poor, dirty, and dangerous conditions in a vandalized and desolate cityscape.[7] At the opposite end of the scale is a Japanese conception of cities which they call "Ecopolis"—the city in which man can live in harmony with nature.[8] Which direction are our cities taking?

A 1991 global study on urbanization and urban development concludes that the only thing we can be certain of is uncertainty in the processes of urbanization and urban growth. "Each decade seems to reveal a somewhat different map of urban growth and to call for a revised set of theories."[9]

Perhaps it depends on what one means by cities. Is a city an agora or an agglomeration? At the same time that most city centers are losing population, the periphery of those cities is gathering masses into its orbit, spilling without limits into the surrounding countryside. The human-scale city centers are losing out to the mechanical scale, which makes it possible for vast distances to be covered by a personal motorized means of transport. It may be argued that we have to accept our life in a modern world and that the traditional city was ripe for destruction. One may even call into question the European and Asian model of a high-density assembly of people. Surely that is not the only model of a large human habitation? Such an argument depends on our point of view about whether modern man is essentially different from the creatures before him.

There are those who maintain such a point of view. They suggest that communities, in the generally accepted sense of the term, are a thing of the past. The only community which counts now is the dinner party community of like-minded people who meet by deliberate arrangement and who do not have to live in close proximity to one another as long as they are connected by a motorway.[10]

While some may agree, the rest of us are social animals beyond the confines of the dinner party. We want to mingle with others, not necessarily like-minded, something we cannot do if we insist on isolating ourselves in a personal transport capsule. We want to go from the bank to the fish market, from the theater to the waterfront, from our houses to our work, from the poor districts to the fancy sections of town, from the decrepit to the spotless—all of it adding interest and stimulus to our rambles. The dinner party community would find its ideal in a city like Los Angeles. The fact that a half-hour walk through streets empty of people is necessary to get a carton of milk would not necessarily bother the members of such a community, since presumably they all have cars.

To take our cities off the endangered species list, however, we must give real flesh and blood creatures, not surrounded by their metal shells, more reasons to be on the street. We can do this in a type of city blessed with what planners call "mixed use."

The End of Urban Apartheid

The mixed-use city is not based on segregation and apartheid, concepts which, politically and socially, have proved to be unworkable. Segregation can be maintained by force, but eventually such a practice creates so much pressure that a society based on it is torn apart.

While we now have ample evidence that segregation is not viable, we still practice it in many areas. We segregate the elderly to live in apparent bliss but actual misery in retirement communities. We condemn the poor to live in ghettos and install the rich in similar but heavily guarded enclaves. We segregate young people in vacation communities and old people in tour buses. We segregate residences and businesses, shops and cultural centers, industrial zones, and, yes, pedestrian zones. All of these are forms of urban apartheid.

In terms of the city, the opposite of apartheid is mixed use, where establishments like shops, offices, schools, theaters, hospitals, concert halls, light industry, cafés, and restaurants act as chessmen (the term used by Jane Jacobs) which control and stimulate the movement of the pawns. If you arrange your important pieces in groups and then space these groups far from each other, you have given up the ability to generate movement and energy between them. In practical terms, the hubs of activity are too far for walkers to move comfortably between them, thereby bringing desertion and danger to city centers.

Although we now have cars, we may not be so very different from our Greek predecessors who enjoyed life in the agora. People there drifted from spot to spot, pausing to chat under the plane trees or by one of the fountains. Public buildings and shrines were in the same agora where meat and fish and the rest were sold. Booksellers had their stalls there, and so did bankers.

To some observers—Aristophanes for one and Aristotle for another—those drifters from spot to spot were vulgar, undesirable fellows. They saw no good purpose served by idlers (such as Socrates). Like some modern planners, they wanted the various functions separated and contained. Aristotle advocated two agoras, one for ordinary commerce, the other of a religious nature, free from idle or vulgar activity.[11] Aristotle no doubt would have approved of the modern custom of putting culture centers and shopping malls in separate areas well away from city centers.

William H. Whyte, who spent sixteen years observing how people move about in a city, sees a parallel between the history of the agora and the direction our cities are moving. In about the third century A.D. the agora began to lose its centrality. It was secluded from the city around it and eventually completely enclosed. According to R. E. Wycherly, a specialist in the agora, city life then lost something of its old quality, and enclosing the center helped lead to the Greek city's eventual disintegration.

Whether we group our amenities in such an enclosed center under one roof, and thereby give up stimulating foot movement within the whole city, or space our amenities far from each other, making it impossible to walk between them, the effect is the same: We keep people off the streets.

But, you might say, we're not living in Greek times. Their cities were small, and the world's population was a fraction of what it is today. What are we going to do with all those new billions?

To solve that problem, mid-20th century city planners put on their thinking caps and came up with two simple (or should we say simpleminded?), though apparently opposite, solutions. The first was to reserve the city center for business, the very rich who could afford luxury center housing, and the very poor who were living in ancient slums. The rest of the people were to be housed outside the city, surrounded by neat little gardens.

The second solution was to save horizontal space by stacking people and businesses up vertically. City planners were given a nudge in that direction by having at their disposal some war-flattened cities and some ancient slums practically crying out for what came to be called urban renewal.

49

God's Little Acre

The decentrists were inspired by Ebenezer Howard's 1898 book *Garden Cities of Tomorrow*. Howard's idea was to repopulate the countryside surrounding London by building a new kind of town—the Garden City—in which the poor might live "closer to nature," theoretically at least a nobler idea than that of the later tower builders who wanted to put their poor at the top of the tower.

What the White King said to Alice in *Through The Looking Glass* might well apply to Ebenezer Howard: "He's an Anglo-Saxon Messenger, and those are Anglo-Saxon attitudes." It is almost a cliché that Anglo-Saxons need more space around them than most other races, and thus planners in Anglo-Saxon countries have a horror of high density and veer toward the mythical ideal of at least a quarter acre per family. The question of density lies at the heart of all discussions about cities, suburbs, and car-dependency. Studies by the Australian researchers cited here earlier have shown that in densities below 30 to 40 people per hectare—about the level of Toronto and Hamburg—automobile dependence soars. In Denver (12 people per hectare) it appears that a 60% decrease in density corresponds with a threefold increase in fuel use per person.[12]

In 1961 Lewis Mumford warned us that "in America space-eating had become almost a national pastime. Standards of one acre per family are taken as universally desirable even if not achievable. As a result the city itself is fast disappearing, its scattered parts lost in space." In cities, where there isn't enough room to surround yourself with your very own God's Little Acre, you could take the next best thing, a house surrounded on all sides by a garden. It was as if the well-known penchant of Anglo-Saxons for surrounding themselves with space extended to their houses. Like their owners, the houses, too, avoided touching each other. Neighborliness yes, closeness no.

But these gardens now immeasurably increased the length of daily trips to work and to shop. One might go so far as to say that a proliferation of personal gardens led to a proliferation of personal transport. It has been estimated that London, rebuilt to the same density as Howard's Garden City, would stretch from Brighton in the South to Birmingham in the Midlands.[13] A sprawl of that size would generate a furious amount of traffic, as like-minded people of the dinner party community go about the business of meeting in their far-flung habitats.

Towered Cities

The tower builders, who thought they were correcting the faults of the low-density Garden City, were inspired by the early work of French architect Le Corbusier, who designed in the 1920s what he called *la ville radieuse* (the radiant city). This consisted of groups of towers which would occupy only 5% of the ground—the rest would be devoted to parkland and a massive motorway system to access the towers. The open spaces around the towers were to be the "lungs" or gardens which the city needed to breathe, an idea that originated with the black smoke of the industrial revolution.

The people who designed these towers often themselves lived in very pleasant 19th century town houses. So they failed to have a clear idea of what it means to live on the twenty-fifth floor of such a development. If you happened to be a mother with small children, you couldn't send them out to play and watch them from your window, but were obliged to go down the elevator (provided it was working) and search out a fenced-in playground. The designers of these towers therefore turned young mothers into baby-sitters, as the designers of suburbs were to turn suburban mothers into chauffeurs.

If you happened to be a teenager, you had no drugstore or street corner to hang out in. If you were an elderly person, you might well be terrified of the long elevator ride with some of these same teenagers, who often had nothing else to do to amuse themselves than to menace the elevator riders. And if you did make it down safely to street level, you would be afraid to venture out into the often fenced-in so-called open spaces for fear of being attacked or inhaling motorway fumes.

Most curious of all, the tower designers failed to achieve their basic goal, that of getting more people in per acre. The twenty-five story Ronan Point tower in East London—built on Le Corbusier's model—contained no higher a density per acre than many four story housing units which follow traditional street patterns. That is because the tower was set into acres of open space while the traditional houses restricted the open space requirement to gardens in the rear. The London authorities were spared the trouble of demolishing this tower (as similar projects had to be demolished in the United States) because Ronan Point collapsed all by itself.

Le Corbusier's radiant city, which Jane Jacobs calls the "automobile freeway version of Howard's Garden City,"[14] did not correct the density problem, but just added many unnecessary problems of its own.

Vienna Surrounded by Phoenix

When New World planners built their cities in the 19th century, they were intoxicated with the idea of abandoning the old unplanned historic European model and building in their stead streets wide enough to turn around a team of horses. The streets were long and straight and laid out in grid patterns. North Americans, perhaps more sociable and less reserved than Europeans, did not foresee that by laying out their cities in that fashion the streets would evolve into obstacles rather than inducements to social intercourse.

Wide and straight streets take up residential space and serve as barriers to social contacts while allowing wheeled traffic to move quickly at the expense of foot traffic. Streets laid out in grid patterns create long, uninteresting blocks, discourage walkers and encourage vehicles, both because a straight line is vehicle-friendly and because a long, boring, and perhaps dangerous block cries out for the quickest possible passage. Unknowingly the New World got its cities ready for the cars which hadn't been invented yet. While the streets in those cities, and the wide straight avenues of European towns, would later carry all the traffic they could bear, the narrow, curved, vehicle-unfriendly streets of European inner cities were to remain comparatively uncongested.

But Europe was not going to be left very far behind the Americans. When the older cities there expanded into the surrounding countryside, the lesson of the narrow curving streets was forgotten, and the new parts of the city became vehicle-friendly.

Most modern cities with an ancient core now deserve the epithet applied by one astute observer to Toronto—"Vienna surrounded by Phoenix."[15] Most American cities might be called Phoenix surrounded by Phoenix.

The Hundred-Year Learning Curve

Human beings are slow learners. It has taken us about a hundred years to discover (or rediscover) a few basic facts about cities. We are only now, for instance, beginning to find out that a small alley opening into a street, a little square suddenly encountered, an avenue divided into different areas, or small spaces cleverly arranged (sometimes called spaces within spaces) gives a better psychological feeling of space than a wide open expanse. It is only now beginning to dawn on us that an American city with its immense freeway and parking infrastructure resembles not so much a city of the 21st century as a city which has suffered saturation bombing. And we are only now beginning to realize that neither the typical suburb, nor the urban sprawl, nor the freeway city is a true assembly of people.

Here are some of the things we have learned (or should have learned) about what makes a city tick: A city should have definite borders, hopefully surrounded by a green space. It should have a definite identity, making its inhabitants proud to live there. It should not exceed a size beyond which its identity gets lost, and beyond which it become too difficult to administer.

It should be roughly round or star-shaped, and compact or dense enough to encourage traversal by foot, bicycle, or public transport. It should have its full share of amenities—shops, theaters, cultural centers, cafés, restaurants, as well as offices, businesses, and light industry—scattered throughout to cut down the need for transport and encourage foot movement.

It should contain a mix of houses, old and new, as much for aesthetic reasons as to attract poorer residents and businesses as well as rich ones; it should contain small, medium, and tall buildings, and many apartments not higher than can be climbed to on foot. It should contain a mix of streets—narrow, wide, curved, and straight—and a mix of big parks and small green spaces.

And finally its inhabitants, administrators, and planners should realize that the physical and architectural layout and arrangement of a city has a profound effect on the social life, welfare, and safety of its citizens.

If we have gone too far to reshape our megacities and agglomerations in the fashion suggested above, we can at least try to make individual centers, perhaps formerly independent towns and villages, as autonomous as possible. In such a city, business activity and social intercourse would revolve around the local centers instead of placing the entire burden of communication on roads and the transport system.

Every concession a city makes to the automobile encourages movement at the expense of access and contact, and roads at the expense of residences and amenities. Such concessions inhibit the kind of city life described by Jane Jacobs, where "multiplicity of choice and intensive city trading depend on immense concentrations of people and intricate minglings of uses and complex interweavings of paths."[16]

If we can bring the car under control one day, we can begin to replace its then obsolete infrastructure. Using the vast spaces now reserved for freeways and parking, we can try to create a series of lively centers or agoras, connected by convenient foot and bicycle paths. It is even possible to imagine that we could make proper parks out of car parks, and use some of the freeways for light rail systems where distances are too great for walking. Perhaps that is an idle dream, but it has the merit of not being in of what Jane Jacobs calls "Le Corbusier's tradition of wishful frivolity."

And it gives us a further reason for curbing cars.

54

4

OURSELVES: THE AUTO AND THE EGO

In spite of all the woes discussed so far, people still love their vehicles. The image we have of them is very different from the reality. It is perhaps a little like the image of the sea as a beautiful expanse of clear blue water with miles of deserted beaches which draws people to the coasts, but when they get there they find the ocean polluted, the beaches jammed, and high rises and cars everywhere.

In spite of this difference between dream and reality, it is sometimes said in Germany that for a husband the car comes first, the wife second. According to the popular French magazine Elle, *the car is the French girl's closest companion, without which she is paralyzed. Fabienne, 32 and single, says that the day her car is being serviced, she has the right to stay in bed. For Danielle, 38 and married, it's drive or die. For Valerie, with three children, it's the only escape she has from the madhouse of home and office. And for Cecile, 27, the car is the great love of her life, her true companion, the being which knows all her little secrets that no one else seems to care about.[1]*

Cars and the Modern Soul

Since we love our cars with such passion, it is only natural that we shut our eyes to their flaws. But those flaws are there and they will not go away. For almost every advantage cars have introduced into our lives, there is a corresponding drawback.

The very cars which have liberated some women by making them mobile and independent have stranded others in faceless suburbs or made them into full-time chauffeurs. The very cars which have been a boon to some of the handicapped have handicapped others for life through accidents. The very cars which allow some of the elderly to get around in ways they couldn't before, trap others who fear even to step outside into a busy street.

The same cars which take some children to Disneyland prevent many more others from playing in their own street. The same cars which make it so convenient for some of us to get to work, make it more and more difficult for others to do so. The same cars which take us to the hospital so quickly are often responsible for such a trip in the first place. And the same cars which have broadened social life for some of us have left others without friends or neighbors in streets and neighborhoods abandoned to automobiles. But beyond these unpleasant side effects of the motorcar there is another and perhaps even more sinister development: the car is beginning to take possession of the modern soul. Increasingly *auto* (the Greek word for "self") is coming to stand for *ego* (the Latin word for "I").

During the 1980s an advertisement for a German car frequently told people that "you are what you drive." The Swedish social psychologist Johan Asplund tells how people are identified by their cars:

> In Scania (where I live) the villagers are often uncertain about the names of people and they identify each other as "he with the red Saab" "he with the old Volkswagen." . . . In Scania there are many retired people without cars, and younger villagers have certain difficulties in distinguishing them from one another.[2]

The Swedish ecologist Emin Tengström writes that "the automobile . . . plays an important role for many people in their attempts to handle their existential problems and the question of their own identity. A threat against the car can, therefore, sometimes be interpreted as a threat against the individual himself." He thinks one of the reasons why cars have become so important may be that the car appears to solve an age-old dilemma: "The will to stay within one's own territory, and the necessity to be mobile outside this territory, both of which can be accomplished in a car."[3]

In the United States the auto-ego connection goes perhaps further than elsewhere. Americans will go to amazing lengths to make their automobiles scream: "Mine, and nobody else's!" For some teenagers, cars are a kind of machine-age costume, and the accessories say something about who they are. You dress the car as if it were you.[4]

The Vroom and the Womb

"Toucha My Car And I Breaka You Face" was the message on one Australian bumper sticker, expressed in the broken English of some Italian immigrants. Touch a man's car and you touch him. Challenge a man's car and you challenge him. The car has become his alter ego.

This process of the car seeping into our consciousness starts very early. According to some child psychologists, today's children can make the vroom sound of a motor before they can form the word "mamma." They identify early on with the power of the car and its driver, and they feel protected by the purring, upholstered, and soft cradlelike rocking of the car interior.[5]

If one agrees with the theory in vogue among some psychoanalysts that birth is a trauma we never forget or forgive, one can go even further and compare the car to the womb in which we were lying so snug, warm, and cozy; therefore the exit from that car to confront a cold, threatening, inhospitable world outside becomes a somewhat similar trauma. People often sit in their cars, refusing to leave the snug womb-car even when not driving, or take long trips "into nature" only to eat their picnic in or just beside their vehicles because they are reluctant to separate themselves from this safe haven.

For the child the car is at once a symbol of wished-for power and the cause of actual powerlessness. Small children must, against their will, hold the hand of a grown-up to be safe from that same symbol of power and security. Their desire to move freely must be subordinated to the orders of parents (who themselves obey traffic lights), making the children stop and go like Pavlov's dog. Such constraints at the hands of their parents may well lead to the children's revenge when they are old enough to drive by stimulating dangerous driving behavior toward members of their parents' generation.[6]

Once children are old enough to go to school, their dependence on automobiles increases if they are driven there. Figures from Britain show an ominous trend: In 1990 three to four times as many children were taken to and from school by car as in 1971.[7] As a result such children do not develop the landscape map they need to carry in their heads for later orientation. They will often later oblige their parents to take them to their lessons and appointments as they will have an irrational fear of public transport. If they are not driven, they stay at home and watch TV like the elderly.[8] They learn early in life that "the car is a most frequent and necessary tool for the organization of everyday life."[9]

When children who have been brought up to regard the car as a symbol of power and speed are old enough to drive, they often do so recklessly. But lecturing such children about their driving behavior has been found of little use by Dr. Till Bastian, a German physician who specializes in drug and car addiction. Dr. Bastian makes the halfhearted suggestion that we must offer these teenagers something positive, a chance to be creative, to have joy in their lives without climbing into their cars. But the good doctor admits that this is easier said than done, and offers no concrete examples of positive teenage joys which are unrelated to the internal combustion engine.[10]

The joys which are so related are all around us. We live in a culture where the acquisition of a drivier's license has been compared to ritualistic practices in technically less advanced societies. Some sociologists take the view that the young person sometimes withdraws to the isolated world of the car in order to reduce the pressure of the modern environment. The habit of young people to "cruise" in their cars is said by other sociologists to represent a method to demonstrate their group identity and status in society.[11]

The child and teenager who has grown up and practically eaten and slept with his modern alter ego, is now ready to be considered a serious potential customer by the automobile industry. Such young people have been nicely prepared, without being aware of it, like a well-spiced roast ready for the oven.

Of Mice and Men

The sexual symbolism equating the automobile with masculinity is well known and frequently used in advertising and automotive literature. In that world there is a lot of talk about wild, untamable animals, power, and technical precision, which is meant to stand for unconquerable dominance (outspeeding the fellow next to you). One automotive writer even speaks of his car's race-tuned engine as emitting a "primal howl."

We are, in fact, so used to the advertisers' constant bombardment of young people with appeals to their masculinity that many dismiss this as a cliché not even worth discussing. Cliché or not, such propaganda does tend to brainwash children. In a recent discussion this author conducted with twelve-year-old school children *all* the boys said they were going to get a car when they came of age, whereas *all* the girls said their acquisition of a car would depend on where they lived.

Some advertising is very graphic, such as the February 1986 German ad "Coleman has the longest." In line with such sexual connotations, one design for the German Opel in which the tailpipe slanted downwards was not accepted by the management. In a Range Rover advertisement showing a scantily clad heftily built young woman wading in the sea with a drawn knife in one hand and a rope in the other, the overt associations are sporting, daring, and adventurous. The hidden command is to "wrestle with the amazon, take away her knife, and put her on her back."[12]

Even if a male wants to fight against such stereotypes, it is not easy in a culture where he is constantly told to be a man, where masculinity must be struggled for and proved anew each day. To be a man means to "burst with energy, power, and sexuality." Often male self-definition is "weak and in need of constant reinforcement," playing into the hands of such advertisers.[13]

Although advertising addressed to men goes through fashions and cycles, its essence remains the same: adventure, risk, attack, conquer, command, tame, confront, lead, act, win.[14] The automobile is ideally suited to these commands. Not only does it give power to those who lack it by the simple act of pressing the accelerator, but it offers the driver a kind of roller-coaster thrill that he may lose control of his vehicle.

The automobile gives power to those who lack it.

A number of writers have described the association in most males of self-control and manliness, and the fear of the "soldier type" to go beyond strict limits. With the car this soldier type can let go of his need for masculine self-control by exceeding the limits (i.e., speed and security) while exercising the masculine qualities of daring, danger, and dominance.

One psychoanalyst has even gone so far as to suggest that an addiction to sailing, surfing, skiing, flying, or speed driving must come under suspicion of being an expression of inner emptiness and lack of human contacts.[15] In such a view, a person who finds it difficult to confront himself or be in a calm environment where he may come face to face with his inner self is obliged to throw himself into frenzied activity to avoid contact with himself or others. While this is perhaps an extreme point of view, it may have a grain of truth in it.

Needless to say, not all driver excesses are expressions of inner doubt and emptiness. Some of the irresponsible driving is quite conscious and deliberate. Many drivers have a love/hate relationship with their vehicles. They are often quite well aware of their behavior but they can't help themselves. We seem to have at one and the same time the two feet nature gave us and the four wheels bestowed upon us by the industrial age, and the two are often at odds.

It is almost a kind of civil war, fought inside the same person. The very same people who, as pedestrians, resent the arrogance of drivers using sheer power and size to have their own way, switch sides when they become motorists. They then consider pedestrians and bicyclists to be obstacles in their path, or vermin to be exterminated.

Accelerate, Darling

Irresponsible driving behavior is somewhat more likely to be male than female, according to one sociologist who shows that women not only pay more attention to traffic signs and signals, but have generally been brought up to be more considerate and more conscious of their fellow humans. Whereas men, for exam-

61

ple, might curse the Ford or Mercedes in front of them, women may try to imagine its driver who is, perhaps, not so different from them.[16]

According to a Belgian study women wanted a car that was "warm, nice, or calm." A Swedish study matched these attitudes to their actual choice of cars and found that women would choose such makes as Renault, Fiat, Volkswagen, Nissan, and Toyota, whereas the men went for the more powerful cars like Mercedes, BMW, Volvo, Audi, and Saab.[17]

The people who write advertising copy for carmakers have been uncertain how best to address women. At first it was easy: cars were bought by men, so women were sex objects draped over, under, or next to the car to attract the ever-virile male customer. Thus Rolls Royce, for instance, pictured an elegant lady in a white fur coat (car advertisers have a natural affinity for other destroyers of the environment), and Jaguar a lady dressed in leather spread-eagled against a wall. Then in the 1980s, the European oil and automobile industry looked at statistics which showed that while 52% of men use cars daily, only 19% of women do. The industry then determined to target women as car customers, the way that cigarette, milk powder, and pesticide industries target the Third World today.

Since the association of cars with power would work less well with women than it had with men, the advertisers seized on the next best thing—women's liberation. The woman of "today" became the new heroine, as active as her male counterpart. Today's woman is, of course, still beautiful, seductive, and secret. But now she is also capable, successful, and independent.

Already in 1970, before the European discovery of women as potential customers, a book called *Gib Gas Liebling* (*Accelerate, Darling*) encouraged women to take the steering wheel into their own hands, something their sisters had been doing in the United States for years. The authors claimed to put an end to the sexualization of the car.

But in an unconscious sexualization of their own (of which the book's title is already clear evidence) they go on to say that the "driving license is the first hurdle which must be overcome in the love affair with the auto. To really love a car a woman must first drive it, otherwise her relation remains platonic." Or, "a driver's license is like a marriage license. Having it doesn't make you an expert, either at the wheel or in bed. The race has only just begun."[18] In other words, the authors are encouraging women to have an intimate relationship with automobiles, meaning to possess one and be possessed by it.

Mildred Pierce, a novel by J. M. Cain, goes further than a mere marriage license:

> She gave the car the gun, exactly watching the needle swing past 30, 40, and 50. . . . The car, pumping something into her veins, something of pride, arrogance, of restrained self-respect that no talk, no liquor, no love could possibly give. . . .[19]

The Wonder Weapon

We have so far concentrated on what cars can do to our heads. But what they do to our bodies has undoubtedly even graver consequences. Helga Rock, for a time a Green member of the Bundestag, holds this "wonder weapon"—the allusion here is to Hitler's V2 rocket—responsible for claiming in this century as many victims as did the plague in the fourteenth.[20] But while the bubonic plague was universally feared as the Black Death, the eleventh plague remains an object of reverence.

Far from being a source of worry, the wonder weapon aspect of cars is, in fact, glorified. A Porsche designer said his cars should "have the winning look that weapons have."[21] In countless films of the James Bond type, it is as if we were depicting the Black Death of the Middle Ages riding forth as a conquering hero, who wins pots of gold and beautiful blondes. In those films the car becomes a symbol of freedom without any constraints, always a powerful desire just below consciousness.

Fashionable writers and actors have continued this worship of the automobile. (Many of them were the same ones who posed in photos with cigarettes in their hands.) The French writer Françoise Sagan objected to being "confronted with figures" (accident statistics) and bemoans "a wretched age in which people are forbidden to kill themselves" (and others, she forgets to add).[22]

Albert Camus, James Dean, and Roland Barthes, all of whom idolized cars, ironically ended their lives as accident statistics.

Motor vehicles worldwide, by one conservative estimate, kill a quarter million people and injure seriously three million people a year.[23] A broader estimate reports the much higher figure of half a million killed annually, and as many as fifteen million total injuries.[24]

Whatever the figures may be, the numbers we read in accident statistics "help us to accept the unacceptable" as Professor John Whitelegg puts it. In the 14th century the victims of the Black Death were lying out in the streets. Car accident victims just show up as little numbers on a page unless you happen to be such a victim yourself. They have this in common with war casualties; but whereas wars raise people's consciousness to casualties, traffic accidents, which demand more victims than most wars, do not. Traffic accidents in the United States produced more deaths in one year, for example, than did America's ten-year involvement in Southeast Asia.

"All of us are immune," writes Whitelegg, "to the road toll, and there is a resistance to fundamental policy options aimed at reducing traffic danger. The car and its promise of freedom and mobility is more than capable of subverting well-intentioned plans to reduce the number of accidents." Whitelegg recently studied the risk of being killed or seriously injured in Cologne. That study showed that the lifetime risk for the general population was one in forty, while in the age group one to fourteen years the risk increased to one in nineteen. "Silly numbers," according to Whitelegg, "are those which purport to show that roads are safe because there are fewer accidents, whereas everyone with a child knows that dangerous roads are avoided and children are forbidden to cross or bike in them."[25] So we have succeeded in making roads safer only because we have scared children and pedestrians off them.

The *Auto-Free Press* of New York puts it another way in responding to a report that appeared in a government publication announcing that Scarsdale (a wealthy suburban community) has not had a pedestrian fatality in seven years. "Who knows," writes the *Auto-Free Press*, "maybe they haven't even seen a pedestrian in seven years."[26]

There Is a Life after Cars

The fact that it is even possible to imagine seven pedestrianless years in suburbia without unduly torturing our imagination shows just how far we have come with our car-dominated world. To wake people up at least to the physical danger of automobiles, our car-addiction specialist Dr. Bastian proposes that the cars of speeders, drunk drivers, and other violators be taken from them on the spot, obliging them to walk home in humiliation. He presumably arrived at such draconian measures because a good talking to or even a dose of psychotherapy made no impact whatever on the motorists.

For the moment there is neither an adequate police force nor the political will to restrain and punish offenders seriously. But Dr. Bastian has a point nevertheless. We may initially have to use compulsory restraints if for no other reason than to show drivers that the world won't come to an end if they can't use their cars on some days of the week. Or perhaps we should put it that the world will come to such an end if they can?

Well, here we go, talking about drivers as a selfish lot who do not listen to reason and are out to destroy the world. But who are these drivers if not each one of us? Each one of us, yes, but with the means of power in our hands and feet to lead us into excesses. What Lord Acton said about power applies most especially to the power of an automobile—power tends to corrupt. And the more absolute is that power—the faster and the more powerful the car—the more absolutely it corrupts the driver.

That is another reason why we must curb cars: as a kind of shock therapy to make motorists realize they can do without them; to save us from ourselves. Once we find out that life is possible without total car dependence, we may even stumble onto a different form of existence in which there is a place for natural activity like walking and bicycling, social and neighborly contacts, birds that sing, and forests which not only have live trees in them but can be walked through peacefully, calmly, and with joy.

5

THE CHALLENGE:
FINDING THE MAGIC WORD

The philosopher and scientist Frederic Vester, who was talking to us earlier about tumors, thinks that we have a lot to learn from biology to understand how an organic system works—and the complex ballet we execute to move from place to place can be said to be just such a system. Vester believes that "interventions in open and dynamic systems tend to entail complex repercussions, only a small percentage of which can be expressed in direct cause-and-effect relationships, and practically none in a straight line."[1] We don't know what chain of events we will set into motion when we intervene in the way people move about, even though our intervention may come with the best intention of nudging people towards a healthier and environmentally sounder way of life.

The Road to Hell

The road to hell, they say, is paved with good intentions. Such good intentions are often proposed by local authorities or traffic engineers, or anyone else for that matter who wishes to get into the act. Transport writer Roger L. Creighton pointed out twenty years ago that "proposals are made and contested, charges and countercharges are hurled; simplistic solutions are proposed with sublime assurance. It is almost as if people delight in having an area in which anybody can speculate because nobody knows anything about the subject."[2]

Let's say, for example, that we severely restrict parking in the center city. We may think and hope that this will make the center more lively by giving what was formerly car space over to playing children and their promenading parents. But let's also imagine that we haven't at the same time paid enough attention to public transport or bike paths, and we now find that drivers who cannot get into town take their revenge by shopping in the suburbs, thereby threatening to bankrupt center shopkeepers and leading in turn to further desertions.

Or say we make a beautiful pedestrian zone, keeping out all cars and leading to a total renovation of the old city center. One result flowing from the very success of that zone may be to draw more cars than ever to the area so that drivers can try to have their cake and eat it too by "driving to walk." And the renovations and accompanying fire regulations have now driven up commercial rents to such an extent that all former small shopkeepers are obliged to quit the zone, leaving the field to luxury stores and big chains. Gone then are the little groceries, book stalls, curio shops, and hidden cheap cafés which made the area interesting. What's left is yet another suburban shopping center, this time in the city.

Or, to take an actual example, consider the case of the Washington Metro, which was extended to the Virginia suburbs with the intention of bringing suburbanites into D.C. What happened instead was that 60% of new development since suburban Metro construction was begun took place around the suburban stations,

67

pulling people from center city to suburb instead of vice versa. And to add insult to injury, only 4% came by rail. The rest—you guessed it—took their preferred means of personal transport.[3]

Throwing In the Towel

In spite of occasional local successes, the complexities of automobile-related problems and the seemingly unshakable position of the car in all our transport and city planning is enough to make the more timid among us despair, throw up our hands, and follow that gesture by throwing in the towel. Perhaps our obsession with cars has gone so far that we just have to give up, do nothing, and let things take their course. In such a scenario we would argue that the world has now been so arranged that we cannot do without cars. That this twilight of the gods has already arrived in some sections of the United States is documented in a booklet from the U.S. Department of Transportation, whose prose is as dense as the traffic on suburban highway system described therein.

According to their figures, the number of suburban residents in three large Texas cities increased fourfold and the number of those residents who also work in suburbs threefold in the period of 1960 to 1980. The resulting "private auto utilization rate" was 93%, and the public transport use (generally called "mass transit" in America) was 1%.[4] Although this booklet talked bravely about such concepts as "ubiquitous and multidestinational routing methods," one is left with the uncomfortable feeling that in the real world the 1% of mass transit users consists of poor blacks, Latinos, and women, a segment of the population which does not necessarily inspire these transport planners to great feats of the imagination.

Most of the children in our Western countries have, in any case, been brought up on cars or the expectation of owning one someday. They live in a world of supermarkets, and sixteen-lane highways which can only be crossed by renting a car on one side and dropping it off on the other.

To them our modern gadgets are temptations they cannot resist. They succumb to gadgetry, and there they stay, alienated little by little from what is called the human condition—a tradition which has not yet come to terms with technology.

A Horse Is at Least Human

"I'd rather have a god-damned horse. A horse is at least human," said Holden Caulfield, talking about cars. Henry Miller, intoxicating himself with words in his usual extravagant manner, puts it this way:

> Besides arms, legs, hooves, claws, fangs, marrow and grit, you've got to throw in the . . . ebb and flow of tide, the conjunction of sun, moon, and planets, and the ravings of the insane. Besides rainbows, comets, and Northern lights, you've got to have eclipses, sunspots, plagues, and miracles . . . all sort of things, including fools, magicians, witches, leprechauns, Jack the Rippers, lecherous priests, jaded monarchs, saintly saints . . . But *not* the motor cars, *not* refrigerators, *not* washing machines, *not* tanks, *not* telegraph poles. [5]

Before we reject such sentiments as these as the ravings of the insane which Miller evidently prefers to refrigerators, before we return to the smug acceptance of the modern world which is our natural stance, let us follow Miller's line of reasoning a little further. Take the case of refrigerators. Aside from releasing chlorofluorocarbons and other gases which help bring on higher temperatures (and consequently a need for even more refrigerators), these cooling boxes entice us into buying huge quantities of food we would not have bought otherwise, just because we can now keep and store them. And to get these quantities we take our cars and shop at the distant supermarket. Instead of making the frequent trips on foot to the neighborhood store which render the town center livelier and safer, we thus contribute to more decentralization and pollution.

Of course, no one is going to abandon giant refrigerators as a result of such reasoning, but to look at the modern world from a different angle can put things into perspective, and help us recognize the complex cycles we initiate by our unquestioned reliance on technology. It is possible that we may not be as different from earlier human beings as we think we are. We have not yet managed to produce the truly modern race envisioned in Huxley's *Brave New World*. But there are signs that we are getting there. That is why we have to try to arrange a world in which we do not allow the mechanical devices which serve us to interfere with basic human values, even if our efforts to do so backfire and occasionally achieve opposite results. We have our failures and our successes, and we learn from both.

What we need more than anything else is the will, the good will from all of us, to help find the magic word which will arrest the course of events the sorcerer's apprentice has set in motion. We are awaiting the master magician to come and give us that word, or more likely the many little words adding up to the magic one which will stop our mad race to destruction.

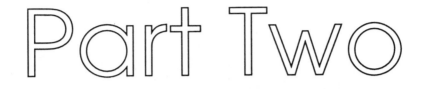

Part Two

How We Can Solve It

To achieve this new and less car-dependent existence, we describe in this second part of the book thirty-three ways in which cars can be curbed or at least be kept from further exponential growth. You might think of them as thirty-three of the little magic words to stop the sorcerer's apprentice.

Many of the measures suggested here to keep cars at bay have been tried somewhere in the world. Many have been in use for very short periods of time often unsupported and in isolation from other measures which should accompany them. It isn't of much use to put speed bumps or flower pots in one street without considering surrounding streets and neighborhoods or even the entire city. And we must never forget that attempts to set things right can often be counterproductive. All are suggestions of ways we can restrain the automobile. The proposals have been grouped into eight different categories or means of attacking this problem.

The objective in the first set of suggestions is to make us recognize that there is a problem. The next group suggests specific ways of controlling that problem. This is followed by three groups of ways to get around car use by choosing an alternative means of transport. We then look at economic means to restrict car use and go on to look into our own lives for solutions to the car problem. And finally we try to see if there is a right place for the car, both in the Third World and at home, and find out how political pressure groups, parents, and children view that place.

Thirty-three is an arbitrary number and in no way constitutes an exhaustive list. Each reader is invited to make personal additions to it—the more the better. But these suggestions point out the general direction we must take to follow the long uphill road toward more moderate car use and a healthier environment. Christina Rossetti has warned us what to expect:

Does the road wind uphill all the way?
Yes, to the very end.
Will the day's journey take the whole long day?
From morn to night, my friend.

LIFTING THE VEIL:
SOLUTIONS 1–3

What prevents us from even realizing that there is a problem with cars?

The fact that motorcars have undergone very few changes in a hundred years has allowed us to get used to them and take them for granted like an old, comfortable pair of shoes. We rarely question what they actually do to us, how they should be designed to fit into our delicate world, or what they cost us in money terms, let alone in other ways.

And those who sell those cars to us make sure that we don't ask questions, by keeping our minds on other things.

> *Siemens engineers have calculated that, if the automobile had developed as*
> *radically as, say, the integrated semiconductor circuit, today it would*
> *weigh less than two ounces, hit over 3000 miles per hour top speed,*
> *travel more than 300,000 miles on a single tank of fuel,*
> *and cost under three dollars.*
>
> Jens Priewe, *Fast Cars Die Sooner*

The Two-Ounce Three-Dollar Car

If governments did not subsidize the motor industry the way they do, and if people had a clearer idea of the car's true economic costs, automakers would be obliged to pay more attention to making their product efficient and competitive. At the 1986 symposium "The Future of the Automobile Industry" in Davos, Switzerland, a member of the audience asked the assembled heads of the automobile industry to answer a question which he considered highly important. What real progress had there been since the automobile was first developed? He confessed that he himself could see no fundamental difference between the modern car and the vintage 1924 old-timer in his garage.

The gentlemen on the podium seemed rattled. Well, uh, they said, what about the new steering axle, the new braking system, lower fuel consumption? In that way they evaded responding to the assertion that, all advertising to the contrary, the auto continues to be a rather old-fashioned buggy. It has not learned anything really new in a hundred years. It still needs roads to travel on, still guzzles only gasoline/petrol, still cannot get by without a driver. Its engine, with its relatively poor combustion and heavy exhaust, has not been replaced by a better drive system, even though far more efficient power sources are known. And its power is still being dribbled out unregulated—through thousands of shafts, pinions, bearings, rings, balls, and joints. Where aircraft construction has gone through three generations, and computer design through five, the automobile has failed to progress beyond its first generation.[1]

The car is thus a machine which could have been designed by the American cartoonist Rube Goldberg, who specialized in inventing absurdly complex contraptions to perform simple tasks.

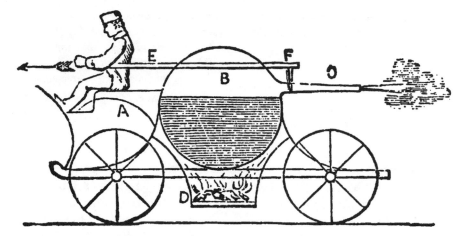

Newton's Steam Car, 1688.

Such a contrivance makes no attempt to correct a basic flaw common to all our energy uses: the unbelievably inefficient way with which energy is converted from primary source to final service.

An internal combustion engine at best converts 35% of the potential energy available in a barrel of oil. But when that 35% is then transmitted to the wheels which move the vehicle forward, at least another third is lost in that transmission. And when heaters, air conditioners, wipers, radio, as well as vehicle aging and malfunctioning are added in, the efficiency of the energy conversion process needed to transport a person in a conveyance ten times heavier than he is, is minimal. Energy analysts have estimated that we in our cars end up using only 2% or 3% of the potential energy in the oil as it comes out of the ground. That would be the equivalent of clumsily opening a bottle of champagne and spilling practically all of it on the floor, leaving only a single sip.[2]

We know that radical new car designs exist but are being held back by their makers until "needed." One mini Honda, for instance, has been tested which gets an incredible 5000 miles per gallon under lab conditions.[3] To accomplish such feats, engineers would have to reduce weights by using plastics, low-alloy steel, and aluminum; reduce aerodynamic drag and rolling resistance of tires; take cylinders out of action when not needed; have dual cooling circuits which allow engines to warm up more quickly; and use more free-flowing oil to reduce heat loss due to friction in the engine.

All of these are within the technical means of carmakers, but they are not regarded as commercially interesting , i.e., profitable. Moreover, making such cars would not necessarily solve all of the problems set out here. Such improvements could create some environmental benefits that might be offset by the additional vehicles enticed onto roads due to lower operating costs. Those lower costs might in turn spur the makers to produce heavier engines, now that those engines could be run on less fuel and money.

Dutch researchers have in fact confirmed such a cycle in the Netherlands. They found that some carmakers used the "excuse" of greater fuel efficiency to increase the power of their engines, since their customers could now drive heavier cars without any additional fuel costs. Drivers of such cars were now tempted to try higher speeds. Where higher speeds were not feasible, as in cities, drivers of these more powerful vehicles would constantly speed up and slow down. This is, of course, an extremely inefficient way of driving, as accelerating quickly must overcome wind resistance and gravity in a sudden burst, while braking quickly fails to let the wind and gravity come to the engine's aid. Much of the environmental advantage of greater fuel efficiency— cars using 45 miles per gallon produce only half the carbon dioxide in their lifetime than do cars getting 18 miles per gallon— was thus lost.

What is doubtless needed is a much more radical approach to car design. We have to overcome four basic faults of the modern car: size, noise, danger, and pollution; and perhaps a fifth fault— excessive comfort inviting excessive use. For this we need not only a complete design rethink but practically a psychological revolution of the kind which has taken place in regard to sun bronzing or smoking, both of which were once fashionable and are now not regarded highly. It would perhaps be better for radical auto design to forget about existing cars altogether and take as a point of departure entirely new concepts such as the little silent, nonpolluting white bubbles shown in Woody Allen's film *Sleeper*.

An attempt along those lines is being made in Chicago with a transportation system concept called Personal Rapid Transit. PRT calls for automated car-sized passenger vehicles traveling on their own grade-separated guideways. Passengers and goods would be transported nonstop from origin station to destination station.[4] Such concepts have been knocking about in research laboratories since the 1960s, but now may be the time to bring them out of the closet and really try to make them work.

The British transport writer and specialist Stephen Plowden has a vision of automobiles in a future world which does not come from a dream fantasy but is realizable within a generation. He proposes a car he calls "The Local Runabout." This is a small, light vehicle (yet to be designed) which runs on electricity, solar power, or hydrogen and whose top speed would be 30 miles per hour. It could be driven by the holder of an intermediate license much easier to obtain than regular drivers' licenses, possession of which would be made much more difficult.[5]

City centers would be closed to the Runabout (as well as to conventional cars, of course) but many suburban and country roads would be restricted to Runabouts and licensed freight vehicles only. Residents in those areas would be discouraged from owning conventional cars, doing all their local driving in the Runabout. If they wanted to own a conventional car for long-distance trips, such a car would be parked outside town limits and accessed with the Runabout.

Long-distance trips by conventional cars would be discouraged by strict and low speed limits, by high eco taxes, and by cheap and easily accessible alternative transport. City centers would rely entirely on public transport, cycling, and walking. There would be few parking problems, since Runabouts would be used only in areas of low-density housing, where private parking would generally be available.

An even more radical idea is that of giving up individual ownership of cars altogether, at least in urban areas. In Amsterdam in the early 1970s, a white car or *Witkar* was put into service which was meant to be used by anyone who was a subscriber to

A Witkar parking terminal.

the system and thus had a key. The Witkar failed, partly because there weren't enough terminals, and partly because the cars were being misused. But it failed above all because people and industry weren't ready for such a concept.

We now have a widely used system of supermarket shopping carts which users release and return by depositing and recovering their coins. Bicycles, using that same system, are to be introduced in Copenhagen in 1991. They can be released by depositing DKr 20 (about $3 or £1.85) in the rack which holds them. The 5000 bikes which will initially be put into service will be financed by advertising on the machines and the storage racks which, if not very landscape-friendly, will at least help fund the system.

The city Witkar of the future, which could operate along similar lines, might be a two-seater the size and type of amusement park electric bumper cars or golf carts. This vehicle would have no radio, no heater, could not go faster than 15 miles per hour, and might have only a canvas top for inclement weather. Such a vehicle could be operated by a plastic "smart card" ticking off the units as the vehicle is driven, clearly indicating to drivers how many units are left on their card. The cards would be on sale in drugstores and news kiosks. These electric carts could be charged at the terminals to which they must be returned to recover the deposit. Some terminals would be situated near conventional parking lots for travel into the city. The carts or carlets would be financed by the sale of the operating cards and would not be parked on city streets but at terminals throughout the city, similar to bus or taxi stations.

This is just one of many ideas that have been advanced for a radically new car design meant to overcome the conventional car faults cited earlier. One thing such a car would not have is a tiger in its tank. It would not even have a tank to house such a tiger.

But what would happen to the carmakers and the people they employ if we really abandoned the conventional car in significant numbers? An engineer with Krupp and I. G. Metall tried to deal with this question in a 1989 meeting in central Europe to discuss "The Psychology of the Automobile Society." He answered his own question as to whether the private car can be converted to a social and environment-friendly product with a resounding *no*.

> We can add catalyzers, but that doesn't solve CO_2, stop-and-go, and cold start emissions; we can make cars more silent, but that would make them even more dangerous; we can use electronic guidance systems, but aside from the added cost, this would not attack the basic problem of hitting people and animals, destruction of cities and street space, social isolation and the rest.[6]

Instead of making a silk purse out of a sow's ear, the advice of this engineer to carmakers was to begin thinking about turning their production to other things: trams, buses, small energy-efficient heating units, service and goods vehicles, solar-powered cars, small and low-velocity true city cars, and new and more efficient bicycles, reversing by this latter means the historical process of turning bicycle factories into car factories.

History has shown that we cannot protect or subsidize an obsolete industry. Rather than save the motor industry we should

CAR PRODUCTION IN SELECTED COUNTRIES

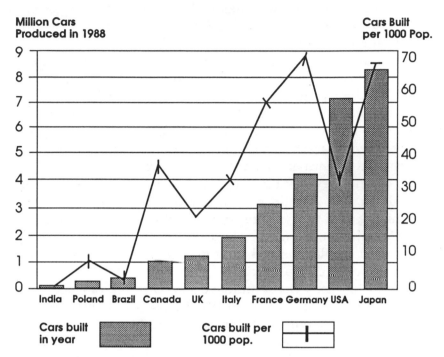

Million Cars
Produced in 1988

Cars Built
per 1000 Pop.

India Poland Brazil Canada UK Italy France Germany USA Japan

Cars built in year   Cars built per 1000 pop.

be sending it a signal that perhaps its days are numbered. We could begin sending such a signal by buying fewer second and third cars and taking better care of our first cars to make them last longer. We could be buying used cars (if environmentally sound) instead of new ones and we could be renting cars when needed instead of buying them. Or we could renounce them altogether by rearranging our lives. All this would send a message to the automobile industry to begin rethinking their products and their long-range plans.

Two years ago BMW's chairman, Eberhard von Kuenheim, said in an interview: "We have only one product, the motorcar. Only with motorcars can you make such a high volume of sales. There's no other product in the world."[7] The car industry has been a single product industry, making more progress on the production side than on the product side. But its heady days of growth appear to be over, and it is now becoming a mature industry, which means it is thinking about survival strategies and boiling down individual makers into fewer but more powerful combinations.

Although the numbers of cars produced are expected to grow and grow, that doesn't necessarily make automobile production a growth industry. The cars they produce are around for many years and the older ones tend to go to Third World countries and satisfy the demand there. The fact that the world is constantly filling up with cars means that production *must* eventually stabilize or decrease even if the numbers on the roads increase.

If the industry—and its single product—were not so heavily subsidized, and if it did not concentrate so much on gadgetry, gimmickry, and the wasteful practice of coming out with new models each year, it might have a better chance to follow the logical product development which is indicated in the Siemens quote at the beginning of this chapter.

But the industry never did have a good record of responding to new ideas. Between 1912 and 1941 thousands of letters begged Ford engineers to put directional lights on the rear of the car to indicate when the driver was about to make a turn. Thirty years had to elapse before the engineers responded to such practical suggestions.[8] Already in the 1970s Lawrence J. White had characterized the American automobile industry as unresponsive to changing consumer preferences and technologically stagnant.[9]

If carmakers were to put their ears to the ground and listen to the coming ecological rumblings, they might concentrate on only two types of cars—a luxury model for those who insist on having such a thing, and a basic car for everyone else. This basic car might look to some aspects of the early Ford days when cars were just a means of transport, and you could have any color you wanted as long as it was black. A further evolution of the industry would produce some of the more radical designs discussed here.

Mr. von Kuenheim seemed to be saying that cars are where the money is. However, it may not be there much longer if those who make them insist on behaving like dinosaurs. The carmakers who have paid very little attention (or rather the wrong kind of

CARMAKERS, ENERGY EFFICIENCY, & THE ENVIRONMENT

A POTENTIAL CONTRIBUTION OF THE INDUSTRY

Technology	Benefits* (%)	
	Min	*Max*
• High-compression lean-burn spark-ignition engines	5	14
• High-speed compression-ignition engines	20	30
• Compression ignition with turbocharging and intercooling	25	40
• Electronic engine management	5	20
• Automated transmission	15	20
• Vehicle weight improvements	5	10
• Aerodynamic improvements	5	10
• Reduction of ancillary power requirements	5	8
• Improvements in tires and lubricants	3	5

*Relative to current design of spark-ignition engine vehicles.

B ACTUAL CONTRIBUTION OF THE INDUSTRY

- Addition of 50 million new vehicles each year, few of which are currently "state of the art" in energy/environmental terms.

- Inertia in developing new designs and technology because of perceived lack of commerical interest.

- Even when available, new technology will apply only to a percentage of new cars produced in first years.

- Because of existing "dirty" vehicles and continued production of some "dirty" cars, it will take at least one or two decades for clean vehicles to make major a impact on the world fleet.

83

attention) to their product may already have found out that cars are not where the money is. In the third quarter of 1990, General Motors reported a $2 billion loss, Chrysler lost over $200 million, and Ford's profit dropped by 79%.

Could it be that what has been called the "terrible triumph" of the motorcar is coming to an end? And if it is, is it really true that millions of American jobs will be lost if we take steps to reduce global warming and, consequently, car production as the president of the United States threatened in July 1990?

Must there always be a clash between economy and ecology or can we think of ways to restructure our economy in a more environment-friendly fashion? Should we not ask our leaders to look up the word "economy" in the dictionary? One of the meanings they will find there is "careful management of wealth, resources, etc; avoidance of waste by careful planning; thrift or thrifty use." How did we manage to stand that definition on its head?

SOLUTION 1
Radical redesign of the conventional car.

✧

Farewell! thou art too dear for my possessing.
Shakespeare, Sonnet 87

Our Dear Companion

It has been calculated that the solo driver-commuter in California spends ten times more for his transportation than the typical public mass transit commuter.[10] But that is not what the average American motorist thinks. His calculations are based on wishful thinking and, perhaps, a certain deliberate blindness. For him, the cost of fuel is only slightly more than the cost of a transport ticket.

The Hertz Corporation (whose calculations are not based on wishful thinking) has estimated that the average cost per mile for a new car in 1985 ranged from 54 cents for a subcompact to 83 cents for a standard car. The median round trip to work in the Los Angeles area is 29 miles, meaning that the solo commuter spends an average of $20 on his daily work journey, or something like $5000 a year for his daily trips to work, not even counting parking.

Commuters, who often do not know (or even want to know) their yearly car outlay, normally will not include their annual fixed costs (spread-out cost of purchase, depreciation, insurance, etc.) in calculating mileage costs, as they consider such fixed costs inevitable for a valued necessity. The Hertz calculation, on the other hand, included depreciation, insurance, license fees, interest, maintenance, and repairs, with the added assumption that the car would be sold at the end of five years and would travel 10,000 miles per year.[11]

A Swedish economist found that only one private car user out of six could estimate the costs of car use in a reasonably correct manner. Although the majority of the group investigated was astonished when the correct figures were presented to them, only one in six said that this information would influence his driving behavior in the future.[12]

According to figures from the British Automobile Association the annual running cost of a properly maintained car is £2985 at 1989 prices (about $5000). This includes the cost of the original purchase, spread out on an annual basis, but it excludes (like the Hertz figures) the cost of garaging and parking.[13]

Even such calculations, harsh as they may appear to be, do not yet include other costs, such as the time spent on car-related items. The radical philosopher, intellectual, and social critic Ivan Illich has given the following estimate of such time:

> The typical American male devotes more than 1600 hours a year to his car. He sits in it while it goes and while it is idling. He parks it and searches for it. He earns the money to put down on it and to meet the monthly installments. He works to pay for fuel, tolls, insurance, taxes, and traffic tickets. He spends four out of his sixteen waking hours on the road or gathering his resources for it. And this figure does not take into account the time consumed by other activities dictated by transport: time spent in hospitals, traffic courts, and garages; time spent watching automobile commercials or attending consumer education meetings to improve the quality of the next buy. The model American puts in 1600 hours to get 7500 miles; less than 5 miles per hour.[14]

Even this recital does not include all car-related costs. There is the matter of time (and its value in terms of money) lost in traffic congestion each year. These costs have been estimated in 1986–1987 for Europe as follows: Belgium (for commuters only) $425 million; France (motorways in the Paris area only) $1.2 billion; Holland (trunk/main roads) $500 million; West Germany (nationally) $8.5 billion; and Britain (nationally) $25 billion.[15]

Such numbers are obviously rough estimates, but to bring the billions down to earth, we might look at the British figure, which tells us that congestion costs work out roughly to $1000 (£620) yearly for every single vehicle in that country. In the United States, it has been estimated that travelers in each of the top 33 metropolitan areas have lost an average of $1 billion a year. The economic costs of congestion on 300,000 miles of primary highways have been calculated at about $150 billion annually.[16]

Whatever the real figures may be, here, as in other car-related matters, ignorance is bliss, and a refusal to confront the facts appears to keep motorists happy. Car insurers are now beginning to relate the cost of automobile insurance to the miles traveled, which is a way to call real costs to the motorist's attention. Families often calculate their food or entertainment budgets, and they would do well to calculate their transportation budget also. To determine the true cost of their car journeys, they would need to keep an accurate weekly mileage chart for each vehicle in their family and multiply each mile traveled by its real cost. Or they can install what is called by its designer an "in-car travel cost display meter," which is currently in the testing stage. This shows the *real* cost of each mile traveled and allows the driver to compare this with the *perceived* cost of the trip (normally only a quarter of the real costs).[17]

They may then find that the car is "too dear for their possessing" and opt for other solutions.

SOLUTION 2

Helping car owners become aware of the true costs of using their vehicles.

✧

A truth that's told with bad intent
Beats all the lies you can invent.
Blake, *America*

The Surgeon General's Warning

Today, when presidents are sold like soap, most advertisers tell the truth with bad intent, whether they sell products or places, ideas or ideals. The tiny fragment of the truth which suits their purpose—not a half truth nor even a quarter but, say, one sixty-fourth of a truth—is all they let us have. That, of course, is a better technique for them than an outright lie, because we recognize and often believe that tiny fragment of the truth.

In the United States, some $5 billion a year is spent on car advertising, more than the total spent on mass transit.[18] Because of this massive amount and because they deal with products which can be life destroyers, car advertisers, like their confreres in the cigarette and gun industries, have a special responsibility not to distort the truth.

In the best of cases, car ads can contain a lot of unconscious irony. When Porsche of North America tells us that "we all have a desire to create something that will show we were here," our impulse might be just to look out of the window for an unintended confirmation. Porsche and all the other carmakers won't let us forget for a minute that their products are on show everywhere. While it is just possible to imagine such copy being the result of a genuinely naive belief in the product, a more cynical approach is revealed by another car ad shown on the U.K. program "The Media Show" (which analyzes television advertising). This one made use of zen terminology telling the viewer that he was synchronized and one, in body/mind/spirit/nature, with his car. Here the advertiser exploits the modern public's yearning for a lost spirituality. Whatever adjective you may want to apply to cars, spiritual would surely not be among them.

Then there is the Mazda ad with its advice not "to let anything come between you and seventh heaven," a message which appears right in the middle of a magazine article on landscape deterioration brought about chiefly by cars. For the seventh

This car is now available with optional breezes, sunsets, and smell of morning dew.

heaven in town we have the Lancia Y10 which, after first having been designated by its makers as "the car of cities," is then endowed with a speed of 90 miles per hour, ideal for "escaping the city." While in the real world of cities there is rarely enough open street space to indulge safely in such speeds, there is in the seventh heaven of our advertising fraternity.

That fraternity is still addressing us as if our earth contained unlimited worlds to be conquered, with open roads on which you can leave the rest of the pack behind while you wend your way through verdant fields and shady woods. Though in real life you are more likely to see trucks, campers, house trailers, and cars of all descriptions through your windshield than woods and fields, advertisers have a very different vision of the world. As concepts like beauty, adventure, distance, and remoteness fade from the real world of nature, they are entering the world of advertisers, who only make us dream of a universe with a few cars—yours and mine.

In the advertising utopia there is rarely more than a single car. Except for the much higher speeds with which one may now quickly reach any destination, we are back on the empty roads of the 1920s. The good old open countryside days which are still being evoked by advertisers were described by an engineer and traffic planner, addressing still another conference on what to do about cars, by quoting a tourist's report from 1929:

89

. . . above all, the poetry of the journey, the fairy tale world of streets in distant parts and their wonders and adventures. The ideals which one encounters: a quiet path along a field, playing children in narrow village streets, blonde young girls nodding a greeting, distant castles on mountain tops, the evening sky in darkened valleys. . . .[19]

While advertisers usually deny the reality of congestion (there are, after all, still some open roads), they have a harder time denying pollution. But they try. An Audi advertisement of 1989 actually claimed that their catalytic converter would transform pollutants into harmless nitrogen, water, and carbon dioxide—the most dangerous greenhouse gas of them all.[20] And there was only a tiny fragment of the truth in the recent claim of a British oil company, in an ad liberally illustrated with trees, that their lead-free petrol was reducing damage to forests.

We have explored earlier the well-known association between sex and cars. Sociologists who study such matters have even found that the shrinkage of huge American cars to more moderate and sleeker lines in the 1970s paralleled the size reduction of bust lines in pinup fashions. Less obvious, however, are the inter-

Associating cigarettes with cars.

connections between what might be called the ABC cartel: Automobiles, Booze, and Cigarettes.

In France, where cigarette advertising has been banned in cinemas, a new film genre has made its appearance under the innocent guise of travel agencies. We are shown a hard-drinking, adventure-seeking male, driving a powerful car in some Third World country under the sponsorship of Marlboro or Peter Stuyvesant Travel. Often a car rallye through swamps and jungles will be sponsored by a product like Camel.

The agencies which design these ads are not content to simply glorify the name of their cigarette, but would like to make sure that we associate that cigarette with the masculine symbols of the car and the bottle, all coupled with the penetration and destruction of the jungle. The French government has finally put its foot down and is trying to restrict even disguised cigarette advertising. Perhaps the agencies will respond by simply showing a driver forcing his car through the jungle and let the conditioned response do the rest.

According to government sources, smoking in France causes 65,000 deaths per year, and alcohol 45,000 deaths. While car-related yearly deaths alone (around 10,000) are not up to these totals, an additional 50,000 people per year are handicapped for life, and another 200,000 are injured. When we put these figures together, we begin to understand the real casualty rate. There are thus surely logical grounds for restricting car advertisements, labeling them with warnings, or both.

In the United States, cigarette packs and advertisements carry a warning from the surgeon general, the highest doctor in the land, that this product may damage its user's health. Some other countries stipulate similar warnings. Car advertisements could contain comparable messages, such as "This product contributes to global warming and may cause health problems and serious injury." Such a warning would establish a connection between car use and unpleasant consequences which not all of us recognize yet.

But perhaps more effective than labeling would be simply restricting car advertising in the manner of a new French law passed in June 1990 (and effective as of January 1993) which sim-

91

ply bans tobacco and alcohol advertising from all media—radio, TV, newspapers, magazines, billboards, and metro posters—as well as banning the makers of such products from sponsorships of sport and cultural events.

Condemning the images created by the advertising agencies to stimulate consumption of their ABC products does not mean that we must be puritans or fanatics about such consumption. It is one thing to take a drink or a smoke after a hard day, or drive to visit a friend, and quite another to associate such actions with adventure, aggression, and risk, characteristics determined by advertisers to be masculine.

What Oscar Wilde said about war can easily apply to the images invented by these advertisers to glorify alcohol, cigarettes, and automobiles: "As long as war is regarded as wicked, it will always have its fascination. When it is looked upon as vulgar, it will cease to be popular." Until the time arrives when motoring is considered vulgar, it may be logical to make the automobile, which poses risks of death and injury not only to its users but to nondrivers and to unborn generations, the target of an advertising ban. That would allow us to take off our rose-tinted glasses and see the car in its true colors.

SOLUTION 3
Place restrictions or a total interdiction on car advertising.

7

CLOSING THE FLOODGATES: SOLUTIONS 4–10

Now that we are beginning to see cars in their true colors, let us see if we can't find ways to control or restrain them.

There have been attempts by cities all over the world to do just that in a great variety of ways, and we will have a look to see how well they have succeeded.

And while we are attempting to close the floodgates for cars, we'll see if we can also deal with the trucks and lorries, the race of giants.

They Curb Dogs, Don't They?

They do, or at least are supposed to, in the United States where curb signifies not only the sidewalk's edge (kerb of the pavement in England) but restraint. This means that people must restrict their dogs' dirty business to one specific area. Cities like New York manage to enforce reasonably strict adherence to this rule without worrying unduly whether they are interfering with the "freedom" of dog owners who, in the end, themselves comply with the rules without undue complaints.

Taking on car owners with equally tough restrictions on the ability of their vehicles to perform their own dirty business turns out to be a more daunting prospect for most cities. Some have tried and abandoned the effort, others do it sporadically, and a few have had the courage to impose their will on the car and have reaped the thanks not only of city dwellers but often of motorists themselves.

One of the earliest and most famous attempts to deal with the nuisance of cars in cities was made in England in 1963 by Colin Buchanan, who used the analogy of a hospital for his idea of dividing the city into areas:

> The basic principle is the simple one of circulation, and is illustrated by the familiar case of corridors and rooms. Within a large hospital, for example, there is a complex traffic problem. A great deal of movement is involved—patients . . . doctors, consultants, nurses . . . food, books, letters, medicines and appliances. . . . A good deal of this includes wheeled traffic. The principle on which it is all contrived is the creation of areas of environment (wards, operating theaters, consulting rooms, laboratories, kitchens, libraries, etc.) which are served by a corridor system for the primary distribution of traffic.[1]

But by comparing corridors to streets, Buchanan failed to draw the correct inference from his own analogy. Hospital corridors are not only conduits for wheeled traffic but also places where people meet and exchange conversation, or store extra file cabinets. It is more useful to think of the urban environment like an open-plan office, where the demarcation between room and corridor is often blurred and overlapping.

Following the Buchanan report, whose diagnosis of the problem—if not the solution—was widely accepted at the time, cities with the political will and enlightened leadership have developed a variety of ways to address our eleventh plague. Some have tried by raising parking fees or restricting parking places; others by something called traffic calming; some by creating pedestrian zones; others by road pricing or licensing fees; and some finally by simply sealing the city off and posting guards at all entrances (as was done in medieval times) to bar access to certain categories of vehicles.

Car bans, which have been tried (among other cities) in Athens, Santiago, Florence, Milan, Rome, and Bologna, risk the ire of car drivers who resemble the gentlemen in Walter de la Marc's "The Huntsmen":

> Three jolly gentlemen,
> In coats of red,
> Rode their horses
> Up to bed

in their desire to get as close as possible to the object of their journey. One way to prevent the jolly gentlemen from riding their horses up to bed is to rotate car access to the city center according to the number plate of the car; this method of restraint has been tried in Athens and Lagos on alternate weekdays, and in Caracas on a once-a-week basis. The Athens restriction, first introduced in September 1982, operates in the central area known as the *dactylios* and is based on odd/even differentiation. Vehicle entry is permitted on a given day according to the last digit of the license plate in such a way that each vehicle is banned on alternate days during the week, i.e., on March 13 only vehicles ending in 1, 3, 5, 7, and 9 can enter. Restrictions applied only to moving vehicles; those parked can stay there as long as they don't move. Although residents were included in the ban, they were later given a dispensation between the hours of 7:00 A.M. to 8:00 A.M. and 4:00 P.M. to 5:00 P.M.

The Athens scheme was introduced because of severe environmental problems and had as its objective the reduction of car traffic by half (i.e., the one out of two alternative plates). In fact, car use inside the dactylios decreased by only 22% because of special permits, rescheduling of journeys, and people buying second cars or obtaining alternate plates; and taxi use jumped by 26%. Nevertheless, vehicle hours initially dropped by over one-fifth, and the pollutant nitrogen dioxide was reduced by over one-third, followed by sulphur dioxide with reductions of about one-sixth. Unfortunately, steady growth of car ownership in the Athens area has erased some of the earlier benefits of the scheme.

Because Greece, which has no local car industry, now imposes a duty of up to 300% on imported vehicles, Athenians tend to keep their old and heavily polluting cars as long as they can, so the import tax has, for the time being, helped make the situation worse. In addition, the odd/even scheme in Greece encouraged a considerable amount of fraud, discriminated against the poor and honest, was instituted without an overall traffic and parking

NITROUS OXIDE EMISSIONS WORLDWIDE

N$_2$0 Concentration (parts per billion)

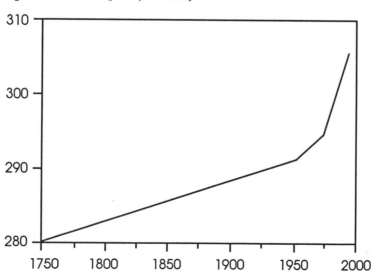

strategy, and did not consider the so-called boundary effect on the areas not covered. Altogether, that makes this particular scheme perhaps more an example of what not to do.

A multiple package of measures finally introduced in 1988 calls for the creation of a ring road, delimiting the central area; improvement of fuels and introduction of cleaner technology; control and inspection of vehicles; construction of two metro lines and extension of the trolley system; and application of varied working-hour schedules.[2]

In Lagos a similar odd/even restriction was introduced in 1977 in response to congestion where a ten- or fifteen-mile journey was taking between two and a half and three hours. The short term results of these restrictions in Lagos were encouraging, with people switching to car pooling and buses on banned days, but within a year the benefits had been lost and conditions returned to their pre-edict level. There were a number of reasons for the scheme's failure in Lagos: affluent families bought a second car; some households obtained two number plates; there was a sharp increase in company and government cars (which were exempt); and 70% of people interviewed thought it would be possible to overcome the restrictions by bribing traffic wardens.[3]

A similar scheme was introduced in Naples and was also unsuccessful because of abuse. In northern Italian cities, where people are perhaps less temperamental than in the south, car bans seem to operate more efficiently. Florence, a city of half a million, introduced traffic restrictions in 1988 for its central area. Only cars belonging to residents, visitors to hotels, delivery vehicles, buses, and taxis are permitted to drive through any one of the fifteen control points which are manned by a total of around thirty police. All other cars are banned between 7:30 A.M. and 6:30 P.M., and again from 9:20 P.M. to 1:00 A.M. Pollution levels have dropped by between 20% and 30% since the scheme's introduction.[4]

The Milan restricted zone was introduced in September 1985 and followed a referendum which supported gradual restriction of traffic in the central area. Unauthorized vehicles may not enter, travel within, or remain parked on the street in the area during the restricted hours (7:30 A.M. to 6:00 P.M.). The restrictions apply to all motor vehicles except the following: registered goods vehicles, buses, trams, taxis, emergency vehicles, motorcycles, cars owned by disabled drivers, by residents of the restricted area, by doctors, and by certain employers (e.g. hotels), and people who own or lease parking space in the area.

Approximately 48,000 permits had been issued in Milan as of March 1989 and about 100 police officers enforce the scheme. Figures provided by the Commune suggest that between March 1985 and May 1988 the number of cars entering the area between 7:00 A.M. and 1:00 P.M. fell from 58,000 to 32,000, but remained stable at other times, giving an overall reduction of car traffic throughout the day of about 20%. Since the effect on other than private cars was very limited, the overall traffic reduction amounted to just 10%.

In fact, to a casual observer who enters Milan, the effect of this ban seems to be nonexistent. Having gone to the trouble and expense of instituting the scheme, the city then watered it down to such an extent that at first glance it seems hardly worthwhile. Still, even a 10% reduction is an achievement and a beginning. Often it is better to start with a small objective, succeed, and then expand, than start out with a grandiose plan which comes to nothing.

And mild beginnings can establish precedents for stricter measures later. In 1990, for the third consecutive year, Milan's business district was closed altogether to cars and trucks on some weekends before Christmas. Shoppers used skateboards, horses, bicycles, or simply walked. Schemes vary in what is prohibited and where. In Bologna the resident permit allows a particular vehicle to drive through all the zones, but it can park only in the zone assigned to it; in Florence the permit generally limits both parking and access to the designated zone; in Rome the ban does not affect parking, only movement in the zone—in practice it is only enforced for vehicles entering the zone.

All the Italian schemes involve substantial administrative burdens: typically 50,000 permits are issued per city and enforcement is a major cost—typically 100 to 200 police officers are involved in checking violations at the cordon or inside the area.

These schemes also have the following points in common: in each case there was a ring road around which prohibited traffic could divert; and in each city the scheme had been subjected to a public referendum where the restrictions won majority support.[5]

The idea of a public referendum emphasizes a point which is now becoming something of a slogan in ecological circles: "Think globally, act locally." It is chiefly at the local government level where an individual can put global thinking into action. The majority—often the vast majority—of voters are not owner-drivers, and making the world safe for automobiles often goes against their own as well as the world's interests.

Lübeck is one of the first German cities to experiment with closing the entire city center to private motor traffic. This ban is in effect on Saturdays only and even so was far from uncontroversial in the city council. The mayor says that pragmatic reasons were mainly what convinced him to ban center-city traffic. "Vehicle emissions and vibration on roads, some of which date back to the Middle Ages, pose a serious threat to the historic building stock." Without denigrating the mayor's scheme, one is entitled to wonder whether the one car-free day per week is going to reduce that serious threat by an appreciable amount.[6]

Nonetheless, one car-free day may lead to more. After the initial Saturday, the mayor noted much less resistance from the traders who found their business pretty much as usual. As in almost all such cases, the shop owners who are initially opposed rally round to the scheme once it is in force, and in the end often find their business actually improved because of easier pedestrian access.

The attitude and turnover of shopkeepers before and after car restrictions has been studied extensively; but in spite of the growing evidence for generally positive effects of such restrictions upon them there is almost always much initial resistance. For example, the German Retailers Association holds firmly to the belief that shoppers with their families—unlike commuters—are seldom inclined to switch from cars to public transport even though in Hamburg three out of five shoppers do so, using buses and trains. Some Lübeck department stores give the carless shoppers an assist by allowing them to leave their purchases in the cloakroom for later pickup. Others are considering free shuttle service to periphery parking lots.

In this they are supported by Volvo chief executive Pehr G. Gyllenhammar who has said that "cities must not be choked by vehicular traffic." Gyllenhammar, who is far-sighted enough to cast around for ways in which his product can coexist peacefully with the rest of us, holds that free parking on the outskirts of town and frequent bus or train service to the center are necessary preconditions to any car-free city center.[7]

While park-and-ride systems on the outskirts protect city centers, they often put an enormous strain on suburban areas, which are saddled with oceans of parked cars. A Paris suburb which built fenced-in pay parking lots found that it had to abandon pay parking when cars flooded streets and fields in order to avoid the charge.

In spite of such unsocial behavior on the part of drivers, Munich town planner Bernhard Winkler, who helped devise the Bologna curbs, learned in that city that you mustn't vilify the motorcar; it simply doesn't work. In Bologna, as in Lübeck, traders who were initially dubious calmed down after the scheme was in operation. In the Bologna scheme, residents were limited to one car per family for city center use. Originally public transport was free, but now a small fare is charged. (Although the point has not been studied extensively, our guess is that some charge is likely to make people value their transport more than if it were entirely free.)

Interestingly, the Bologna traffic restraint policies are *progressive*, continually tightening up as public transport is improved. Thus it becomes ever more difficult to travel by car to the central area as more pedestrian streets are created, trolleybuses are introduced, and the twelve-kilometer long metro system is completed.[8] As a result of these restraint policies, cars using the city center declined from 160,000 to 35,000 per day, and a further decline to the level of 28,000 is anticipated. In Bologna, unlike in Milan, the casual visitor is immediately struck by the comparative absence of vehicular traffic.

As a result of the Bologna scheme Professor Winkler, who calculates that a car takes up fifty times as much space as a pedestrian, has had a great many callers from other cities interested in instituting similar schemes, though none as yet from his native Germany. Germany has gone a long way with traffic calming and integrating the car in its city centers as an invited guest, but total car bans there are still considered too radical.

Nevertheless, even mild measures like temporary citywide bans for specific occasions can turn out to be very important. The canceling of 100,000 on-street parking places by the mayor of Paris is said to have originated in the bicentenary celebrations of 1989 when the government enforced severe traffic restrictions in most of the city, demonstrating to the mayor and many others that a different way of life was possible.

Because of the potential importance of any kind of car ban as a measure to save motorists from themselves, we list such bans here as

SOLUTION 4
Carefully designed total, partial, or temporary car bans in city centers.

✧

101

> *Ne'er saw I, never felt, a calm so deep!*
> *The river glideth at his own sweet will:*
> *Dear God! the very houses seem asleep;*
> *And all that mighty heart is lying still!*

Wordsworth, *"Composed Upon Westminster*
Bridge, September 3, 1802"

Woonerfs and Traffic Calming

More than a century and a half was to elapse before anyone attempted to restore to cities the calm which Wordsworth had observed from Westminster Bridge. The idea of calming a street started in Holland about thirty years ago. After the third child had been run over in a residential neighborhood of Delft, and after the authorities refused to take action, local residents took matters into their own hands. They organized a night raid with picks and shovels to reconstruct their street in line with a new idea, the concept of a *Woonerf* (literally, a "living-yard"). When the authorities arrived with police and bulldozers to reconstruct the street, the residents stood their ground and protected their new layout.

After that event, the term Woonerf became a collective noun for a wide range of often very divergent solutions aimed at making a residential environment more agreeable and safer. Then, in 1976, the Woonerf was given a legal basis in the Netherlands; in 1988 traffic rules were legally amended to take account of Woonerfs, including some in new shopping, village, and city areas which were not principally residential in nature. Inevitably, some of the spontaneous, meek-shall-inherit-the-earth quality of people designing their own streets was lost when the government codified it into law. In some cases policy was applied blindly and without local participation.

The principle of a Woonerf is that a street is valuable public space and should be shared by all users. Thus streets may be altered to allow walkers, bicyclists, and leisure seekers to share the space with cars safely and without conflict. That means that street space should primarily be laid out for slow traffic. Conditions should be optimal for walking, playing, shopping, and so on. The motorist is only a guest. Or, to put it another way, the car is not the enemy; overspecialization of street space for car use only is.[9] The Dutch recognize that streets which bear a traffic burden of more than one hundred motorcars per hour are not suitable Woonerf candidates, which rules out routes with through traffic, trucks, or large buses.[10]

The limitation of driving speeds within the Woonerfs is often enforced by the provision of physical elements, sometimes called sleeping policemen. The Woonerf designers believe that you can regulate traffic conditions more effectively with the architecture of a street than with cops or traffic signals. Such architectural modifications concentrate on obliging a car to slow down. This means that a fast passage is to be obstructed in some way: by strips of different paving, width restrictions, speed bumps, single lanes of moving traffic, offset center lines, placement of trees, landscaping, benches, lamp posts, and the use of features already present such as a staggered line of house fronts. A Woonerf is thus a complete architectural concept, not just a couple of tubs and some white lines.

In the original concept, the entire street space was put at the disposal of pedestrians and was therefore not divided into carriageway/road and sidewalk. Research showed, however, that this posed a problem in some places, especially to the elderly and disabled, who now had the impression that the entire street was a carriageway. To get around this the Dutch suggested planting a row of trees rather than, for instance, the use of elevated sidewalks. The Dutch did not want to give up the idea of a one-level roadway which is there for all users, including, of course, the handicapped who thus avoid getting on and off a higher level. Woonerf users even include parked cars which also have their place in some of them. Such places are often distinctly marked or paved differently. Again physical obstacles like benches and flower tubs act as sleeping policemen to prevent illegal parkers.

In Germany the first generation of *Verkehrsberuhigung* (traffic calming)—using many of the same principles as the Woonerf—was initiated in 1976 by the state of North Rhine–Westphalia, which asked cities willing to participate in an experiment of traffic calming and *Wohnstrassen* (living streets) to nominate residential areas where this could be tried. Traffic calming uses such features as chicanes, rumble strips, speed brakes, traffic throttles, width restrictions, entry treatments, road closures, footway widening, and staggered parking. Since its origins in 1976, it has evolved from a revolutionary and utopian concept to become official policy in Germany.

As might be expected, the Federal Ministry of Transportation was the last to advocate the new direction for traffic in cities. Initiatives in Germany, as in most countries, are almost always taken at the local level. "Think globally, act locally" applies to traffic calming as well as to most other environmental issues.

In the North Rhine–Westphalia experiment the cities received guidelines and strong logistic support from a steering group, and citizen participation was encouraged by many public meetings. This first large experiment was universally recognized as a success. Its principal result was to realize a better partnership of all traffic participants and thus to achieve greater safety for pedestrians, especially children, the elderly, and the handicapped. The most important measurable effect was an increase in road safety. The total number of traffic injuries annually was reduced in the thirty participating areas by an average of 44%, and the number of serious or fatal injuries was reduced by well over half.[11]

A second generation of projects and approaches in larger city districts began in 1980, and this time was not restricted to residential areas but also extended to the reconstruction of major roads. Now, after a decade of small successes, a third generation of traffic calming in Germany focuses its efforts on cities as a whole. Programs for 30 km/h (18.5 mi/h) speed limit areas or *Tempo* zones, are not restricted to local areas but applied to entire cities, as seen in Aachen, Bonn, Bremen, Hamburg, Heidelberg, Kassel, Kiel, and many others. This is in spite of a conflicting German regulation that a Tempo 30 zone may not be longer than 1000 meters.[12]

In this new approach not only residential streets were to be rethought, but also collector roads, main streets, and through roads. To accomplish this, traffic development plans did not spring entirely from the head of a traffic planner but started to involve all those affected by the new measures—residents, businesses, public

Chicanes   Speed brakes

Road closure

Entry treatment   Traffic throttle

transport companies, bicyclists, and emergency services. In other words, traffic planning became democratic instead of being imposed from above, as had been the custom before.[13]

Areawide traffic calming has been carried out on an experimental basis in two large German cities, Berlin and Mainz. Berlin is (or was) one full step ahead of the rest and is now aiming to limit traffic speeds to less than 30 km/h in the subordinate road network of the areas chosen as models. To accomplish this, Berlin has made use of speed tables or speed brakes, which are created by narrowing the street width to 4 meters (13 feet) and laying a band 1.6 meters (5 feet) wide of a rougher paving and texture in the narrowed section.

These narrow speed tables make cars slow down and drive much more cautiously since there is only just enough room to pass each other; they leave room on each side for level bike paths; and they don't disturb ambulances the way speed bumps do because ambulances need not slow down to go through a brake, which is more of a psychological than a physical barrier.

Great importance in Berlin was attached to green areas. Tall trees were planted where streets were narrowed, along with sturdy shrubbery and robust grass on the edges; and grass was also used in between flagstones, suggesting a private and little used drive. The modifications were coordinated with the curator of monuments in order to maintain the historical character of the streets. "Dreary street gorges, tempting drivers to rush through them at dangerous speeds" have thus been transformed into "pleasant avenues which appear spacious and have enough room for numerous purposes."[14] Cars now drove at considerably slower speeds, with less braking and accelerating. One must always remember that cars are not mindless mechanical objects, but are driven by people who are subject to physical and psychological stimuli.

The Berlin traffic-calming experiment was interrupted by the fall of the Berlin Wall, an event which, though universally applauded, had an unforseen effect on this experiment. A West Berlin traffic police official declared, a few months after that event, that "we are on the verge of collapse." He and his East Berlin counterpart estimated that over one million additional cars had joined Berlin's carfleet in 1990. Before the wall's opening there were 700,000 cars in West Berlin. Both men said that the euphoria over the collapse of communism in East Germany had made it almost impossible to police the streets. The chaos in Berlin is such that German drivers, usually obedient, now regularly park on sidewalks or in bus lanes, and disregard traffic signals. "That little word 'freedom' has threatened to overthrow all our traffic rules," the official said.[15]

But when sweeping historical changes don't interfere, serious conflicts between road users such as those requiring sudden braking or evasive maneuvers occur much less frequently in a traffic-calmed street than otherwise. According to one analyst, the number of accidents in which persons were injured decreased by 60% on streets with traffic calming, and the cost of personal injuries and car damage decreased by more than half (from DM 4.6 million in 1982–1984 to DM 2.4 million in 1986–1988).[16]

If traffic calming is planned for major roads—and that is where most of the accidents and environmental problems are— the usual instruments for calming residential streets cannot be used. In Borgentreich, one of the German cities chosen for traffic calming experiments, a major road has been "reconstructed," a

word the very sound of which was shunned by traffic engineers until political intervention forced them to consider it. Initially the results of the Borgentreich reconstruction were mediocre: a carriageway width of 6.5 meters (about 3.5 car widths) remained for motor vehicles, plus broadened areas on curves. One-meter-wide paved side strips are supposed to lead drivers closer to the road center and give space for bicycle riders. Trees border the streets, and roads at city entrances are accentuated by different pavings and occasional tree-planted traffic islands. In spite of these features drivers still tended to enter the city at high speeds, as the average driving speed decreased only from 53.3 km/h to 47.7 km/h, with one out of six drivers going in excess of 60 km/h.

Borgentreich then continued its reconstruction and gave up the previous rule that two trucks should be able to pass one another on a major road, thus allowing that city to narrow the carriageway to 4.5 meters (not quite 15 feet) at some points. The incidents which were anticipated when carriageways were thus narrowed did not occur; waiting situations were resolved without traffic lights or yield signs. This was accomplished with a traffic volume of 6500 vehicles per day including 9% of truck traffic.

Now that traffic calming is accepted and practiced in many

parts of the world, one tends to forget the revolutionary change in thinking about traffic movement which it represents. Up to now traffic engineers had automatically thought that the solution to better traffic movement was to make a road wider with fewer obstacles. Traffic calming reversed that approach in suggesting the opposite, to make a road narrower with more obstacles.

That is not to say that traffic calming is the answer to the car plague in cities. Visitors to German schemes are usually shown prestige areas like the Agnes Viertel and Nippes in Cologne, rather than the miserable few plant tubs and chicanes in the Applerbeck suburb of Dortmund. Also, studies on the effects of traffic calming on surrounding areas—the so-called boundary effect—are still rare, so we can't be certain whether its effects on the whole city are benign.

One often-overlooked reason why Germany has been in the forefront of traffic calming is the cost of making the physical modifications; Germany is one country which, in addition to having the political will to do so, also has sufficient means to convert traffic calming ideas into facts. Traffic calming costs, according to experience gained in the model cities, are estimated to be as follows: for the first stage—30 km/h speed limits and temporary

measures—$0.35 per square meter (a little more than a square yard). For the second stage—partial reconstruction, trees etc.—$25 per square meter. For the third stage—total reconstruction as evidenced in Borgentreich—$100 to $200 per square meter. This last and very costly third-stage reconstruction is only necessary at certain points, often on major roads, where more than mere traffic calming is called for.[17]

In spite of all this traffic calming, Germany is a long way from condemning the car or even reducing motor vehicle use on a significant scale. But the discussions and trials on traffic calming for the last fifteen years have considerably modified the conception of motor vehicle use in that country. It is now seen more critically than during the 1960s, despite the fact that car ownership is still rising and the car is still Germany's "best-loved pet."[18]

At least German planners, and increasingly the population as a whole, are beginning to understand that their cities cannot be adapted to motor traffic without losing their identity—a point amply proved by many an American city. One could argue that even in Germany traffic-calmed areas represent only a tiny percentage of the total road network, but perhaps fifteen years is not a long time to rebuild a civilization based on the motorcar.

According to a book called *Cities Are Good for Us*, the greatest single failing of new, car-based civilizations is that "traffic has taken over city streets which used to be meeting places, and places where children could play."[19] There is no question that solid progress has been made to address that failure. David Engwicht, a member of an Australian group known as Citizens Advocating Responsible Transport (CART) describes his visit to Nuremberg as follows:

> On my trip I walked across a bridge which once carried 30,000 vehicles. Now up to 25,000 pedestrians use it every hour. Approaching this bridge I joined a crowd listening to some musicians. On the bridge itself were brightly colored market stalls. On the other side I was drawn into a side street by the laughter and shrieks of children. A little further up the street a number of people stood around a dramatic sculpture and fountain depicting the up and downs of married life. This roadway, which once roared with the sound of 30,000 vehicles now resounded with the sound of children, laughter, music, chatter, and the soothing murmur of water. The planner showing me around Nuremberg indicated a street which had just been converted to a mixed use street with a 20 km/h speed limit. Pointing to a sidewalk café surrounded by planter boxes of vibrant flowers and people chatting under brightly colored umbrellas he said: "See that? A year ago none of that was there. It is only after we calmed the traffic that the people and the flowers appeared. It was only then the people felt they could come out and enjoy their street again."[20]

That is a good beginning. And it seems now that the ever greater urgency of environmental concerns and the ever increasing awareness of the general public will achieve much more solid progress in the fifteen years to come.

SOLUTION 5
Traffic calming and street modification to give noncar users a greater share of street space.

✧

> *Expatiate free o'er all this mighty scene of man;*
> *A mighty maze! but not without a plan.*
>
> Alexander Pope, *An Essay on Man*

Dead Ends and Live Centers

We have now looked at outright car curbs and at traffic calming which uses street modification to slow down vehicles. But another way to keep unlimited numbers of cars from entering a city area is to divide the city into self-contained cells which make penetration by through traffic difficult. And a closely related and quite ingenious approach is to turn a neighborhood into a maze in which only local traffic can find its way.

London is fortunate to possess examples of both cells and mazes which were not put there deliberately by traffic planners but were leftovers from the great estate system that was chiefly responsible for the way London grew from the 16th century onwards. The English historian Gillian Bebbington has shown how what she calls the "pigheadedness" of landowners in the 16th century is strikingly visible on the map of London's West End. She explains how the ancient estate owners planned and built only for their own estate and demonstrates that there is an almost total lack of communication, for example, between adjacent Grosvenor and Berkeley lands, each of which were planned as self-centered estates. She goes on to complain that

> London is a maze of pointless cul-de-sacs, winding lanes, streets at oblique angles, and streets with a kink in the middle, which far outnumber the direct routes from A to B. Such has been the course of English history, that London never had the chance of other world cities of forming on a logical grid.[21]

In a book called *The Mews of London* the authors answer Bebbington's complaint by saying, so much the better! They point out that the "maze of pointless cul-de-sacs and winding lanes" is also London's great strength. They cite the example of a shopper emerging from Macy's in New York after having exhausted both cash and patience, being confronted by crowds, honking cars, and unrelenting traffic. The logical grid has made certain that every single street in New York is a through street, holding as much traffic as it can bear.

The same shopper emerging from Selfridges in London is in a more fortunate position. He can soon escape the crowds and traffic by ducking into one of London's thousands of quiet alleys, lanes, or mews. The cars avoid these lanes because they have no reason to use them; because, not leading anywhere, they are in fact "pointless."[22]

The five hundred-odd mews of London form a discreet, hidden, and almost secret network of narrow streets containing mostly two-story stable houses. They were placed there by the builders of the great London estates to attract persons of quality who would usually need the provision of adequate stabling. But the historical accident which deposited the mews in London's midst in such generous quantities has also provided early and quite stunning examples of what came to be called traffic cells and mazes, later to be superimposed quite deliberately on cities that had had the "chance " of forming on a logical grid.

The cell concept originated in Bremen and has since been taken up by Besançon, Copenhagen, and Groningen, among others. Vienna now treats the whole of its historic center as a cell which can be entered and left but not traversed. All cells have in common the interdiction to traverse them—a vehicle user has to exit onto a ring road and then reenter the desired cell.

Perhaps the best-documented cell system is the Göteborg, Sweden, scheme where the inner city is divided into five zones, with trams forming boundary lines in some cases. The zones are more or less sealed off to traffic wanting to pass from one to another. During the first few months of the scheme there was a 50% reduction of vehicle flows on some roads that were previously main routes through the central business district; and while there were corresponding increases of 25% on the ring routes, such traffic moved faster because of simplified flow patterns. After two years, accidents had dropped by 10% on ring roads and by 40% inside the cells, with fewer serious collisions.

113

The Delft, Holland, scheme is based on four traffic cells, with the cells being semipermeable. It is possible for local traffic to travel between adjacent cells (for instance, goods vehicles making deliveries) without going on lengthy detours, but through traffic is discouraged from entering the area. There are a number of bus gates, allowing public transport access from one cell to another, and a comprehensive cycle network connects all the cells and the central area.

A traffic maze is literally that: Any vehicle other than a local one will quickly lose itself in a series of one-way streets and cul-de-sacs from which a driver without a local map can rarely find an exit. London lends itself quite naturally to the maze system, and traffic planners there have cleverly enhanced the natural isolation of parts of London until there are very few major roads going from west to east or from north to south. Drivers on these few and usually heavily congested main roads trying to find shortcuts or rat runs to beat the congestion will usually end up losing more time in finding their way out of the maze than they would have lost by sticking with stop-and-go traffic.

Both cells and mazes are based on the concept that such areas are backwaters—in the best sense of that word—to be used only by the people who live and work there, and no one else. They are not an example of the architectural segregation we discussed earlier, since, in themselves, they contain or should contain the mixed uses which enhance any neighborhood. What they segregate is only the through traffic which has no business there in any case.

It is true that such a system places an added burden on the major and ring roads which must now carry a greater share of the traffic and that vehicles which cannot pass from one cell to another must go greater distances with somewhat greater resulting pollution. But it is also true that by concentrating through traffic on the major roads with the resultant congestion, some motorists will have been discouraged from taking their cars and will have switched to other means.

Is it better to let the floodtide of automobiles sweep over the whole city, even in somewhat diluted form, or create islands of calm and safety where people can go about their daily lives in comparative peace?

SOLUTION 6
Using cells and mazes to protect local areas from through traffic.

✧

She had very nice feet and plenty of money.
Daisy Ashford, *The Young Visitors*

A Zone of Your Own

The feet *and* the money would be useful in many modern European pedestrian zones.

When such zones work well, as they do in many cities like Hamburg and Munich, they are a marvelous improvement over traffic-choked streets. In Munich, center-city stores declined in the early 1960s, and the city council decided to revitalize the central district by making streets easier to walk around in. The Altstadt or Old City was redesigned primarily for pedestrians. Before the redesign, an estimated 70,000 people visited that area. Today it is said that 400,000 people go there each day.[23] In both Hamburg and Munich extended walking areas connect with public transport stops and stations and thus encourage walking and leaving the car at home.

If we look at these zones carefully, however, we find that they may not be the ultimate solution to the car problem that people often think they are. On being asked whether he approved of the extensive pedestrian zone which Montpellier's colorful mayor Georges Freche had created, the local representative of an organization called *Droits des Piétons* (Pedestrian Rights) replied:

115

I hardly ever go there. Since I don't drive, I need my bicycle to get there, but there are no bike paths in Montpellier, and the boulevards surrounding the zone are so charged with traffic that a bicyclist cannot safely venture upon them. Once you do get there, there is little to interest a walker except watching people peering into shop windows displaying items with high price tags. There is no special reason to traverse the zone, as one would just emerge onto the inner ring roads; some of the once ancient winding streets have been disfigured by modern storefronts; and in the evening parked cars and motorcycles invade the precinct. And when you do get to the central square, it is either filled with tables bearing pamphlets advertising some scheme of this same colorful mayor, or with demonstrators against him.[24]

This somewhat one-sided lament comes from a member of a generation for whom walking meant more than a means of locomotion from the underground parking garage to the nearest luxury shop.

The primary objectives of pedestrianization are safety and environmental improvements: to remove traffic from historic or central areas and main shopping streets in order to create a more pleasant and safer environment for people on foot. With the growing competition of out-of-town shopping centers, there is now even more of an incentive to do this.

West Germany has a strongly developed system of pedestrianization in its towns and cities, networks often five kilometers or more in length. The creation of such a zone is usually resisted by shopkeepers before implementation, but in fact trade often increases because of the improved shopping environment. In France, Rouen had one of the earliest pedestrian networks, followed by Colmar, Strasbourg, Aix-en-Provence, and Montpellier. In Britain, most towns over a certain size have introduced some degree of pedestrian priority, whether simply by pedestrianization of a main thoroughfare or a more extensive scheme. Among the more recent zones are those established in Leicester, Covent Garden–London, York, and Wolverhampton.

Although most of these pedestrian zones are a vast improvement over earlier car-choked city centers—the Montpellier cen-

tral square is, in spite of its critics, a very pleasant place to be in—
it is difficult to rid oneself of a suspicion that pedestrians are
treated like children by the city planner. They are given their
zone, where they can play. Having put pedestrians in their place
as it were, such paternalistic planners seem to be saying: We have
done all we can for you, now go ahead and enjoy yourselves. The
suspicion that transport planners still don't take people on foot
seriously is reinforced by a publication such as *The National Travel
Survey*, a yearly statistical compendium of all journeys made in
Great Britain. The journeys recorded there exclude all trips of
under one mile because "most of these are made on foot" and
presumably don't count.

Elsewhere in the transport literature it is grudgingly admitted
that "94% of all journeys" begin and end on foot. How the remaining 6% begin and end is not explained, and one is left to
wonder if they, by chance, were the three jolly gentlemen cited
earlier who rode their horses up to bed, or if they, like old Father
William, stood incessantly on their heads?

Transport officials, who presumably begin and end their own
journeys on foot, seem to be treating the pedestrian zone as a precious gift presented to the foot-powered minority, with the string
attached that these nonmotorized beings must now shop for luxury goods and sit in high-priced cafés to pay for the luxury of not
being hunted down by cars.

Perhaps cities should address themselves to walkers, rather
than pedestrians. Such persons usually want to cover some distance instead of going around in circles within a limited area.
Such persons want to explore odd corners and distant areas of a
city rather than stay in the reservation or ghetto which has been
neatly prepared for them. Finally we are back to the evils of
urban apartheid: an exclusive pedestrian zone, all dressed up
with no place for pedestrians to go, will initiate the rising rent
and gentrification cycle we have discussed earlier, so that true
walkers are driven from such a scene.

Ideally pedestrian zones should be connected to through
walkways and bicycle paths coming from and going to distant
corners of the city. Ring roads and parking lots must be kept as
far outside the city as possible, or they defeat their purpose by

117

drawing large numbers of cars into the center. What one might call the "chain-storization" and "boutiquization" of pedestrian zones is one of the trends currently working against these precincts. Such trends are plainly visible in most of them, from Leeds to Bologna, and from Nîmes to Modena. In this latter north Italian town, a recent two-hour walk through the beautifully restored inner city failed to turn up a single corner grocery, reasonably priced restaurant, sit-down café, or even snack bar.

A second, and equally alarming trend, perhaps also a legacy of such architectural segregation, is the tendency of certain zone sections to attract a particular social group to the exclusion of all others. A section of Les Halles, the modern mall which replaced the elegant art nouveau fruit and vegetable markets of old Paris, tends to be a focal point for a number of shady characters who feel quite at home there (perhaps attracted by the aesthetic pollution?) and who, by their menacing presence, exclude many ordinary strollers.

In the case of the K Street Mall in Sacramento, pedestrianization failed to attract suburban shoppers downtown as long as existing groups of teenagers and groups of elderly found the mall to be comfortable for hanging out. In 1982, after a decade of debate, merchants and planners agreed on a plan that sacrificed pedestrian improvements and the "undesirable" users they bring by restoring street traffic to K Street.[25] They thus began a process that in the United States is assuming rather alarming proportions:

> The latest panacea for downtown retailing is to bulldoze the pedestrian malls created 10 to 20 years ago and put cars and trucks back on the streets. Financially hard-pressed cities are committing between half a million and two million dollars to shorten or remove pedestrian features that were considered commercial successes when they were installed.[26]

The article which describes this new trend puts the failure of the inner-city malls down to suburban competition which, it holds, provides better access and more variety. On weekends, shoppers abandon the town center to the poorer inner-city residents, who don't find anything to buy there. Fresno, Tampa,

Miami Beach, Kalamazoo, Oak Park, Eugene, Norfolk, and Santa Cruz are among the American cities which have already modified or eliminated such areas, or are considering "retrofitting" them.

Bulldozing pedestrian malls is a panic move, caused by seeing too many vacancies in the former zone, vacancies which are not, incidentally, very frequent yet in the European zones. Neither paternalistic city fathers nor bulldozers can solve the social and demographic problems which lie behind the pedestrian-mall vacancies. It is a problem which needs patience and more study. A 1981 study investigating the effects of pedestrianization on traders in eighteen locations showed seventeen of them with beneficial effects on trade, and only one with negative effects. Two of the schemes which had positive economic effects were in the United States in Atchison, Kansas, and Pomona, California.[27]

For the moment, however, the problem of the pedestrian zone is complicated by the fact that such zones don't seem to cater to a true mix of shoppers. They either attract the tourist and carriage trade, or they fall on hard times and are taken over by venders of cheap stereo equipment, T-shirts, and souvenirs. This latter is true of Memphis, where the Mid-America Mall contains a retail mix which is somewhat sleazy and not upscale enough to attract tourists or suburban shoppers. Yet were the upscale shoppers to arrive, they would drive out the poorer inhabitants who live there and who must also shop there to make the zone lively.

Neither in Europe nor in America have we been able to work out a satisfactory mix for these zones. The Europeans have the advantage of possessing cities which are naturally walker-friendly—compact and interesting for someone on foot. In the United States the pedestrian zone is often grafted on a walker-unfriendly environment as a quick fix to stop the flight from city centers, and as a way to champion local businessmen.

Neither "pedestrian zone" nor "mall" are accurate designations for such areas. Pedestrian is a boring-sounding, latinate word, and zone suggests a restricted area with an uninviting function as in industrial zone. The American word mall is almost exclusively used for shopping areas. A term like "walk city" might be more appropriate.

The problem in all its complexity cannot simply be solved by running a two-mile trolley line through the mall, which the city of Memphis is now bravely planning to do. That is again a "construction" solution, a building-your-way-out-of-the-problem solution, though it is at least a move in the right direction.

The ideal role for public transport in pedestrian zones is to provide efficient access to the zone, and to provide a discrete means of circulating within it. In many cases, neither function has been resolved satisfactorily. In Portland, Oregon, almost three buses per minute on some roads produce noise levels of 75 decibels, and in Philadelphia's Chestnut Street, marked crossings had to be introduced to protect pedestrians from the 120 buses per hour. The Bavarian city of Würzburg is trying to solve that problem by equipping its trolleys with digital synthesizers which play tunes ranging from Beethoven to the Beatles to warn pedestrians of approaching trams.[28] In the days before digital synthesizers, an old-fashioned "ding" not only warned pedestrians but was background music for a lively city.

Although there are now pedestrian zones in almost all of the world's cities, a totally peaceful coexistence between people on foot and mechanical conveyances has so far eluded us. In the end we may have to apply the German citywide traffic calming approach to these foot precincts in order to get away from the concept of the reservation or the luxury shopping center.

Such an approach seems to have been taken by the French city of Bordeaux which in 1988–1989 instituted a policy to restrict car traffic on most of the old city's road network. The idea of the mayor and the energetic counselor in charge of the program is not to ban cars totally but to make it difficult for them to gain access to the area. This is accomplished by a combination of street modifications, speed limits, traffic light controls, and parking policy; residents are urged, for instance, to share their nighttime places with daytime shoppers.[29] The project's aim is not a one-time modification but an ongoing program, which is coordinated by a team consisting of an economist, an architect, an urbanist, a landscapist, a transport specialist, a traffic safety expert, and finally a psychologist to make sure the program sits well with the local people, whose own representatives do not seem to be included in the team as yet.

The ideal city would be designed for people—be they walkers, bicyclists, horse riders, or automobilists. In such a city all these groups would learn to live together without the evils that segregation brings in its wake. But until we get our true city mix, we may have to make do with pedestrian zones, with all their weaknesses, as being a more human environment than a traffic-choked city, where one single mode of transport dominates to the exclusion of all others. Perhaps we went awry, as Jane Jacobs has said, "by replacing, in effect, each horse on the crowded city street with half a dozen or so mechanical vehicles, instead of using each mechanical vehicle to replace half a dozen horses."[30]

For the users of those mechanical vehicles who complain that they don't have a zone of their own, a Green traffic specialist in London has suggested what he calls "car precincts." In these automobile zones car lovers could overtake each other to their heart's content, knock down plastic old ladies, hear the sweet music of an idling engine, take deep drafts of nitrogen oxides and hydrocarbons, and have accidents ranging from dented bumpers to the kind of *autos-da-fé* depicted in Godard's film *Weekend*.[31]

SOLUTION 7
The creation of mixed-use pedestrian zones.

✧

> *This England never did, nor never shall*
> *Lie at the proud foot of a conqueror.*
>
> Shakespeare, *King John*

The Conqueror

In spite of Shakespeare's noble sentiments, England lies today at the proud foot of a conqueror. There is an army of occupation on the streets of English cities more numerous and more powerful than any conquering forces in history. Soldiers of this army are at their posts morning, noon, and night, day in and day out, summer and winter, and year after year. If one soldier leaves his post, that one's place is immediately taken by another. And if the local people try to interfere with the occupiers' rights and privileges, they do so at the risk of their lives.

Up to a third of the average city's land area is taken up by its street system, and a large portion of that third is in turn occupied by these conquering battalions, standing guard in front of almost every building in the city. What shall we do with this army of occupation? Shall we "throw the rascals out"? Could we? Or would they then take their revenge on us by seeking their work, their pleasure, and their necessities outside our city? And, if we really managed to remove all the stationary tin soldiers, would the moving ones then exercise their passion for speed on the now empty and open streets?

Professor Winkler, the Munich planner responsible for the Bologna car restraint scheme, warned us not to vilify the motorcar. In the interest of all concerned, we must learn to live with this army of occupation until the tin soldiers themselves discover that they may be better off somewhere else. To help them to such a discovery, we must understand what parking is all about. Making parking free, easy, and plentiful encourages car traffic. Making parking expensive (that is, charging market prices for a space), difficult, and scarce, discourages car traffic. In our modern, car-dependent cities, either one of these policies contains risks, both for the cities and for the drivers themselves.

We have discussed earlier the devastation which a car-friendly infrastructure can wreak upon a city. But allowing un-

122

Paris street illustrating pay parking on both sides and bottleneck crosswalk treatment.

limited on-street parking also makes it difficult for the drivers themselves to circulate in their city. Such a policy removes, willy-nilly, over half of a city's street space from any other use, including that of the circulating cars themselves. The city becomes a giant garage. Many city streets which are not boulevards or major thoroughfares are just wide enough to accommodate about three cars side by side, thus allowing one line of parked cars on either side and a comfortable lane for moving vehicles. Any obstruction, like a car waiting to park, will effectively block the center (and only free) lane.

Such a street may be compared to a heart patient's clogged arteries which allow the blood to circulate through only a small portion of what should be an unobstructed pipeline. Any obstacle like a clot can block circulation with fatal results. With heart patients we use drugs or major surgery to clear the artery; on city streets we could begin by eliminating one line of parkers which would free that lane for deliveries, pickups, and emergency stops (with strict time limit enforcement); and it would also free it for

123

bicycles, hand-pushed trolleys (such as are still in use on Seventh Avenue in New York), and pedestrians overflowing the sidewalk. At the same time this lane would allow space for any temporary obstruction which would otherwise cause a "car arrest."

Much can be done to discourage parkers by painting lines and messages on the pavement, and while such lines aren't very pretty, they are certainly an improvement over the cars which would otherwise be there. Drivers do often respect lines indicating exactly the place they must occupy. Moreover, warning lines, like zigzags, are rarely violated. City authorities can entirely change the character of their streets merely by painting a row of four L- or T-shaped corners to assign vehicles to specific places. If they put the word "pay" next to those lines, the street will gain an open look even before machines dispensing park-and-pay tickets have been installed.

Eliminating one line of parkers on city streets is a first step with which motorists could learn to live. What happens, you might ask, to the cars which used to park there? Presumably the same thing that happened to the Central Park ducks in winter that Holden Caulfield wondered about in *Catcher in the Rye*.

To continue a proper strategy, the other side of the street would then have to be converted to metered parking. Surely we ought to apply to city streets (which weren't made to be parked in for nothing) the same principle Lewis Carroll applied to waxworks: "You ought to pay, you know. Waxworks weren't made to be looked at for nothing."

It is no doubt ironic that the motorcar, superstar of the capitalist system, expects to live rent-free, although a French group called "Auto Defense" (dedicated to the car above all) fails to see the irony. Their lawyers are diligently searching the Napoleonic code for obscure loopholes to prove that on-street parking should be free.

Opinions are divided on whether the sudden imposition of parking charges will make matters better or worse. On the one hand studies in Germany have shown that traders there tend to underestimate the role of transit-using, walking, and cycling customers and to overestimate the purchasing power of the car-bound shoppers.[32] On the other hand, a study of large parking increases in four city centers showed that the imposition of parking charges to restrain car use may have serious unwelcome side effects on commercial activity, diverting many shopping trips to suburban locations.[33]

Because the results of any parking policy are difficult to predict, the key to any parking policy is to put it into place gradually, thereby giving drivers a chance to make alternate arrangements, and to make sure that such alternate arrangements are available to them. In Paris, for example, 85,000 on-street parking spaces had been converted to pay status by 1990; by 1992 there will be 120,000 of them. And there is adequate public transport for those who want to leave their cars at home or even get rid of them altogether.

Ideally, both on- and off-street parking should be the subject of a comprehensive policy instead of a patchwork of conflicting interests. The city of Hamburg, for instance, has fixed the number of parked vehicles it can accept at 20,000. After that number has been provided for, the city spends its money and energy on outlying park-and-ride systems (often paid for by developers).

Nevertheless, there are limits to the effectiveness of measures restricting parking availability. There is, to start with, noncompliance with parking regulations. Then there is the pressure from residents for more parking places near their homes; such pressure leads city authorities to relax restrictions on total parking stock and often results in increased center circulation. The principle that city residents should be entitled to parking spaces is taken for granted by most local authorities and is even enforced by some of them. It is, however, debatable. People who choose to live in cities are generally much less car-dependent than suburbanites or country dwellers and should trade easy car access for the privilege of living in city centers.

In any case, most city authorities are only able to control a proportion of the parking stock; the rest is in private hands and experience shows that it tends to be used more intensively as city stock becomes scarcer. To address that problem, private parking operators might think about trying a new Swiss system called *Schur Park* which would benefit them and the city. In that system, parking spaces obey the law of supply and demand. A computer calculates how many spaces are available in a given lot or garage and varies the price of parking according to the spaces available. The fewer spaces available, the higher their price will be.[34] This application of free market principles to parking lots would discourage drivers from entering the city at heavily used times when they know prices would be higher. As city parking gets scarcer, the private places would go up in price, constituting the restraint mechanism over which the city authorities, without the cooperation of private-parking operators, can only exercise limited control.

To avoid traffic congestion and pollution caused by drivers cruising the streets to search for a parking place, new technologies called Parking Guidance and Information (PGI) systems are being developed by some cities in England, Germany, and Japan. Such systems incorporate roadside message signs announcing available spaces, a counting mechanism which keeps an up-to-the-minute record of all free spaces, and a control center which relays that information to the roadside message display units.[35] But the flaw of any PGI system is that by making it more efficient for drivers to find parking spaces, they encourage rather than discourage car use. Like "smart streets," automatic guidance, and many similar technologies, the basic assumption here is that people will take their cars, and that we must make it easy for them to do so.

Finally we must address a point often overlooked by authorities using parking scarcity as a traffic restraint measure. Such authorities may be inviting traffic rather than restraining it because through traffic in central areas tends to take up any capacity released by parking restraint. There are sections of central London where parking restraints, by the promise of faster movement, encourage vehicle traffic which has no business there. In London's case, that is well over a third of total traffic flow.

The city of Zurich, among the most environment-friendly cities in the world, has cleverly turned the tables on such through traffic by using cars parked side by side (in blocks of four) as an actual car restraint measure. Such a "parking block" is marked by painted lines at each end of a street, creating a one-lane bottleneck there which discourages through traffic, yet leaves the rest of the street open.

If we restrict center parking, we must provide adequate periphery parking and public transport to entice people into town without their personal transport. And at the same time we must abolish all center parking subsidies, such as free parking for executives, company and city employees, or apartment dwellers. It is instructive to note the experience in Canada when the government discontinued free parking in 1975, even though parking was still subsidized. As a result, single occupancy vehicle use dropped by 21%, while public transport, pools, and other means increased by 24%.[36]

In another study, 275 county and federal workers commuting to Los Angeles' Civic Center were compared. The federal employees paid for their parking while parking was free for county employees. In all other respects the two groups were equally matched. Use of cars with single occupants dropped by almost half for federal employees, while car pool use in the same group increased by two-thirds and public transport nearly tripled.[37]

A transport researcher in California bemoans what might be called forced parking subsidies in his native state. He was obliged to work in crowded conditions because the city refused his company permission to occupy a building with more space across the street. The reason for the refusal was lack of parking spaces. Their current parking lot was only two-thirds full, and our researcher, like others, cycled to work. To make the new building legal a huge hole had to be cut into one wall to create more unneeded parking spaces, which in the end remained empty when the company did occupy the building.[38] Along with the two-bedroom apartment which this researcher rented, the city forced two parking spaces on him which he did not want and which, by raising his rent, subsidized car users.

While permission may often be refused for the conversion of a house into flats on the grounds that there are insufficient parking spaces to accommodate increased demand, there is no restriction whatsoever on the house's existing occupants to create similar parking problems by the acquisition of additional vehicles. In an attempt to reverse this kind of Alice-in-Wonderland planning in which logic is stood on its head, John Whitelegg argues that cities, instead of requiring free parking spaces in commercial and residential developments, should on the contrary charge the developer a high rent for such places, an amount Whitelegg suggests as $5000 per space per year. This would force the developer to pass such costs on to the car user. Unfortunately, in practice, the developer would undoubtedly raise apartment rents and then offer "free" parking, just as supermarkets provide "free" parking and pass the cost of such spaces on to the customer in the form of higher prices, which even noncar users have to pay.

Nondrivers not only have to pay for parking lots, they have to look at them. Aside from the other evils the permanent army of occupation brings to the city under siege, cars are one of the major contributors to the aesthetic pollution we discussed earlier. So existing parking lots, which are not only eyesores but pedestrian stoppers, must be made more attractive. The first prize in a 1988 competition called "carscape" for Columbus, Indiana, envisioned a park, an urban plaza, patterned pavements, and pear trees which mark the season with white blossoms in the spring and orange leaves in the autumn. Such ideas have been tried in Europe, for instance in Zoetermeer, Netherlands, where parking areas are combined with playgrounds, and in Nice, France, where floral borders line the public car park.

To play the parking card most effectively, local authorities might consider the following simple rules: (1) Automobile users *only* should be made to pay for supermarket, office, and residential parking, at least within city limits. If there is to be privately subsidized parking, it must be heavily taxed by the city. (2) Parking regulations have to be strictly enforced or be self-policing wherever possible. (3) Parking policy has to be worked out between local authorities and private enterprise. That means that a proper balance has to be found for the optimum number of private places necessary to replace on-street parking, without providing so many subsidized or private spaces that excessive car use is encouraged. (4) Governments must withdraw or severely limit tax breaks for work-related parking. The World Resources

Institute suggests an equal tax-free travel allowance for all forms of transportation which would in fact favor public transport since an allowance for bus, metro, or pools would not begin to cover the much higher free market parking charges.[39] (5) Finally, the co-ordinated parking policy must be put in place gradually and must be progressively tightened to achieve its ultimate goal of decreasing the number of cars circulating in a city without losing the economic and cultural stimulus which car drivers bring to it.

SOLUTION 8
Using parking policy as an instrument to restrict car use in cities.

> My object all sublime
> I shall achieve in time
> To let the punishment fit the crime.
> W. S. Gilbert, *Mikado*

Punish or Perish

All the controls we have discussed here won't work unless there is reasonably strict enforcement. But at present the attitude most countries adopt toward traffic violators is lax and listless, which is due partly to the elevated status of the motorcar and partly to the cost of enforcement. A study of Pasadena's city budget for the years 1983–1985 showed that 40% of the budget allocated to police was automobile-related.[40] Usually there is neither enough money nor enough police to apply to traffic violations, even if the political will to do so were there. For these reasons any device which is self-policing and prevents the violation before it occurs, and any device which discourages infractions, is far better than setting in motion the cumbersome machinery of the law after the offense has been committed. Administrative simplicity should always be a major factor in determining any control policy.

What are the most commonly committed offenses? In a study on urban traffic regulations in the United Kingdom it was found that while virtually every driver breaks traffic regulations at some time or another, some regulations are much more highly respected than others. No Entry and No Right Turn signs were rarely violated, whereas most drivers admitted occasional speed and parking violations.[41] The public in this survey considered the No Entry and No Right Turn violations, along with stopping on a zig-zag line, the most serious of ten sample offenses shown them, suggesting that people violate most often the rules they themselves consider the least important. The fact that speed and parking regulations—the ones which do the most damage to nondrivers—were low on the scale of importance for most of the respondents would suggest that motorists worry chiefly about dangers to themselves, like driving the wrong way in a one-way street.

We hardly need a survey to prove what we see with our own eyes. Speed limits are routinely violated in all countries. In Germany, the 50 kilometers per hour limit in cities is exceeded by six out of ten drivers; and in an ironic illustration of the German penchant for speed, the East German government, even before economic or political union, raised the previously strictly enforced 100 km/h limit on that country's motorways to 130 km/h, in preparation for following West Germany's example of doing away with speed limits altogether.

(In another ironic footnote to history, East and West Germans, though politically in agreement, have been crashing into each other at record rates since the Berlin wall fell. The road toll for East Germans was 70% higher the year after the wall fell than the year before. The traffic police chief of Brandenburg—formerly DDR—has said that the Easterners suffer from a kind of "motorized inferiority complex" and want to outrace the Westerners.[42] The East German police in their old Wartburg cars, who cannot even catch the Eastern drivers in their powerful new Western makes, would be better off relying on self-policing devices.)

Effective self-policing devices to enforce speed controls are of two kinds. One kind modifies the car itself, the other the roads cars travel on. One way to modify the car is to install a speed governor which cuts the motor at speeds over certain limits or at least flashes warning signals when those limits are reached. Such governors exist and could be made mandatory for cars and trucks. But because sudden speed cutoffs may be dangerous in case of emergency maneuvers, adequate warnings and time delays would have to be given by such monitors before cutoff. In cities, cars should be limited to 30 km/h (18 miles per hour), with a combination of speed governors and calming techniques to ensure driver adherence. Experience suggests that once drivers have no more choice in the matter of speed, they will accept the 30 km/h city limit with little resistance and perhaps without even the need for speed cutoffs.

Until manufacturers abandon the practice of making their city cars capable of 90 mi/h there are many street modifications which can discourage drivers from using excessive speeds. We have discussed some of these in the section on traffic calming; much depends on making drivers realize that they have entered a speed limit zone. Signs alone are generally not enough to accomplish this; it takes special paving, well-designed arches and entrances, speed brakes, curves, trees, obstructions, road narrowings, bottlenecks, and physical barriers.

With illegal parkers, as with speeders, a penny spent on prevention is worth a pound of cure. Sidewalks used to be self-policing restraints, until cars discovered that they could jump them. So now some cities use bollards to prevent cars from parking on the sidewalk. These bollards are about 12 inches in diameter, 20 inches high, square, hexagonal, round, or rectangular in shape, and are usually made from cast cement. They are placed close enough together to prevent entry of a car. When placed in narrow streets in some of the older cities, bollards often lend a medieval castellated look to the street and are an attractive architectural feature. They are totally effective in streets narrower than two car lanes, as drivers, unable to park on the sidewalk, will not dare block moving traffic. Bollards are often placed at pedestrian crossings as well; if the roadbed at the crossing point has also been narrowed to one-and-a-half-car widths by extending the

131

Narrow street with bollards to keep the street clear
of parkers.

sidewalk, no driver is able to block such a crossing, and pedestrians are safer in having less road space to cross.

We have already seen how the city of Zurich places a block of two-by-two parked cars at the end of a street, thus creating a speed bottleneck and a narrow pedestrian crossing at no cost whatsoever, and even adding four parking spaces—not enough to attract masses of cars into the city, but a bone thrown to the hungry motorist. There are other self-policing measures against illegal parkers such as counterflow bus lanes or slightly sunken or elevated public transport lanes, which we will discuss in Chapter 10.

Because drivers are usually law-abiding citizens, more than half the respondents in our U.K. study were in favor of additional traffic regulations and stricter enforcement. The study suggested several factors that can lead to better compliance. First came self-policing measures, followed by clear and unambiguous sign posting. After that, respondents thought it important that the reasons for a regulation be self-evident, well understood, and have local support. Next, positive alternatives need to be offered such as recommended alternate routes or parking. And finally, enforcement needs to be conspicuous, so that road users realize regulations are taken seriously by the authorities. Unless the authorities punish, and punish effectively, their safety or car curb program will perish. Such effective punishment as towing away an offending vehicle—for example those parked in a bus lane or on zigzag lines—had strong support in the U.K. survey, whereas wheel clamps (the Denver Boot) were thought just to prolong the offense since the vehicle would remain there, perhaps for days, until the owner claimed it.

In many countries the police have neither the money, nor the time, nor even the inclination to punish driving offenses. The police like to maintain good relations with the public, and in spite of these survey results which suggest public support of stricter measures the public often sides with the drivers and against the police when they witness an enforcement action. A case in point which recently made newspaper headlines involved a woman shopper in midtown Manhattan who had left her car in an illegal spot for a few minutes. When she returned to her vehicle and found a truck about to tow it away, she broke into uncontrollable sobs. A crowd of hundreds soon gathered pleading her case with the police, who promptly arrested one of the pleaders. When the officers didn't relent, the crowd collected the considerable sum needed to release her automobile. For such reasons towing and other punitive functions may be more efficiently performed by private companies, who are immune to complaints and are eager to punish simply to reap the financial rewards.

A special category of offenders omitted from the U.K. survey cited above are drunken drivers. Some progress in enforcement against this most dangerous group of violators has been made in the United States, especially in response to public pressure by such groups as Mothers Against Drunk Driving (MADD).

Drunken drivers cost the United States an estimated $23 billion a year in property damage and lost productivity. They kill 23,500 people annually—half of all yearly accident fatalities—and thus cause more deaths than even guns (20,000) in a country where guns are readily available.

To make some inroads against this unnecessary slaughter, Aetna Life Insurance began a program in 1989 in partnership with MADD, in which video cameras were mounted on many police patrol cars in the Columbus, Ohio, area to film drivers right after they were stopped. A driver who shows up in court three months later all reasonable and contrite, in a three-piece suit, with kids, devoted wife, and mother in a wheelchair, now makes little impression on the jury. All videotaped drunken driving arrests that came to court in the participating county ended in guilty pleas before the case consumed costly court time.

In Iowa, voters have approved a new law that requires repeat drunken driving offenders to get new automobile license plates which carry special prefixes, alerting police to the driver's status. The law permits police to stop such cars at random. A six-to-three U.S. Supreme Court ruling upheld a sobriety checkpoint program in the State of Michigan and, by extension, in most other states.

The French are considering legislation to lower the permitted alcohol content per liter of blood from 0.8 grams to 0.5 grams to bring them in line with other European countries. This would be the equivalent of one aperitif or two glasses of wine with a meal. The average alcohol content per liter for drunken drivers involved in accidents in France has been 1.2 grams, or more than double the newly proposed restriction.

The lowering of the alcohol content may prevent some accidents, but for the moment it won't do much to change the fact that there are some 600,000 drunken French drivers out on the roads every day, of whom only 200 are apprehended. Here, too, the proverbial ounce of prevention would save much needless suffering. What can we do to prevent drinkers from becoming drivers?

The obvious answer would be to arrange a less car-dependent social life for ourselves, where parties and pubs can be walked to or are within reach of public transport. Is it really beyond our capacity to arrange the kind of life where we can drink a bottle with our friends and not have to worry about any consequences more serious than falling down and skinning a knee? But until we can do so, we must think of other measures to prevent people from holding a wheel in the hands which have just held a whiskey.

One such measure is the idea advanced by the Harvard Alcohol Project for what they call The Designated Driver Campaign. This is a campaign involving the media including no fewer than fifteen Hollywood studios, advertising agencies, MADD, and the National Council on Alcoholism and Drug Dependence. The idea of the designated driver is a simple one: a couple or group of friends selects one person to abstain from alcohol and to be responsible for driving. The others are free to drink or not as they choose. The Harvard Project is convinced that this positive approach is more effective than the negative "Don't drink and drive" command. The designated driver is chosen by a group and is therefore supported by that group. In addition the concept is easily communicated and diffused by the media. They point to a successful operation of such ideas in some Scandinavian countries. The project claims that over $100 million in prime time exposure during the 1988–1989 television season has made "designated driver" a household word in the United States.[43] In addition, they advise those who intend to drink at a gathering to plan their journey home in advance, either by public transport (if they are lucky enough to find it at that time of the night!) or by arranging sober transport by nonpartygoers in advance.

In a variation of the designated driver program, some youngsters sign a "contract" with their parents which will exempt teenagers from parental blame for staying out late at parties, provided one in each group stays sober for the drive home.

No doubt it is also possible to prevent many accidents by much stricter testing procedures for issuing driver's licenses, and periodic testing of driving ability. It is perhaps no exaggeration to say that half the people on our roads shouldn't be there, because their skills are not up to modern driving conditions. If half of all present driver violations could be prevented by tests, education and cleverly designed self-policing measures, and a further quarter could be rigorously punished—both attainable goals—that would leave us with only a quarter of the current infractions to deal with.

If, at the same time, we managed to lessen our dependence on cars, that remaining quarter would shrink to a nuisance we could live with.

SOLUTION 9
Formulate policies to prevent or punish infractions effectively.

Theirs was the giant race, before the flood. . . .
Dryden, "Epistle to Mr. Congreve"

The Race of Giants

So far we have been trying to get vehicles off the road and make city and countryside more environment-, walker-, and cycle-friendly. But to achieve this, the private car is not the only obstacle we have to overcome. We must also do something about giant trucks/lorries. Trucks pose something of a dilemma. We apparently need (or imagine we need) the myriad goods they bring to our doors. But while they fulfill this welcome function, their drivers have become a power to be reckoned with. In Alfred de Vigny's words about the army, they have become "a nation within a nation . . . one of the vices of our age."

In Chile they helped topple the government of Salvador Allende. In the United States the all-powerful truckers union defied even the popular Reagan administration when that government wanted to ban the "Bobtail 2000" tractor races. In Japan they are nicknamed "Tarmac Warriors" and organized into clans, with codes of honor, rites, symbols, and economic interests. Their jug-

Giant trucks blocking crowded city streets.

gernauts are covered with decorations of ancient temples, fire-breathing dragons, sea monsters, gem-encrusted Buddhas, and popular film stars. Thousands of little lamps light up the body work. Much of this, like the once-a-month nighttime tractor races, is strictly illegal, but the government is powerless to prevent it.

In France, the truckers have threatened to block the German border because the German government wants to impose a tax on heavy trucks for circulating on German roads, a tax the German truckers themselves can deduct from other taxes they pay to their government. In Hungary, truckers in 1990 blocked the border for three days until the government agreed to halve the projected 65% increase in the price of fuel, a measure which might have made alternate means of goods transport more attractive.

In such trials of strength between the trucking industry and national governments, it is far from certain that those governments will emerge victorious. Austria has had a running battle with international hauliers, eight thousand of whom use that country to avoid neighboring Switzerland, a nation which has courageously banned lorries over 28 tons. The Austrians want to ban heavy lorries on roads between the hours of 10:00 P.M. and 5:00 A.M.

In the early days of the European Community the trucking industry pushed European lorry limits up to monster size: 16 meters long (soon to be 16.5), 2.5 meters wide, and a gross weight of between 40 and 50 tons. The British lorries, for the time being, are restricted to "only" 38 tons, a circumstance which leads some traffic engineers to worry whether Britain can be competitive with the continentals, or whether it should allow trucks even longer than the 16.5 meters which will be permitted in 1992.[44]

Advocates of even more giant trucks have perhaps never stood on the Roman bridge of a medieval European town and watched what happens when these behemoths try to pass each other or negotiate a right-angle turn at the bridge's end. The walking paths on either side of one such narrow bridge in Sommières, near Montpellier, which contain throngs of pedestrians streaming to the open-air market in the town center, are less than a yard wide and broken in numerous places. The trucks race over such a bridge at the rate of one every three minutes on busy days and cause mile-long traffic jams and spread diesel fumes as they negotiate turns which were made for Roman chariots. Similar scenes are enacted in countless other towns and cities.

The surprising thing about the truck lobby's advocacy of weight and size extensions is that it appears to go counter to the industry's own interests. Delaying 40-ton vehicles in Britain for a further nine years is, in fact, no disaster for the haulage industry, because hauliers take the view that the lower the weight limits, the greater the number of journeys required, for which they can

INCREASE IN TRUCK TRAFFIC

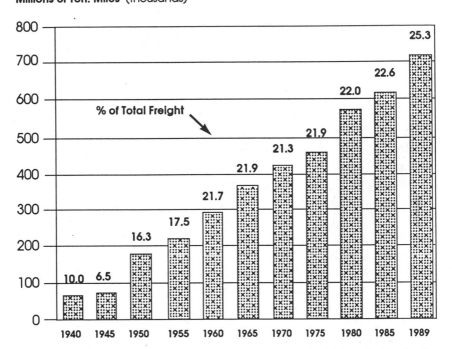

Millions of Ton. Miles (thousands)

The figures given here represent the percentage of total freight carried by trucks. Because this is expressed in ton/miles, heavy goods like sand and coal and oil which are usually carried by barges, rail, or pipeline, make the truck share appear to be lower than it actually is. Trucks usually carry lighter and bulkier goods, and this requires many *more trucks than would appear in a ton/mileage chart.*

presumably charge additional fees. Moreover, whenever weight limits rise, operating costs do as well.[45]

Whatever truckers conceive their interests to be, they will defend them truculently, and governments are afraid to lean very hard on this nation within a nation. A German researcher has estimated that lorries in his country pay only one-eighth of the costs they incur and this in a country where they are already more heavily taxed than elsewhere.[46] In France, the Pedestrian Rights Organization reports that trucks roar through villages in that country in spite of nighttime prohibitions, gladly paying the small fines which are, in any event, infrequently applied.

On British dual carriageways 87% of rigid vehicle drivers and 92% of articulated lorry drivers exceed speed limits. Some 20% of lorries fail the annual tests carried out under the Department of Transport's testing schemes, although the operators know in advance when the test is due and have time to prepare for it.

In the United States in 1986 there were 278,000 accidents nationwide involving trucks, an increase of 22% over 1982. Because trucks are bigger, it was nontruckers who bore the brunt of such accidents. If single vehicle accidents are eliminated, only 3% of heavy truck accident fatalities involved truckers themselves.[47]

In England, a 38-ton vehicle overloaded by 10% for a year will produce additional receipts of £10,000 (almost $20,000) and is fined a mere £160 when caught, which isn't often. And overloading persists even though it was shown in some areas of England that overloaded trucks there accounted for 60% of the road damage.[48]

If trucks have an incentive to overload, which they do routinely, they underload as well. The operators usually equip themselves with the largest vehicle that the law allows in order to be ready for any job. Once they have the big vehicles, they are obliged to use them even if the load is small.

The trucks therefore have it all their own way; they overload, underload, push for larger sizes, and in the meantime make more frequent trips with resultant diesel pollution and accidents in which they themselves don't suffer much.

Grim as all of this sounds, there are things we can do to lessen the menace of this giant race. Though in general the measures advocated in these pages are either self-policing or involve means of reorganization that correct the offending situation without resort to penalties, trucks have gone so far that we are obliged to be strict with them. The following is a list of suggestions to control the trucking menace:

- First, we can try to establish a dialogue with the truckers themselves to find out whether they really enjoy negotiating narrow turns with their huge articulated vehicles, spewing noise, diesel fumes, and confusion in all directions, in addition to destroying roads and historic houses along the way.

- Second, countries need to be firmer in their dealings with the haulage industry. Switzerland went the right way to ban lorries over 28 tons, a ban which should eventually be followed by other countries. The more frequent journeys necessitated by smaller vehicles can be compensated for by making them fully (though not over-) loaded.

- Third, we must institute stricter spot and weight checks and heavier penalties for speeding, overloading, and underloading. Technology already exists in which sensors, built into the road bed, pass weight and speed information to a roadside computer which in turn triggers a camera to record the license plate of the offending vehicle.[49]

- Fourth, a system in use in the United States could be copied more widely. This is the Intermodal (piggyback) Rail System which involves transporting loaded truck trailers or containers by rail for the portion of the trip for which a rail line exists. New York's Railmaster Intermodal Transportation System uses "bogies" (wheel units which fit on rails) onto which the entire trailer can be put without any loss of time over ordinary truck journeys. The trailer is picked up on the other end of the run by another truck cab, eliminating hundreds, and sometimes even thousands, of road haulage miles. When higher fuel taxes come into force or the price of oil goes up, such rail haulage may become (if it isn't already) more economical than straight runs.

- Fifth, city deliveries should be strictly separated from long-distance hauls, and should be made from small vehicles after the big loads have been broken down at the city's periphery. City deliveries, especially in pedestrian areas, should be effected before 10:00 A.M. and much more hand trolleying should be used (as is the case in Cologne). In the future, electric trolleys such as are used in train stations could make city deliveries from designated central points which would avoid the use of big trucks on most city streets. Small, electric flatbed vans are already being used for that purpose in St. Moritz, Switzerland.

141

- Finally, haulage distances must be shortened. In terms of tonnage, the quantities trucks haul have remained stable because when people get richer, they buy higher quality goods and services rather than quantities; and static populations do not generate the same needs for buildings and equipment that growing ones do. But because we have a motorway system and because permitted truck sizes get ever bigger, operators are more likely to take on long-distance runs.

The single market in Europe and the associated deregulation of lorries will bring about a 70% increase of ton/kilometers on the roads of Germany. This is partially due to the enormous profits to be made by industrial organizations and retailing businesses if production strategies concentrate on a small number of dispersed sites to reduce expensive inventory. Trucks then become the new warehouses, and the entire burden formerly carried by inventory is thrown on the transport system.

To correct this, a weight/distance tax has been proposed which would reduce the reliance on distant suppliers and increase the attractiveness of local suppliers. Perhaps an even better tax would be a weight/volume tax because the problem increasingly has to do less with weights than with the enormous volumes created by modern packaging methods. Because packaging gets ever bigger and more wasteful to attract the customer, a volume tax might discourage manufacturers from inefficient and wasteful packaging.

Increasing the cost of road transport would have the effect of obliging hauliers to make greater use of alternate modes, such as rail and water. In Portugal road haulage is discouraged by doubling the tax for trucks operating on routes competitive with rail services. A weight/volume/distance tax would force truckers to make shorter runs, consolidate their own loads, and share space with other truckers. The effect on industry would be to encourage greater reliance on local suppliers, and consumers would be forced to pay the full cost of truck transport. In all cases the net result would be fewer trucks on our roads.

We have not even mentioned the aesthetic pollution introduced into cities and countryside by these giant trucks, which would surely lose a beauty competition with the ships of the old nursery rhyme which were "all laden with pretty things for thee" and had "sails all of silk and masts of gold." If our present means of goods delivery is disagreeable, dirty, and dangerous, let's at least make it shorter, sweeter, and scarcer.

SOLUTION 10
Stricter regulation and higher taxation of trucks.

8

CHOOSING HUMAN POWER: SOLUTIONS 11–13

Now that we have considered curbs which physically restrain motor vehicles and curbs which discourage their drivers, we are ready to look at other ways those former drivers can use to get to where they are going. We will start with the cheapest, easiest, and most environment-friendly way to do this—putting one foot in front of the other. After that we consider another "innocent" means of getting around—the bicycle. And finally we'll see how we can give boots and bikes some routes of their own.

Where'er you walk, cool gales shall fan the glade,
Trees where you sit shall crowd into a shade:
Where'er you tread, the blushing flowers shall rise,
And all things flourish where you turn your eyes.

Alexander Pope, *Pastorals*

The Cobbler's Nags

It is something of a comedown to make the jump from Pope's idyllic walker to the pedestrian environment of the modern city.

The problems that face city walkers were tabulated in one recent English survey which brings the modern would-be walker down to earth. This sampling found the condition of sidewalks to be their most serious problem, with 46% citing cracked or uneven pavements; next came what was euphemistically called dog dirt with 42%. This was followed by 37% who complained about too much traffic, 32% about uncleared snow, ice, or leaves, 24% about vehicles on sidewalks, and 23% about inadequate pedestrian crossings.[1]

According to this English survey, it isn't much fun walking in many a city, though some give walkers protection from snow, ice, leaves, sun, and rain by the use of arcades and sheltered passages.

But what about the cool glades, the shady trees, and the blushing flowers? Well, while we pay lip service to the joys of walking, and while we all tell each other that, oh, we love to walk, we seem to have developed a distinctly negative attitude toward it nowadays. Like many another activity of modern life, we have managed to take walking out of its natural context and put it into a kind of package to be sold separately. So someone will think nothing of driving a car to the local health club, do an hour on a machine called a walker, and return home by car. He surely got his walk in that day, but instead of things "flourishing where he turned his eyes," his eyes are more likely to have been turned on other sweaty exercisers. Is it because there are no interesting things to look at on our potential walks that we must take our big riding machines to reach the walking machines? And are there no interesting things to look at because those riding ma-

145

chines have blocked the view and the space for the potential walkers?

Oh, we're still walking, even today, but most modern walks are car-connected or car-engendered. According to Ivan Illich, modern Americans walk as much as their ancestors, but most of it now is through tunnels, corridors, parking lots, and stores. There doesn't seem much point in trudging along a dreary street gorge when the same journey can be accomplished so much faster and in so much greater comfort by car.[2]

We now walk only where we cannot get close enough with our vehicles, or where walking is a recognized activity, like a Sunday hike by a group of ramblers. This is in consequence of what our friend John Whitelegg calls the "car's parasitic pollution of space, time, culture and mind."[3] The knowledge of having a means at hand which can cover a distance quickly and with ease "spoils" any other form of locomotion because it makes such a form unnecessary, save for exercise or in circumstances where such a means is faster or easier than driving.

Surveys from Germany, a country which has been called "a republic on wheels"[4] have shown that people there are not entirely ignorant of the car problem. A great majority of its citizens are now finding traffic conditions and environmental damage related to cars increasingly intolerable. But are these same people walking or cycling? No, quite the contrary. Statistics in that country show that the cars which those honest burghers buy and use are ever growing in number and size and power. There is evidently a big chasm between the perception and the will to do something about it.

The reason that attitudes towards walking are so very important is that fully one out of three car trips in Germany is under two miles in length, and many of them could therefore have been walked or cycled.[5] In France such short journeys constitute an even higher percentage, almost half of all car trips undertaken.[6] Beyond all statistical, sociological, and philosophical analyses, dare one accuse modern folk of being just plain old lazy?

Analysts divide modern city walkers into three groups: the brisk walkers, who just want to get where they are going; the loiterers, who have no goal and just want to kill time; and the largest group, the meanderers, who have a goal but take time out to look at interesting things along the way.[7]

To get people back on their legs for journeys less than ten or fifteen minutes of walking time, all three groups must be given incentives, shortcuts, interesting things to look at, cafés to loiter in. And we must stop calculating the time advantage gained by driving. We must look upon walking as an independent means of locomotion, and a very special one at that. Put into the colorless language of transport specialists, walking "incurs by far the lowest expenditure; provision for it is very cheap, and capital and running costs are very low. Its efficiency is very high, environmental impact negligible, and use of fuels zero."[8] Voilà. While that doesn't exactly inspire us to go for a day's walk the way Pope's lines might do, it may be the best we can do in the 1990s.

In earlier times, boot-enclosed feet were sometimes called the pony's shanks in England, or *Schusters Rappen* (cobbler's nags) in Germany. When people said you had to make do with the cobbler's nags, it meant you couldn't afford fancier transport, implying that such transport (even then) would have been better, had you only been richer. In the old German tales, the cobbler's nags were often used to refer to the mode of travel used by artisan apprentices going on their *Wanderjahre* to seek a master or to establish themselves in their trade. Not being able to afford a post chaise, it could easily take them months or years to get where they were going, if indeed they had a precise goal; more often they would let their boot-enclosed feet carry them where they might.

On the way they would see sights they could not see from the seat of a post chaise. They would notice every flower in a hedgerow, every rabbit crossing their path; they would see strange old men with long white beards; they would encounter good-natured women who gave them bread, cheese, and wine; and they would be cheered on their way by the pretty girls at the village fountain. These were often the happiest and most memorable years of their lives, years they would have missed had they been able to afford a carriage, with its own, albeit very mild, form of parasitic pollution.

Later, the tradition established by these early wanderers was

147

carried on by artists, writers, poets, and musicians, from Goethe and Mendelssohn to Rilke, D. H. Lawrence, and Simone de Beauvoir. All of them made foot journeys through Italy, Spain, and the south of France. They, who could have afforded a fancier means of transport, chose their feet to get to know the world intimately, which you can do much less well from the seat of a carriage.

Walking may be an activity slow to yield immediate satisfaction and must therefore be entered into quite thoroughly before its full benefits can be realized. Putting one foot in front of another for a period of time produces a rhythm, and one ends up marching to one's own inner drum which can go a long way to sustain a walker. But people who walk also need to see and meet interesting things along the way, and it is just there where the modern world fails them.

In some cities and in some wildernesses the walker now has, like the American Indian, a few reservations. But in the countryside, there where the artists and artisans used to wander, the modern walker has to make do with the shoulder of the paved road—if there *is* such a shoulder, and if it isn't being used by bicycles. There is nothing more dispiriting than to see a forlorn walker brave oncoming traffic, danger, and pollution.

So fares the walker in the three "necessary" environments (city, country, and wilderness) which we discussed earlier. In the fourth, the suburban, walkers have for the time being nothing much to look at and risk being confronted by uncrossable intersections. As long as we cannot do more for them, they too will become an endangered species. To keep that from happening, we must begin to calm country roads as well as city streets to make them more walker-friendly.

In the older countries of the world, villages were often spaced out according to a walker's scale, one hour's stroll from each other (or five minutes by the space-and-time-eating car). We can take our cue from such foot-scale distances and locate our new towns and communities an hour's walk from each other, and our city attractions within a fifteen- or twenty-minute stroll, hopefully with shady trees and blushing flower-bordered walks between them. In such ways—admittedly utopian for the moment—we may help to bring walking back to city and country as an actual means of transport instead of a leisure-time activity.

SOLUTION 11
Make cities, suburbs, and countrysides more walker-friendly.

✧

The wheel is come full circle.
Shakespeare, *King Lear*

The Virtuous Cycle

After the many vicious cycles connected with motorcars, it comes as a relief to talk about a virtuous cycle. How truly virtuous that cycle can be is spelled out by a 1980 Chicago area transportation study which found improved bicycle access to public transport to be the most cost-effective way to reduce auto emissions. In this study it was found that bike-and-ride access would cut hydrocarbon emissions at a public cost of only $300 per ton, compared with almost $4000 per ton for a commuter rail-car pool, close to $100,000 for express park-ride service, and over $200,000 for a feeder bus service.[9] In Japan and Holland cycle parks around train stations and public transport stops allow people from outlying areas carless access to city centers and make the bicycle in those countries an important means of transport.

The bicycle is efficient, nonpolluting, healthy, environment- and user-friendly. As a way of getting around, it is also in most countries considered marginal and unimportant, and few places bother to collect transportation data that count bicycles as transport means.[10] In spite of official disdain or indifference, the two-wheeler is alive and well in many parts of the world. But to do anything concrete about the dominance of motorcars, bicycles

The bicyle is efficient, nonpolluting, healthy, environment-
and user-friendly.

must become more than a pastime for children and a leisure sport
for adults. They must take their rightful, practical place alongside
cars, public transport, and walking, as a legitimate means of getting around.

For many Third World countries bicycles are as important as
cars are for us. In the Western countries it is often supposed that
bicycle use thrives only in flat terrain and temperate climates.
However, as many studies show, an enlightened public policy is
much more important as an element of success. Not merely important, but perhaps even critical. Cyclists in southern European
countries for instance enjoy little official support and are therefore fewer in number, in spite of clearer skies, than their confreres
in colder and rainier climates but warmer official attitudes.

When officials do their best to further bicycle use, such transport thrives. In Groningen, Holland, a city of more than average income and car ownership, fully half of all daily journeys are made by people on bicycles. In Erlangen, Germany, where the mayor rides his bike to work, a quarter of all commuting trips are made on bicycles, and the same percentage holds for Tokyo and parts of Denmark.

In London, on the other hand, capital of a country which was once known for its bicycle friendliness, only 2% of today's daily trips are made by that means of transport.[11] In the bicycle-oriented university town of Cambridge, England, which has bicycle paths and a bike bridge over the railway, the county council is even considering a bicycle *ban* on three main shopping streets between 10:00 A.M. and 4:00 P.M. But interestingly enough, this is to improve the environment for pedestrians; cars are to be banned during the same period. Cyclists claim that badly parked goods vehicles force them to use footpaths, hence the pedestrian-cyclist conflict responsible for the ban.

From a pedestrian point of view, a bicycle ban can be quite understandable and perhaps even desirable. We have already seen how the scorchers scattered and terrified pedestrians in the 1890s; today's equivalent are mountain bikers, who invade wilderness trails and threaten hikers to such a degree that California State Park employees do not remove fallen logs over trails just to discourage those modern scorchers. Many wilderness trails have been closed to mountain bikers who often disregard such closures. (It is interesting to note that Lord Acton's maxim about power corrupting applies not only to politicians and motorists, but to any group more powerful than another, as are mountain bikers vis-à-vis mere hikers.)

But Groningen, the largest city in northern Netherlands, and the Dutch government behind it, is not thinking along those lines. That city makes every effort to encourage bike use by working in close cooperation with cycling and public interest groups, and by providing cycle routes, bicycle-friendly travel planning, and bike parking. There are eighty covered and guarded stations to park some 90,000 cycles in Holland, a powerful inducement to encourage bicycle use in getting to trains and public transport stops.

Dutch cyclists now have at their disposal something on the order of 13,500 km (8500 miles) of cycle paths, many of which are directly connected, giving riders uninterrupted access to reach their destinations. Cycle-path planning in Holland is thus viewed in its entirety rather than, as in many countries, a bits and pieces strategy.

Such piecemeal planning all too often produces scenic bike routes which start and end nowhere and are used only for leisure cycling. And sometimes you even need your car to get there. The cycle paths in Holland cover over 12% of that country's road system, and following that example countries like France and Germany should have 30,000 miles of bike paths each, and the United States 450,000 miles. You are invited to guess whether even one-tenth of that figure has been provided in those countries.

As long as officials consider cyclists (along with pedestrians) marginal, it has to be up to individuals, groups, and societies to see to it that this underused means of transport regains the respect it once had, before it was overshadowed by its motorized big brother. What will it take to realize the bike's potential and regain some of its lost eminence? To gauge the bicycle's chance of making a major comeback as a means of daily transport, let us for a moment leave bicycle-friendly societies like Holland and Denmark, and consider the extreme opposite—car-friendly California.

Most of the advances the bicycle has made in the San Francisco Bay Area have been due to the actions of individuals and small groups of enthusiasts. In 1974, after the Bay Area Rapid Transit System (BART) had been built, bicycle activists made a major effort to talk BART into allowing bicycles on its trains. They more or less achieved their objective, within some limits.[12] Today bicycles are permitted on BART trains in reverse commute direction during rush hour, and in all directions at other times. The bikes are transported free of charge in the last car of a train. Buses on some routes in the Bay Area are now equipped with bike racks (in front) which accommodate two bicycles, and such cycle transport may be extended to other routes in the future, again in response to pressure from cyclists. Ferries, some of which owe their very existence to the last major earthquake, usually take bicycles unless they are full.

Of the eight bridges in the Bay Area, only two have unlimited bicycle and pedestrian access, while a third (the Golden Gate) has restricted hours. On some other bridges the California Department of Transportation (Caltrans) operates a free shuttle van which can be called from telephones at either end of the bridge. Because the Bay Area is crisscrossed by wide bodies of water, bridge access is absolutely essential for work-related trips.

Caltrans has finally realized that in the 1990s it must become a true department of transportation rather than a department of highways, a step which has yet to be taken by most other local authorities. In the past, Caltrans had not bothered to apply for a $4.5 million federal aid highway fund for bicycle projects, but a recent vote which focused the attention of Californians on clean air and the environment changed that attitude.

A survey of cyclists made by the Metropolitan Transportation Commission in Berkeley, California, gives some idea how such funds should be spent, and on what type of campaigns. The survey suggested that local authorities should:

> require deposits on bottles (to avoid broken glass on roads); allow bicycle access on freeways and bridges; set standards of bikeway construction and maintenance; include bicycle safety in driver-license examinations; include bicyclist and motorist education in school curriculums; allow tax credits for bicycle commuters; eliminate free parking for commuting motorists; and provide reasonable insurance for bike theft and accidents.[13]

In the same survey cyclists were asked what they considered high priority projects to encourage bicycle rather than car use for transportation. The highest priority was given to continuous bike travel and the elimination of specific barriers such as bridges, rail crossings, and dangerously narrow roadways. Next came bike lanes, bike paths, the sweeping of such paths, and clear route markings in urban and suburban areas. This was followed by bicycle parking facilities at employment and shopping centers, and transit terminals. Lesser orders of priority were provision for carrying bicycles on transit vehicles, information on existing bikeways and route maps, education programs for cyclists and motorists, and bicycle-trained law enforcement officers.

The responses in such surveys are not just wishful thinking. The ever-growing cycle movement in California is making its weight felt. For example the eighteen-year-long struggle to allow bicyclists on expressways may soon be won, though one might well wonder about the pleasures of cycling on an expressway. There has also been much argument whether to allow cyclists to ride on bridge and road shoulders normally reserved for incapacitated vehicles. Here, too, highway officials are slowly being prodded into recognizing the bicycle as a possible alternative to the car rather than an unwanted obstacle to traffic.

Such surveys make clear what it is that cyclists want in order to take to the road in large numbers. Most of the items Californians requested have already been achieved in bicycle-friendly societies. Such societies include the bicycle in all their transport planning. Moreover, they keep accurate statistics on bicycle use (frequency of use, accidents, theft, and other problems), encourage and develop a bicycle constituency (bike clubs, transport groups, school and business associations), and monitor, modify, and expand their programs to further bicycle use.

Communities without such programs have not understood that "each time a driver makes a trip by bicycle instead of by automobile, not only the cyclist but society as a whole reaps the benefits."[14] On today's congested roads, bicycles provide not only mobility, they provide access, which is something their big, noisy, smoking, four-wheeled relatives do not always manage.

SOLUTION 12
Making bicycle use more appealing by creating a bicycle-friendly infrastructure.

✦

Humpty-Dumpty sat on a wall
Humpty-Dumpty had a great fall.
All the king's horses and all the king's men
Couldn't put Humpty together again.

Putting Humpty Together Again

Many of the world's road systems, often built years and years ago, have fallen into disrepair, and it seems beyond anyone's power to put them together again. Such is certainly the case in the United States, where the government concentrated for decades on building a mighty road system without giving much thought to how such a network was going to be repaired and maintained. As a result, America's road and bridge infrastructure is slowly falling apart. Today almost half of U.S. highway bridges need replacing, and many bridges have half their width closed for fear of excessive strains. There are surely as many potholes in the U.S. road network as there are stars in the sky. Nay, some would say, more!

Since our economy is so arranged that money and facilities can always be found to make something new and repair is somehow not economically viable, the potholes remain, furnishing comedians with material for their jokes. What can we do about this?

We have three options: We can build new roads or freeways to replace the old, which is usually the preferred option in a culture where the hope for the future resides in the young, the new, and the shiny. We can repair the existing roads if we can find the will and the means to do so. Or we can choose a third option which is rarely considered: Close some of them altogether to motorized traffic.

Many studies have demonstrated that new roads create new traffic. But much less work has been done to show the obverse: how the closing of existing roads can possibly eliminate existing traffic. Still, we have a few examples of such processes. Many years ago Jane Jacobs told the story of how, in the 1950s, the residents of Greenwich Village in New York were threatened with a plan to build a highway through Washington Square Park to replace the small local streets which were handling traffic flows.

155

The park commissioner at the time, Robert Moses, had the rather un-parklike idea of putting a major traffic artery through the center of the elegant square so beloved by Henry James. Instead, the residents managed, after a protracted political battle (in which this author participated), to have even the existing road closed. The chaos that was to result on the surrounding streets, as predicted by the traffic engineers, never materialized. But there was a rather unforseen result: traffic not only didn't increase but actually diminished. Every traffic count taken around the park perimeter, and lower Fifth Avenue which led to it, showed a slight reduction. Nor was there any sign that traffic went on more distant alternate roads. Traffic had simply *disappeared.*[15]

Some decades later, on the other side of the ocean, the Greens, who held the balance of power in Nuremberg in 1989, forced the closing of the last road carrying through traffic in their city's central district. Again there were predictions of chaos. And again the traffic simply disappeared. Like the rain of the nursery rhyme, it had gone away, but unlike the rain, it had not come another day.[16]

Similarly, one of seven bridges in Munich was closed to traffic while repairs were going on. There was an outcry by motorists, but the city authorities cleverly took no notice. When the uproar died down, the authorities decided never to open the seventh bridge to motorized traffic again although they wisely didn't publicize their decision. In the end, the closure of the seventh bridge was accepted and helped to make that city a haven for pedestrians.[17]

When engineers and city planners look at traffic, they often regard it as a river, a fixed quantity which comes rushing by, do what you may. It's a problem of hydraulics: You can dam it or divert it, but you can't stop it. But traffic is not such a river. It is nothing but a lot of individuals who have decided to go somewhere with their chosen means of transport. If roads are too narrow, if parking is too scarce, if traffic moves too slowly, or if the road is closed altogether—well, they will reconsider their decision to go somewhere or use an alternative means of transport. And the rushing river suddenly becomes a trickle.

So that means that in some of our communities we could exercise our third option. Instead of building new roads or even repairing the existing ones, we could simply close the potholed road to motorized traffic and turn it over to hikers and bikers. Such users can make do with gravel-filled potholes, since their feet and slender wheels put so much less strain on the road surface than the cars and trucks before them.

Is this a viable option? Well, it is certainly a cheap one for the local authority. One could even consider potholes a poor man's traffic calming. And if you present drivers with a fait accompli, there is little they can do about it except to grumble and take the nearest available replacement. Or perhaps take to the cobbler's nags or the virtuous cycle themselves?

The roads we didn't build, and the traffic we discouraged by putting Humpty together again only lightly (without the investment of all the king's men), will make its small contribution toward global cooling. And nonmotorized transport will have an artery of its own.

SOLUTION 13
Close damaged roads to motor vehicles and turn them over to nonmotorized transport.

9

FIGHTING FIRE WITH ICE:
SOLUTIONS 14–17

Since cars have taken over so much of the world, the easiest way to make alternative arrangements, after walking and cycling, is to start with the cars themselves. That means fighting our firebreather with the ICE (Internal Combustion Engine) itself. As long as we are stuck with cars, let's at least fill those cars and make them into semiprivate (or semipublic) transport.

Our best chance of doing this is to use taxis, car pools, hitchhiking, and something called paratransit.

The Second Oldest Profession

There is one means of public transport and a potential competitor for the private car which is practically never thought of in those terms: the taxi. In cities, people think either that there are too many of them when they clog city roads, or not enough when you really need one in the rain. And in small towns and the countryside they are often perceived as waiting sleepily in front of the local train station (where such stations still exist), but if you need one elsewhere, the wait may be very long indeed. In spite of their importance, or potential importance, as providers of transport, taxis have received little attention from analysts and policy makers and are rarely integrated into the overall transport policy of a city or region.

Yet in western countries the taxi business accounts for close to one million vehicles, provides paid employment for nearly three million people, transports more than ten billion passengers annually, and offers its service to the public on a twenty-four hour basis, including emergency situations where no other service is available; all of this without the subsidies which often are necessary to keep public transport afloat.

In spite of these impressive accomplishments, taxis, as used today, are even less efficient than private cars in terms of the street space they take, the energy they use, and environmental impact they make. Most of the time taxis operate as single-occupancy vehicles, spending their time cruising up and down city streets and contributing to congestion and pollution. In addition, working conditions for the drivers are unsatisfacory; they are often poorly paid and exposed to danger. In many places, instead of providing a solution to the problem of cars in cities, taxis add to the problem.

Moreover, taxi services are very unevenly distributed; there are vast differences in taxi availability from one country to another, within different areas of the same country, or even within the same city. Thus, although Greece has about one taxi for every 300 inhabitants while North America has only one for every 18,000, you would never know this on the streets of New York City where taxis often take up more space than even private cars.

159

But if you try to find a legal cab a couple of miles outside the city, you might have very poor luck.

There are a number of ways to integrate taxis into the overall transport picture so that they can make a more useful contribution toward replacing private cars. Because the taxi industry is so poorly understood in most places, the first step must be to improve our understanding of the job that taxis actually do in a given community. How many are there? How many people do they transport? How much do they charge? Who uses them and why? Who owns them? Who drives them and how much are they paid? What are the problems of taxis—for the users, the drivers, the owners, the police, and the local authorities? How does your community compare with places which have good taxi service? Getting the answers to such questions would not be a monumental task for most communities and could be accomplished in a matter of weeks. It does not need years of "study," usually a code word for no action in transportation circles.

Once the local situation is understood, the first issue to consider would be removing the barriers to group riding. Taxi sharing is a powerful way to attack one of the most flagrant shortcomings of cabs, the fact that they carry even fewer passengers than private cars. It is possible that the era of the single taxi client, like that of the single occupancy vehicle, is drawing to a close. In many cities taxis are still prohibited from picking up groups of passengers who may be going to the same part of town, but in others—such as Washington, D.C.—this is common practice. In such places taxis are more economical, more environment-friendly, and more efficient users of street space. And they promote social contacts and a sense of sharing.

Some people will always have reservations about cab sharing, and there is no reason why individuals should not be free to choose their own level of taxi service. Private or premium taxi transport will of course be more expensive (like first-class train travel) but there is no reason to make it obligatory for everybody, which is the current practice. For many, the overriding argument in favor of group riding will be its low cost to the user since it can be several times cheaper than single client service. Moreover, taxi

160

sharing has the effect of increasing the number of vehicles available to the public.

Sharing will be easier to organize where there are many people out on the street seeking taxis as is the case in dense city centers or along major streets and arteries. In such situations, the taxi may operate as a jitney or line taxi, picking up passengers either on being hailed from the street or at designated stop points. In a novel by Peruvian writer Mario Vargas Llosa which came out in the 1970s, all the characters continually use a jitney, for both center-city and countryside transport. This jitney was a kind of shared line taxi, usually an old vehicle, charging no more than buses. The jitney, in fact, appeared to be the principal form of public transport in Lima at the time.[1]

Calculating proper fares could be a problem, though not an insurmountable one. In many developing countries where such taxis are called by names such as *Por Puesto* (Mexico), *Dolmus* (Turkey), or *Kri-Kri* (Nigeria), the fare can be the subject of lively negotiation. In other places it may be an amount well known to users of the system.

Technology can help to turn a more lightly settled area into an "electronically" dense one. One system called TaxiCom links each participating taxi to a central computer via onboard radio and the taxi's own microcomputer.[2] Systems of this sort have been in service in many Scandinavian cities for years, and a number of them have recently been instituted in the United States and Canada. In TaxiCom systems, the central computer keeps empty taxis positioned strategically around the city so that the nearest one can be dispatched as soon as a call for service is received. Orders can be made in advance, on a standing basis (convenient for regular community or school trips), or within minutes of desired service. Rides can be either on a premium or a cheaper shared-ride basis. By using such systems, communities can get much higher levels of taxi service at substantially lower costs. They also eliminate cruising taxis and allow the taxi trade to make considerably more money, which in many cases allows it to pay back all of its investment in computers and other equipment within a short period.

Taxis should also be used for the transport of the elderly and handicapped who otherwise have difficulty using regular bus or train services. This is a standard transportation option in much of northern Europe these days and is worth considering in other places. If in addition we count all those who for reasons of age and health are not physically able or fit to drive cars and shouldn't be out in the deadly roller derby which is our road system, the potential market for such services becomes really considerable.

One major barrier which keeps the taxi sector from innovation and expansion is the way the business is run: something like a local monopoly, intransigent labor union, or corrupt political party, firmly set against trying anything new or different. To make more and better use of taxis, we would have to wean the sector away from such rigid attitudes and allow those directly involved to view themselves as part of a growing business with a social purpose, public recognition, and a chance to make more money.

To accomplish that, it will be necessary to sweep away and rationalize existing constraints and practices which are, in most places, heavily antiquated, chaotic, excessive, and counterproductive. That means reorganizing the local taxi business not around large fleets but with individual owner-drivers grouped into cooperatives with areawide coverage. International studies of the industry have shown that this is the most effective means of organizing the sector, both for those who work in it and for the public. Each taxi driver will then be an independent businessman, operating within an alliance of like-minded citizens offering much needed public services.

The final step in this process is to link the taxi cooperative directly both to local government and to groups and institutions with whom it can work and to give it a role within the community's transportation planning and policy process. That would mean that in addition to group rider services, greater use could be made of taxis in rural areas, transport for the elderly and handicapped, and sweeper services which connect with car pools, public transport, and employer-organized transport.

Once cab drivers abandon the cumbersome way they cruise

the streets to attract their customers, we'll stop calling this the second oldest profession.

SOLUTION 14
Integrate taxis into overall transport planning.

✧

> *Surprised by joy—impatient as the wind*
> *I turned to share the transport.*
> Wordsworth, *Miscellaneous Sonnets*

Para Is Fairer

To get more cars off our roads in the immediate future, especially in places where public transport and taxis are insufficient, we have to look at all other available means of communal transport. The family of transport services which fall in between the private drive-alone car and fixed route public transport is sometimes known as "paratransit," a term which was invented back in the early 1970s in the U.S. Department of Transportation's back offices. One problem with paratransit is the word itself, which has never gained much currency and is practically unknown in Europe. This may be due to its association with disagreeable terms like paramilitary. (*Para* comes from the Greek and means "beside" or "beyond.")

Perhaps someone should invent a better term for this important transport concept, but whatever its proper name, paratransit represents a different philosophical approach to transport. It serves as a catalytic agent that forces us to rethink all aspects of transportation. It is not so much a service concept as a mind-set, which revolves above all around the idea of sharing as the only way to increase vehicle occupancy rates.

Paratransit therefore stands for a host of shared transport arrangements, all of which take less road space and cause less pollution, congestion, and danger, than private cars. Such arrangements can include short term or group rental cars and vans; gypsy, ghost, and shared taxis; jitneys; group limousines, dial-a-rides, private minibus services; handicapped transport; work, school, mail, community, and tourist buses; van and car pools; and hitchhiking. (Because of their special promise, the latter two will be considered separately.)

Paratransit, more often than not, is uncodified, unofficial, unconventional, unincorporated, and unrecognized by transportation planners and policy makers, who have trouble relating to something not subject to rigid schedules, not cataloged, and not enshrined by laws. Paratransit services can be run by a regular public transport operator (as a sideline), by a community or group of individuals, or by private operators.

Often local regulations and planning are slanted in favor of the private car, which can make these in-between services "para-legal" in addition to being paratransit. Aside from their shaky legal and official status, there are other reasons for the high failure rates of such services: being innovative and often makeshift, they are cut off from mainstream transport experience and expertise.

Like many people who open restaurants, private bus operators may initially know nothing about the business. Not being subsidized they are often cramped by budget considerations; they pay insufficient attention to their market; they suffer from technical problems such as vehicle breakdowns and insufficiency; and they don't keep accurate records and thus are slow to learn from experience.

But in spite of these failures, paratransit can act as a kind of gadfly to both public and private transport, springing up wherever there is a need for it. If nothing else, it points up the shortcomings of existing arrangements and provide planners with new ideas. In the United States, for example, community buses have raised real estate values in the towns where they have been tried because they made those towns or neighborhoods more livable and desirable.

There are many buses making empty runs now which could

carry passengers. In Switzerland and Scotland, instead of running empty, postal buses are used extensively to transport passengers. School buses could be used in a similar fashion. Many are idle when not used for school transport, or only half full when so used and could be put to use along routes not served otherwise. In the United States, the yellow school buses are the only form of transport other than private cars which are in general evidence among the numberless back roads of that vast country.

One system called CHARMS has been proposed to help nondrivers in rural areas find the near-empty vehicles which may be going their way. The acronym loses some of its charm when given in its spelled-out form of Computer Helped Areawide Rural Mobility System. The idea of this system is that rural dwellers use their TV, equipped with a special "black box" and telephone (or a Minitel, the French electronic phonebook, if they have one), to register their transport demands with a central office, which has a computerized schedule of all empty vehicles passing the area that day who are willing to take passengers. Such vehicles can be school buses, vans, delivery vehicles, trucks, intercity buses, taxis, and even private cars. All participants are compensated for their services, and the nondriving country dwellers can get to where they want to go.

There is also a whole new generation of minibuses which are attempting to shed the image which buses have acquired through the years, expressed in A. D. Godley's little rhyme:

> What is this that roareth thus?
> Can it be a motorbus?
> Yes, the smell and hideous hum
> Indicat Motorem Bum

These new buses, many of which are low in cost to acquire and run, could be put into service in many areas. They might function as connecting links between towns or suburbs without rail service and the nearest station or as shuttle lines from regular bus stations to industrial zones; or perhaps along highways connecting towns and villages not served otherwise. Because of their

1903 Dion Bouton sixteen-place minibus.

flexibility, much more use could be made of minibuses as "demand-activated" vehicles or dial-a-rides. All you have to do then is to pick up a phone or press a button, and the bus calls for you at your home or the nearest bus stop.

The electronics for such systems exist and are in operation in a number of places, but operators, perhaps weighed down by traditions of fixed routes and rigid schedules, have been slow to try them. Dial-a-ride operators who tried such systems under present conditions in London found that the cost of picking up single riders was too high to make them commercially feasible, partly because of insurance, licensing, and maintenance costs, partly because there weren't enough customers for properly shared services.

To avoid the chaos of Santiago, Chile, where some fifteen thousand unregulated, unscheduled buses—many unsafe, some half-empty, and all spewing pollution—follow any route the owner chooses, the public authority and the private operator should work together. If they don't, as happens frequently in the deregulated United Kingdom, there is too often fierce and destructive competition, with companies more concerned to drive each other out of business than to increase total ridership. Buses are scheduled to run in bunches, and timetables and routes are changed so often that passengers get confused, annoyed, and discouraged. The Germans put some of their transport routes out to tender in a system where private operators carry out the work on a contract or percentage basis, and the central authority maintains some control over the line.

The effectiveness of any shared and not regularly scheduled system depends on the way such rides are organized: whether riders are collected by way of technology from their homes or at prearranged stops, and whether they are given incentives such as low fares, good timing, and comfort.

And beyond that, its effectiveness depends on people's attitudes toward shared rides or for that matter, shared anything. Although conventional transport is also shared, it is shared—like sidewalk space—with a large number of strangers. Paratransit is somehow more intimate and obliges small groups of riders to talk to each other if they don't want to sit in an embarrassingly stony silence as happens so frequently in elevators. This may be a reason why paratransit has not taken off in Europe where people tend to be more "private" than in America and less inclined to talk to strangers. Although there is a European tradition of sharing café or restaurant tables, this does not extend to a private space like a car.

Aside from attitudes, paratransit also has to overcome resistance from established operators who consider this a competing service; from insurers who have never heard of it; and from employers who will not allow transport subsidies for this unconventional form of transportation.

The paratransit concept is best explored by individuals or municipalities who see an unanswered need in their communities. Anyone wanting to start an environment-friendly business could do worse than consider a minibus service, perhaps in cooperation with a local authority. Small buses, seating between fifteen and twenty-five people, can be had new for $25,000 to $30,000. According to British figures, they need to carry an estimated thirty-two passengers per bus hour (or 380 per day) to break even.[3]

As long as public transport is poor in many cities and almost nonexistent in the country, paratransit could do its bit to restrain the automobile. To do that job properly, we would have to restructure our transport systems to give paratransit an officially recognized place. Come to think of it, such restructuring might suggest still another name for this in-between transport idea. Why not call it Parastroika?

SOLUTION 15
Semipublic paratransit services to provide a real alternative to private car use.

> Then feed on thoughts, that voluntary move
> Harmonious numbers . . .
> Milton, *Paradise Lost*

The Prisoner's Dilemma

One form of paratransit which has been highly successful is the High Occupancy Vehicle (HOV). High occupancy vehicles are cars or vans which carry three or more people who share a ride to a common destination. HOVs are an important development because even a slight boost in car occupancy, an increase from 1.5 to 2 persons per average car would bring down carbon dioxide emissions from transport by more than 15%.[4]

One of the first successful pooling projects was started by an innovative traffic engineer in 1973. The prototype for such pools is probably the jitney which dates back to the early days of the automobile. Jitney was the slang term for a nickel, because jitney drivers used to charge a nickel for each shared ride. In a modern refinement over the old pools and jitneys, HOVs are now often accorded special privileges like express lanes on motorways, free bridge crossings with avoidance of tollbooth lines, and free parking privileges.

To study how pools are organized, we have to turn to the United States, the country of their origin, where people have been diving into the pool without reservation. In Europe the attitude has been to stick one's toe into the water and find it too cold, for three principal reasons: distances from home to work are usually shorter, public transport is often available, and Europeans are on the whole more reserved and less inclined to share a stranger's car.

A study by the Swedish Association of Local Authorities proves the point. After having found that seven out of eight motorists in that country travel to and from work alone in their cars, the Association tried to organize carpooling. Several years ago almost half a million motorists in the County of Stockholm were invited to take part in a carpooling experiment. They were given computerized help with arranging groups to occupy the cars. Only 1700 (out of a half million!) eventually registered their interest. No passengers could be found for 500 of these. The remaining 1200 received lists of names and a mere 100 began to travel together. Of these, 50 had traveled previously by public transport.[5]

In the United States, where commuting distances are often considerable, and where public transport is rarely available, car and van pools are becoming increasingly more common. To give a graphic idea of how common they are becoming, we need merely contrast the Swedish figure of a hundred pools with that of southern California, where there are now no fewer than two hundred thousand of them.

Both car and van pools are based on sharing commuter expenses and reducing congestion and pollution. But while car pools generally use an individual's personal vehicle whose riders compensate the owner for such use, a van pool, normally consisting of from seven to fifteen persons, may be personally operated (for which local grants are often available), employer sponsored, or operated by a third party. Such third parties are called van pool management companies and work somewhat like private bus operators; they are usually under contract to individuals or employers.

To shed a little more light on high occupancy vehicles and pools, concepts which may be unfamiliar to people living outside the United States, it may be interesting to look at the results of two surveys on attitudes and preferences of potential ridesharers conducted in different areas of the United States. The first survey comes from Tennessee. Of the 1800 employees in the Brentwood area surveyed, about half expressed a willingness to change their travel modes in order to reduce congestion and enhance safety. However, when the idea that this meant doing without their personal transport sank in, they thought of all the little things they might not now be able to do and thus indicated a need for daycare, lunchtime meals, and convenience-shopping transport.[6]

People weren't willing to give up their cars without strong incentives. Three out of five mentioned such ideas as park-and-ride lots near home, lunchtime shuttles, flexible work schedules, employee cafeterias, company van pools, bus services, and rideshare match assistance. Women were more likely to consider alternate modes (almost 60%) than men (53%). The higher the commuters' income level, the less likely they were to consider ridesharing. Commuters aged thirty-nine and under, who were production, technical, professional, and clerical workers, were more likely ridesharers than executives and sales and service personnel over forty. Perhaps the older and better paid men felt less sociable and inclined to share and more deserving of their cars than people below them on the career ladder.

A common reason given for switching to ridesharing was stress. Half of the Brentwood respondents said that commuting to work is as stressful as anything else they do all day. A further quarter thought that their commute was "more to much more" stressful than anything else. The fact that commuting is so stressful even in a medium-sized community where traffic is supposedly less heavy than in large urban centers does not speak well for our transportation systems.

The second survey, in Washington, D.C., found that about a third of rideshare applicants with one-way commutes longer than twenty miles formed pools while only 13% of those traveling under ten miles did so.[7] Potential ridesharers who are hesitant to try this new travel mode may fluctuate in their willingness to experiment from day to day, so it becomes important to catch them when they are in the right mood. In this survey, over one-third formed pools when a match letter arrived within three days after a pool request while their eagerness to dive into the pool was reduced to a mere 10% when the match letter arrived two weeks later. Two-thirds in that sampling said that they ride-shared to save money. Convenience and time saved by using HOV lanes were the second and third reasons. In this survey, too, more women applied than men.

The Washington survey is interesting in revealing economic considerations as the principal reason for most ridesharers, followed by time saving and personal convenience. Thus time and money, considerations which have been important for people since time immemorial, counted for much more than saving air quality or the environment, let alone considerations for global warming, none of which even figured as a reason. Such surveys would suggest that people don't know or don't care about the numbers given by the U.S. Environmental Protection Agency which show eighty-one urban areas (containing 100 million people) exceeding ozone health standards. Perhaps the designers of these surveys did not even pose such questions, being themselves unaware of them. Environmental considerations are on the back burner of people's minds, a long way behind time, money, and comfort.

There may be a lesson here that pocketbook issues always take precedence over environmental concerns, which intrude less on an individual's daily existence. If that is so, we may have a better chance to achieve car independence in the immediate future with economic arguments. In the long run, however, such arguments tend to shift and fluctuate, whereas the environmental argument gets stronger every day.

An Association of Commuter Transportation (ACT) was established in 1986 in Washington, bringing under a common roof previous associations of van-pool operators and rideshare professionals. ACT's membership grew dramatically in 1989 due to mounting concerns over traffic congestion and air quality and now includes many members from large corporations such as McDonell Douglas, Hewlett Packard, and AT&T. ACT has a variety of committees which focus on special functions and issues and help with providing information and putting people in touch with each other. It has established special councils dealing with employers, public policy, van pools, and transport management. It promotes partnerships with business leaders, public policy makers, legislators, planners, and representatives of the media.

ACT has also given birth to Transport Management Associations (TMAs), of which there are now fifty operating nationwide (up from twenty in 1987) and whose numbers are ever increasing. While ACT is a central policy making body, the TMAs are local, often semi-independent groups executing such policy. TMAs do at the local level what their parent group does nationally; they are partnerships between business and local government whose chief goal is to help solve transportation problems associated with rapid suburban growth although some of them deal with other community issues also. TMAs enable developers, employers, and property managers to pool resources and address transportation problems on a joint basis. While all TMAs are grounded on the principle that the private sector must share responsibility for dealing with traffic congestion—a sound principle not much practiced in the rest of the world—each association responds to the special needs of the area it serves. Some TMAs are private, receiving no government funding, while others are supported by a mix of private and public funds.

Transport Management Associations also differ in the way they view their missions. Some TMAs focus on policy leadership and advocacy and aim primarily to influence public decisions about transportation. Others assume a more operational role: they facilitate ridesharing, coordinate alternative work or staggered work hour programs, administer parking management, operate shuttle buses, and help their members comply with local traffic mitigation requirements. Some second-generation TMAs have evolved into broad purpose organizations which, in addition to their transport functions, manage a wide variety of shared services such as day care, security, and telecommunications. Thus the TMAs have almost assumed the role of mom and pop, making sure that the kids get off to school on time with clean shirts and noses, hats, gloves, and duffle coats. Using such things as car and van pool matching, transit information, and personalized assistance, often by using computers to match riders, the TMAs send the children off without tears or coming to blows.

Having begun their job by providing direct commuter services, the TMAs can then devote themselves to acting as a forum within which business and local government can discuss an area's transportation needs, trends, resources, and plans. The business community gains the ear of local officials on transportation concerns while those same officials have an opportunity to invite private sector comment and participation to improve mobility. Whatever the individual's motivation to share a commute with others, local governments and the TMAs can do much to encourage such sharing by instituting HOV lanes on all commuting routes, giving HOVs parking and toll-free privileges, and publicizing the advantages of ridesharing. California, as usual, is in the lead here, organizing events like a rideshare week, with accompanying group and media campaigns, celebrities, prizes, and a demonstration of an open road "Keep California Moving Day." Such publicity may also stimulate casual pools—good neighbors or friends sharing a car for economic, environmental, or merely social reasons.

While this American-style hoopla may tempt more drivers to give ridesharing a try for economic or convenience reasons, the question of whether to take the car (and be its only occupant) at bottom comes down to a moral choice. John Adams, of University College, London, has compared this motorist's dilemma to the so-called Prisoner's Dilemma from the Theory of Games.

In the Prisoner's Dilemma two companions, A and B, are in separate jail cells, suspected of collaborating in a crime. Each is encouraged by the jailer to abandon the other by throwing the entire blame on him. If A yields to that temptation, he will be rewarded with $5000 and freedom while B, the sucker, will get fifteen years for being solely responsible for the crime. If B blames

A and A remains silent, then it will be B who gets freedom and money, and A the fifteen years. If neither keeps silent and both abandon each other, they will get a reduced sentence of three years for giving helpful information. If both cooperate (unknowingly) by keeping silent and counting on the other one to keep silent as well, they will get freedom for lack of evidence, but no money.

There are four choices open to A (1) Temptation: A defames B hoping B remains silent, thus giving A the jackpot of freedom and money. (2) Reduced Punishment: A betrays B with the expectation that B will do likewise. (3) Just Reward: both A and B remain silent and win freedom, though no money. And (4) Sucker's Payoff: A remains silent even though he fears B will betray him.

Translated into commuter terms, it comes out in the following way (1) The temptation: A drives to work while all the B's take the van pool, bus, or train. The roads are free and A takes the jackpot by not only getting to work easily but stopping off to shop and visit friends. (2) The reduced punishment: Most of the A's and B's take their cars on the road. Congestion, danger, and pollution are terrible. (3) The reward: The A's and B's cooperate and take pools or public transport. It's less convenient than being the only car on the road, but can be clean, fast, and efficient. And (4) The sucker's payoff: All the B's take their cars and one single A waits forlornly for the bus which, if it shows up at all, will be dirty, infrequent, unreliable, slow, and expensive.[8]

Choice three is, of course, the preferred one for all the reasons given in these pages. But opting for pools or public transport no doubt involves agonizing over all the moral and practical choices given in the Prisoner's Dilemma. Should I or shouldn't I?

SOLUTION 16
Using pools and high occupancy vehicles for commutes to work where walking, cycling, or public transport is not practical.

The Auto-Stop

For many drivers, the idea of picking up a hitchhiker carries with it the notion of danger or excitement, depending on whether that hitchhiker turns out to be a young man or a young woman. The sexual connotation of picking up female hitchhikers goes back all the way to the beginnings of the automobile and beyond. Already in 1909 a Thomas Mann novel called *Koenigliche Hoheit* (*His Royal Highness*) described a man whose favorite occupation was to "speed in a crazy fashion about the countryside" looking to pick up peasant girls on streets and beside fields. The car is often associated, consciously or unconsciously, rightly or wrongly, with sex, risk, and adventure, all of which come into play when a perfect stranger is invited into the car's interior.

To go from these fancies to the prosaic task of turning hitchhiking into an acceptable form of transportation is a tall order. We must learn to look upon hitchhiking as a kind of neighborly and civilized behavior before this very much underused and underrated form of ridesharing can play an important role in our transport system. There are more sober historical antecedents for hitchhiking than sex and violence fantasies. During the Depression, harmless tramps often "bummed" a ride. During the war, virtually everybody felt obliged to pick up soldiers. In the 1960s students were considered "safe" to give a ride to. And even today motorists will often take pity on farmworkers who have no other means of getting around.

Psychologically, it helps both the driver and the would-be passenger if the hitchhiker indicates that he has a definite reason, goal, and destination, which can be shown on a clearly written sign. Motorists will often give a ride to a driver whose car has engine trouble, because the stopped car supplies reason and goal for its driver's journey and makes that person respectable.

Hitchhikers, to be accepted, must take their place alongside all other transport passengers so that their trip becomes no more controversial than a bus or train journey. To achieve this, it is probably necessary for local or government agencies to intervene. The French word for hitchhiking, *auto-stop*, suggests one way in which local communities can regulate this activity. In suburban and rural areas, where there are few alternative means of transport, local authorities could designate a series of auto stops, similar to bus stops, in which hitchhikers would legally be entitled to hail a car. Drivers picking up hitchhikers would be encouraged to drop them at another auto stop.

There is, of course, the danger that such auto stops could become teenage hangouts or even gathering places for automobile-related drug dealing and prostitution. Much would depend on how quickly a community can make hitchhiking into a routine travel option, as is already the case at the University of Lancaster, England, where they have built two special well-lit and covered shelters called hitching posts, one of which is at the university, the other in downtown Lancaster, five kilometers away. About five hundred people a day make use of this route.

Both auto-stoppers and drivers could be part of a voluntary registration system which might even use computers to match them in the way carpoolers are matched. And the police could routinely keep an eye on the auto stops. In some cases, local authorities could suggest a payment rate (so many cents per mile or the equivalent bus fare) to lessen the obligation the hitchhiker may feel to pay for the ride. The driver can turn down the proffered payment, but such a rate puts their relation on a paying basis. To avoid resistance to auto-stop schemes from competitive public transport and taxis, auto stops would originally have to be restricted to routes or times of day and night when there are no alternatives.

Something of a precedent for such a system was tried in the 1960s in Berlin during a lengthy public transport strike. In a campaign called *Aktion Roter Punkt* (Action Red Point) drivers who were willing to pick up commuters put a plainly visible red disk in their windshield. They would then pull up to a bus stop where the passengers had already grouped themselves according to destination. The drivers would take, without charge, as many passengers going their way as would fit in their cars. Similar systems could be of great value in suburban areas, at present poorly served by public transport.

If auto stops were widely distributed, they could provide transport for work-related trips, converting single occupancy vehicles to HOVs, with the attendant HOV privileges such as express lanes and free bridge crossings. These privileges would be a kind of payment to cooperating "red point" drivers. This is already working in places like California where drivers often pick up hitchhikers to convert their cars into HOV vehicles in order to benefit from HOV advantages. In a refinement, local authorities could sell tokens or tickets to hitchhikers, which the driver could exchange for cash or free parking. To facilitate the pickup of passengers, each auto stop could be equipped with retractable or electronic direction signs which the auto-stoppers could activate to let the driver know where they are headed.

At the moment the attitude of the authorities toward hitchhikers is that they, like bicyclists or pedestrians, are marginal characters, only more so, as they are sometimes even subject to arrest or police harassment. To give hitchhiking a new image, it may be advisable to change its name to something like "autostopping."

Because of congestion and environmental constraints, official attitudes toward hitchhiking may well change in the 1990s. But, as is the case with bicyclists and pedestrians, it is not enough to tolerate hitchhikers; they must be integrated into an overall transport plan where they should have an established, legal, and respected place.

SOLUTION 17
Allow hitchhiking to take its rightful place in an overall transport strategy.

10

UNDAMNING THE PUBLIC: SOLUTIONS 18–21

"The public be damned!" said W. H. Vanderbilt in reply to a question whether the public should be consulted about luxury trains.

Well, in many countries the public is still damned where their own transport is concerned. So the final group of alternate transport means we look at is the most obvious and often the most neglected—public transport. For the many places where public transport does not exist, it is also the most expensive to put in place, which is the reason why we started with feet, bicycles, and the cars which exist already.

To work cars out of our transport systems, public transport offers the best hope since it can move the largest number of people. We first will look at trains and the problems associated with high-speed systems, and then consider trams, buses, and the magic key which opens the gate to all transport systems.

Now here you see, it takes all the running you can do to stay in the same place.
If you want to get somewhere else, you must run at least twice as fast as that.

Lewis Carroll, *Through the Looking Glass*

Running Twice As Fast

Whenever we decide to leave our cars at home and go for longer distances than boots, bikes, or car pools can easily cover, our natural instinct is to think first of the old-fashioned iron horse, still the most environment-friendly alternate transport means for covering those distances. Trains have seemingly made a comeback in some parts of the world recently, and the new fascination with high-speed trains is seen by many transport specialists and even some environmentalists as a good thing. The usual argument is that they may draw passengers away from highly polluting cars and planes to a more mildly polluting means of transport.

High-Speed Train (HST) facilities exist or are being planned in many countries. There is the Very Fast Train (VFT) project in Eastern Australia, the "Fastrain" in the United States (to be put into place initially in Florida and California), the *Shinkansen* in Japan, and the *Train à Grande Vitesse* (TGV) in France. Since the French system is today the most advanced and visible, both as it already exists and as it is to be, let us look at that system first.

We will shortly be discussing Lille, a town whose idea it was to create rather than merely to satisfy transportation demand. Such an idea may work when its goal is to revitalize a city center, but it becomes somewhat debatable when applied nationally and internationally. The French consider a virtue the very quality which is now recognized as a vice in connection with new roads: their propensity to generate new traffic. This is what the French appear to have in mind with the TGV system.

The passengers attracted to a train system which would put Paris within an easy morning commute of even the furthest French city will not necessarily be people who have switched from cars, vans, or trucks (the TGV's freight capacity is negligible). According to figures from National Institute for Research on Transport and Safety only 10% of TGV passengers are former road users. The remainder are plane users (20%), former existing

179

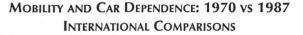

MOBILITY AND CAR DEPENDENCE: **1970** VS **1987**
INTERNATIONAL COMPARISONS

Average Kilometers Traveled per Inhabitant

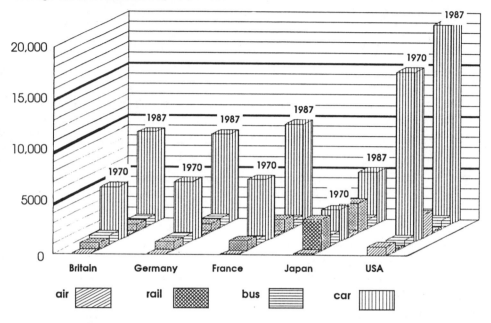

rail users (40%), and *new* travelers (30%).[1] As if to supply the proof that the French expect little transfer from road to rail, they announced in 1988, simultaneously with the TGV plans, a high-priority road and airport expansion program. This called for expanded annual expressway construction, bringing the high-speed interurban road system to 11,300 kilometers compared with a mere 3700 kilometers in 1980 and 1000 kilometers in 1970.

In other words, the French government doesn't look at trains as a cozy, safe, and comfortable way to go see grandmother in the country, but as part of a modern high-tech, high-speed transport system whose task it is to move people as quickly and as furiously as possible, by road, rail or air, it doesn't matter which. The choice seems less important than the movement itself.

Many of the new passengers may be those who are tempted to jump on the fast trains simply because they can get to Paris in two hours whether they have business there or not. And a further and more serious problem is posed by those who decide to become long-distance commuters, thinking nothing of installing themselves 300 miles from their work. Both of these categories constitute new traffic rather than transferees from other means.

High-speed trains do not cater to people like Marcel Proust with his "love for fairylike journeys by train." The TGV instead recalls the airplane, by arranging its passengers stiffly in rows while a disembodied voice in the carefully calibrated cadences of the international hostess style announces overpriced bar snacks and wishes you an agreeable journey. Gone are the old European compartments where people faced each other and often carried on lively discussions, or the plush American dining cars where an actual flesh and blood person played the piano. A German high-speed train goes so far as to offer its passengers idealized video images of the landscape they are passing through, which presumably are more "beautiful" than what they could see out of the window.

In the meantime, while France is spending what is now 2% and will soon be 2.5% of its gross domestic product on high-speed transport, a magnificent train station housed in a building of classic proportions lies derelict with grass growing between the tracks, in the traffic-choked town of Sommières in southern France. Some of the truck traffic asphyxiating that ancient town could have moved by rail, and some of the passengers in the thousands of cars which clog the Roman bridge there could have walked in comfort through the symmetrical portals of the now abandoned local station. The same situation exists in hundreds of towns all over France, and indeed, all over the world. Local train stations are either derelict or have been turned into museums, restaurants, or private residences. Train tracks have been picked up, abandoned, or sold off.

What is the rationale for favoring high-speed transport that caters to the exceptional travel of international business and tourism over the much more highly frequented local transport devoted to the welfare of the people?

In France the idea of high-speed transport is undoubtedly linked to the fear that, without an adequate infrastructure, the economic center of gravity in Europe could shift north and east, leaving France out in the economic cold. "If we don't want the major European traffic flows to avoid our country, it is urgent for us to provide systems that are modern and competitive," said the transport minister in 1988. So France has watched in considerable dismay and envy the expansion of West Germany's motorway system, which is almost three times more extensive than that of France. That could be why the *cour de comptes*, an independent state court that audits government spending, says that "the French highway system is managed and developed outside all economic, legal, financial, and accounting logic." The same lack of logic is now applied to the TGV.

Although France is far ahead of West Germany in high-speed rail transportation, the French government believes that it must push hard to develop the TGV to give the high-speed train technology the best chance to compete in export markets. The French thus follow the logic of Alice in the Looking Glass, by doing all the running they can do to stay in the same place, and running twice as fast to get somewhere else.

To find out what high-speed trains have actually accomplished, we can look to Japan, where high-speed lines were completed in 1969. The Japanese idea was to break up the enormous population centers of Tokyo and other agglomerations and disperse people throughout the country, so they built a system of high-speed rails, and later, expressways. Did that do the trick?

If the goal of this enormous infrastructure was to induce people to move away from agglomerations, it probably served the opposite function just as effectively. Many Japanese experts think that the high-speed trains and motorways have had no effect whatsoever on dispersing urban centers, which have continued to grow; and though others say that without such infrastructure the situation would have been even worse, that is certainly no proof that high-speed trains and expressways have made the situation any better.

One thing is certain: high-speed transport stimulates movement almost, as it were, for its own sake. It could even be said that a high-speed rail line, far from drawing passengers away from cars, deposits more cars on the highways in stimulating general movement throughout the country and across its borders. Making it easy for people to commute to distant places sets up a cycle in which many of these people's friends, colleagues, and family may take their car instead of the train. We have seen the effect near the suburban metro stations in Washington, D. C., where the development meant to serve train passengers finally drew a much greater number of car drivers. The movement generated by the TGV does not, unfortunately, include the hiker who needs local trains to the countryside, and the biker whose machine is not even allowed on the Fr 190-billion TGV system.

But, some may say, though this movement doesn't do much for local people, it is at least democratic—which is often said of the automobile—creating a mobility that helps to break down class differences. Such is not the view of Ivan Illich, who makes the following analysis:

> Beyond a critical speed, no one can save time without forcing another to lose it. The man who claims a seat in a faster vehicle insists that his time is worth more than that of the passenger in a slower one. . . . This time-grab despoils those who are left behind, and since they are the majority, it raises ethical issues of a more general nature than kidney dialysis or organ transplants.[2]

Professor Whitelegg puts the argument against high-speed transport in more practical terms:

> Why do we need to travel from A to B at a saving of X hours? What do we do with the time saved? What is the effect of conquering distance by destroying time? Transport has to serve the interests of sustainable developments within communities across the whole spectrum of passenger and freight movement. Walking and cycling are far more important than HST projects, as is the organization of a space economy so that milk and vegetables travel fifty kilometers and not a thousand to their final destination. The High-Speed Train project is most definitely not part of the solution, and hence must be regarded as part of the problem.[3]

Unlike some of the American high-speed trains which will operate over existing lines and negotiate curves with the help of

183

hydraulically assisted springs, the French are proposing to construct new tracks for their high-speed rail lines since the track
curves built in the last century are considered too abrupt for the
enormous speeds of the new TGV engines. This has led to considerable local opposition against the wide, pylon-lined trackways
which often traverse formerly unspoiled countryside. While the
government is casting around for the lines of least resistance,
protesters frequently block trains, especially in Provence, with
slogans such as "Arise, Cézanne!" These tracks, which will bisect
the rich vineyards of southern France, not only pollute arable
land but create what might be called time and space pollution.
Time and space are following air, water, and earth in being
fouled. These are new forms of pollution we can live without.

If, as projected for the 1990s, America is really going to have
ultrahigh-speed train systems from California to Nevada, from
San Francisco to Los Angeles, and from Miami to Tampa, there
may be some way to integrate local stations along the way and
allow the trains to compete with the motorcar and not only with
airplanes. It is not even certain that high-speed trains divert
many passengers from airplanes. Professor Whitelegg makes the
point that the introduction of the telephone did not diminish the
post. Now people are constantly on the phone *and* receive stacks
of mail. What high-speed trains appear to do is to concentrate the
economy on several chosen centers at the expense of disinvest-
ment in the normally much more extensive nonfavored areas,
with resultant losses in jobs and quality of life. It is the old story
of ghettoization, this time applied countrywide. These trains also
encourage a high-speed mentality since the new rail customers
won't want to lose the time they gain on these trains by walking
or biking to the station. In addition, high-speed trains create 40%
more noise than conventional trains and consume double the energy.

One is left with the feeling that these high-speed trains are
profitable mainly for the people who manufacture them and for
the developers who buy up the land they are to run on. Would it
not be better to spend some of the energy and money now devoted to high-speed transport on local, commuter, and rural rail
lines and reap rewards in terms of reduced car use and an im-

proved environment, which could be considerable? But that would mean heeding Herbert Spencer's warning about time: "That which man is always trying to kill, but which ends in killing him."

For the time being, we are concentrating our energies on killing time and being killed by it, rather than on the joys of taking the local train to visit grandma in the country.

SOLUTION 18
Restore local rail for efficient freight and passenger movement and as a car restraint measure.

> *O how I long to travel back,*
> *And tread again that ancient track!*
> *That I might once more reach that plain,*
> *Where first I left my glorious train . . .*
> Henry Vaughan, "The Retreat"

A Desire Named Streetcar

To those who knew streetcars in their childhood days there is something very nostalgic about them—as if they appear in a dream of a distant land and a distant time. This author remembers his grandfathers by the colors of the streetcars one had to take to visit them. Those were the days when the yellow and green trams went about their business in Berlin to reach the yellow and green granddads. They were also the days when The Royal Commission on Transport in England stated quite categorically that tramways caused much unnecessary congestion and considerable danger to the public.

Likewise in 1937 Sir Charles Bressey and Sir Edwin Lutyens, two of the most illustrious engineers and architects of that time, declared that the removal of tramways was highly desirable and should lead to an increase in traffic speeds of around 15%. In

New York, Mayor Hylan (1918–1923) maintained that streetcars were "useless junk" and the immensely popular mayor Fiorello La Guardia (1934–1945), nicknamed "The Little Flower," said that they were "as dead as sailing ships."

La Guardia was fanatically opposed to trolleys. He felt they "can only be discarded as an obstruction." Mayor La Guardia co-erced private companies and city-owned lines into converting to buses.[4] He did so despite technical reports demonstrating the better economy and operating characteristics of the modern trolleys which the industry had finally galvanized itself into producing in the 1930s. He and others of that period had absolute faith in automobiles as the measure of progress, and rails in the street interfered with this program.

Jane Jacobs advances an interesting psychological reason for La Guardia's attitude. The mayor had a personal need to distance himself from his immigrant origins and define himself as a modern American. Thus, along with streetcars, he also banned organ grinders (a symbol of the Old World) and ended the city's extensive outdoor street markets.[5] With the hindsight of history, we are beginning to realize that The Little Flower, considered a hero by his contemporaries, had a sure instinct for destroying anything that was even vaguely people- or environment-friendly and replacing it with the deadly monotony of the modern age which he so worshipped. Even now he haunts the sleep of thousands of people who live near the busy airport named in his honor.

Modernists and car enthusiasts like The Little Flower gave a

Electric street car with buried third rail, Nice 1900.

tremendous assist to General Motors who—together with counterparts in the oil, steel, and tire industries—acquired more than one hundred electric rail systems in forty-five American cities only to dismantle the electric lines and pave over the track. By the late 1950s, 90% of America's trolley network had been eliminated.[6] It is now forgotten that the United States, land of the automobile, possessed 45,000 miles of trolley tracks as early as 1917, and that they attracted more than 15 billion passengers per year as late as the 1940s. That they disappeared so quickly and thoroughly was not exactly an accident.

A present day transport researcher looking back with nostalgia upon that trolley-rich past has given the following account of life in the United States around 1920:

> In towns and cities, folks went about on trolley cars that ran at frequent intervals throughout the day and took people everywhere for a nickel. Everybody lived within an easy walk of a car line. Suburbanites took commuter trains to their daily work in the city—reading newspapers and chatting en route. For out-of-town trips trains offered Pullman and diner luxury in addition to plush-seated coaches. Railroads also handled the nation's freight. Factories were located along the tracks, permitting direct delivery by train. Because trains could handle heavy passenger and freight loads easily, few lines were needed to meet the needs of fair-sized cities. So, rather than spreading tracks every where, it was advantageous to group the communities and factories in traffic-concentrating nodes, an urban shape which resulted in efficiency and convenience. As a pleasant consequence, outlying land was spared for open space, farms and forests. Urban dwellers had but to walk, bicycle, or ride a trolley to get away for a day's picnic.[7]

Well, it is too late to remake America in this undoubtedly idealized image, but we may perhaps dethrone the prophets of the modern age and henceforth cease to regard the likes of Lutyens, Le Corbusier, La Guardia, Robert Moses, Henry Ford, and Charles Lindbergh as heroes and see them instead for what they were: people who believed that human happiness is dependent on ever better machinery.

A group of "Eco-scientists," more concerned with the *conse-*

quences of scientific thought than with the thought itself, has been coming down rather hard on older thinkers like Francis Bacon, Descartes, and Galileo, as being concerned only with progress for progress' sake without giving thought to the practical consequences of their work. According to this point of view the new channel tunnel, for example, would not be regarded as an engineering marvel but as an environmental disaster.[8]

In spite of the rather lethal combination of brutal scientific progress and business interests, trams did survive in a few American cities like San Francisco, Newark, Toronto, Boston, Philadelphia, Pittsburgh, and Cleveland. Until fairly recently, however, such systems were barely surviving, waiting for the other shoe to drop. After the oil shocks, interest in tramways began to pick up considerably in America. Since 1978, when the first new line opened in Edmonton, there has been a burgeoning of interest in what is now called "light rail," and new systems have already opened in Calgary, San Diego, Portland, Sacramento, and San Jose, and are being considered in Los Angeles, Seattle, Denver, Dallas, Houston, St. Louis, Minneapolis, Baltimore, and Hoboken. And there is even talk of running tram lines on New York's 42nd Street and in Brooklyn, with The Little Flower, no doubt, turning over in his grave.

In view of America's disenchantment with the streetcar, it is ironic that it was the United States which produced the model tram that went to Japan, Canada, and Europe after its abandonment in the country of its origin. This model tram was the Electric Railway Presidents' Conference Committee or P.C.C. car, essentially invented and tested in Brooklyn in the early 1930s.[9] These cars had much quicker acceleration than buses, used fuel more efficiently, and rode quietly and fumelessly on smooth welded track. They were spacious and comfortable and their wide double doors, close to the ground, allowed quick entry and exit.

In the rest of the world, trams were never really abandoned, with only England following the American example (a lone system survives in Blackpool). There are as many as three hundred streetcar systems left in the world, well over half of them in the Soviet Union and Eastern Europe. There are tram systems in

188

Antwerp, Brussels, Ghent, Ostend, Amsterdam, The Hague, Rotterdam, Genoa, Milan, Naples, Rome, Turin, Graz, Salzburg, Vienna, Grenoble, Marseilles, and many other places. In West Germany there are no fewer than twenty-nine cities with such systems. Today the tram, or light rail if you prefer, has gained a firm foothold in the world's cities. Systems are planned or under construction in Copenhagen, Brest, Reims, Rouen, Birmingham, Bristol, Edinburgh, Leeds, Manchester, Sheffield, Bologna, Florence, Lausanne, Stockholm, and Valencia.

Transport specialists make countless references to other systems which are true light rail systems, among them the one which was built for London's Dockland Development and the one in Lille, France. Both of these systems are also part of a new transport generation sometimes called smart transit systems or people movers, most of which are transport systems automatically controlled over guideways for use in places like airports, fairs, and resorts. Unlike trams, these systems usually do not require operators.

For many decades there has been a fascination with futuristic transport systems running on monorails or suspended from cables. The designers of these systems print glossy brochures showing gleaming cities with sunny skies and happy people entering wide-bodied "horizontal elevators." The inventors of such systems see no problems with the huge pylons and tracks necessary for their installation, or the useless shadow spaces thereunder. There may be acceptable ways of incorporating such a system into an existing city such as running it on arcades which give pedestrians underneath all-weather protection, but there is rarely enough money or understanding for such subtleties.

The Docklands Light Railway in London won out over underground rail construction to serve the newly developed Docklands complex not because it was futuristic, but because it was far cheaper to build (£77 million as against £325 million). In addition, it did give a smart city-of-the-future look to the new development. The system is fully automated, the two-vehicle trains can carry some two hundred seated and standing passengers, and the trains arrive at 7.5-minute intervals. But the system has some of the aesthetic flaws of many people-mover schemes. In addition both the capacity and the waiting times are subject to complaints, and passengers are not happy about fare collection and ticket validation. Critics point out that the so-called turnkey contract forced the builder to stick to the original budget with resultant initial economies limiting future expansion.

The Lille light rail system, called *Vehicule Automatique Léger* (VAL), opened in May 1983. Experts had estimated that the number of passengers would reach 35,000 a day, but when the whole east-west line opened, the number of users was more than triple the estimate. The trains are fully automatic and operate at intervals of 1 minute at peak times, 2 minutes in the daytime, and 5 minutes at night and in the early morning, whether there are passengers or not.

The 2-minute interval between trains fulfills an ideal condition sometimes associated with the old trams: when you turn your head after having longingly followed the missed one with your eyes, the next one is already in view. According to a survey by the French National Institute of Transport, what people mind most about public transport is the waiting.

The VAL system was designed to create rather than to satisfy demand, and in this it has been successful. We have criticized roads for creating travel demand, but when the added travel is done in a local train with the object of reviving a city center, it is acceptable or even laudable. In the past, many people used to visit Lille by car from Calais and from Belgium for shopping, but their numbers declined when the city's roads became congested. Moreover, many of the spinning factories closed in the 1970s and workers left. Lille's economy stagnated. The hope of Lille's planners was that the VAL system would provide an incentive for the regeneration of the city, a hope that appears to have been realized. Many credit the new transit system with having saved the city from crisis, which, by itself, is perhaps an exaggeration. But when planners take time and money to invest in a good transport system, they at least have their priorities right, and they often help the city to succeed in other areas.

Efficient as the VAL system is, making it fully automatic also meant that it had to be accident-proof since there is no operator onboard. This means that it must have its own track, leading to additional costs, and often aesthetic pollution and wasted space under elevated tracks. One might question if the labor costs of running the system manually would actually have been higher than the amortized cost and interest payments on the heavy initial investment of the fully automated system.

Even manually operated tram systems sometimes have their own trackways. Some trams still make part of their runs across city centers at ground level, but many others go in tunnels, cuttings, or elevated tracks. In suburban areas they sometimes run on a central reservation with one or two lanes of traffic on either side. The light rail vehicle is fitted with an electronic device which automatically turns the traffic lights in the approaching tram's favor, except where traffic is already crossing.

Hannover experienced a 46% increase in the use of public transport when light rail started running, but this was also due to the fact that the city coordinated the new light rail with existing bus and rail lines and park-and-ride systems. In central Hannover, light rail tracks have been put underground at great cost, which has tended to make streets above ground dead in the evenings. Streetcars can and should be used to make streets lively, a function that the French VAL system also fails to fulfill.

Some transport specialists think that priority tramways and light rail systems are the only way to deal with city traffic. They did the job pretty well once upon a time before they were chased out by cars. Unfortunately those cars not only chased the trolleys but destroyed denser settlement patterns, which makes the installation of new streetcar lines more problematical. Nevertheless, light rail is feasible even in medium and low density areas and city-to-suburb routes, especially if it receives, as it should, a subsidy from the local government. If we have made some critical remarks here about some of the light rail systems, it was to point out weaknesses to builders of future systems, not to criticize trams, which offer perhaps the very best hope for city transport.

To understand the difference between trolleys and other forms of transport like metros, buses, or airplanes, one need

191

merely look at the faces of the people hanging onto the San Francisco cable cars, or watch old European movies, most of which star a tram or two.

SOLUTION 19
The use of trams and light rail systems to replace private cars in cities.

✧

> *He shall separate them from one another,*
> *as a shepherd divideth his sheep from the goats.*
> Matthew 25:32

The Sheep and the Goats

Mayor La Guardia and his other forward-looking contemporaries had little use for streetcars because they impeded traffic. Yet their dearly beloved buses not only do so as well, but the traffic impedes *them*. To solve that little problem, we must follow Matthew's suggestion and separate the buses from the flock of sheep in their cars. One system for doing just that which was already in existence in the days of Matthew has been almost totally overlooked by the world's cities. Many cities have a major river, lake, canal, or waterfront, but very few make use of these for public transport. These are at present used almost exclusively for tourists, even though fast waterbuses and hydrofoils exist for transport purposes.

In 1988 London opened a waterbus service which is twenty miles long and makes eight stops along the Thames, including one stop at the new Docklands Development. Weekday service is from 7:00 A.M. to 10:00 P.M. with boats every 20 or 30 minutes. It presently carries about 1500 commuters per day.

Paris will have such a service in 1991. The Paris waterbus will make twenty-seven stops, of which twelve are in outlying areas,

192

thus giving suburbanites access to downtown. And passengers on the Paris boats will be able to use their magic fare card (the *carte orange*) to travel on the waterbuses.

The waterbus, along with the streetcar, is a joyful means of transport, and one should see many fewer long faces, furrowed brows, or characters out of Dante's Inferno than is the case on underground trains. It seems simplistic to say so, but people feel a lot less well underground than they do in God's open air polluted though that open air may be. Why should public transport users be forced into dingy, smelly, noisy, and dangerous underground passages when they could be listening to the clang of a trolley or watching the ripples left in the wake of their waterbus?

On terra firma, too, we find special independent lanes and trackways for buses are important in the competition with private cars. If buses themselves are stuck in traffic, they invite their riders to give personal transport another try. Such riders would argue that if you must be stuck in traffic, you might as well do so in comfort. That is often the argument used to make cars more luxurious inside and equip them with bars, telephone, and television. In 1989, a dozen women even felt comfortable enough to give birth on a congested Washington Beltway.

To convince such riders that public transport could be faster (even if somewhat less comfortable) than private transport, we must separate the sheep from the goats, something even transit-friendly cities have been slow to do. The city of Paris has 190 miles of reserved bus lanes, but the majority of these flow with the traffic; and even though such busways are clearly marked, they are subject to many obstructions such as deliveries, emergency stops, and private cars using the lanes illegally and often getting away with it. Such concurrent lanes would be more effective if they were constantly filled with buses, because that would leave less room for illegal users, and because car drivers would see that buses are plentiful, quick, and worth switching to. When Thackeray moved to Kensington in 1846, bus services were good enough to lead to his delighted exclamation: "and omnibuses every two minutes . . . what can mortal man want more?" What indeed, except such services today!

A more effective method than concurrent lanes is the counterflow in which buses only (and sometimes taxis) go against the normally one-way traffic. No one travels in such lanes illegally as a car would immediately be noticed. And nobody dares to obstruct such a lane, as to do so would force the bus into the stream of oncoming traffic. Manhattan's one-way avenues might be candidates for counterflow bus lanes.

Three decades ago Jane Jacobs had already expressed disapproval of these one-way avenues since they obliged passengers to walk long and sometimes dangerous crosstown blocks to reach their buses.[10] Ridership did drop (as it generally does) after avenues were made one-way. Some traffic planners suggest counterflow *and* concurrent flow for one-way avenues so that buses do not have to take different routes coming and going. In 1982, New York did manage to develop ten concurrent flow bus lanes covering a total of eleven miles, and these have increased bus speeds by 15% to 25% and even speeded up nonbus traffic by 10% to 20% due to the separation of the sheep and the goats.

In Pittsburgh a counterflow lane was implemented in 1981 to carry buses diverted from a parallel street under construction. The lane was created simply by removing parking along that

Concurrent bus lane in Paris.

stretch of downtown artery. This special bus lane was so successful that it has been made permanent. The lane currently carries approximately fifty to seventy buses in peak hours, and is in effect twenty-four hours a day. Turns to and from the counterflow lane have not been a problem. The lane is marked with overhead signs, double yellow line, and the diamond symbol. The success of this lane is attributed to cooperation between the city and the transit operator, to good driver training, to its self-enforcing design, to travel-time improvement for buses, and finally to the city's ability to remove parking—presumably without disgruntled would-be parkers holding protest meetings in front of city hall.

In spite of the success of such lanes and suggestions that a network of counterflow bus lanes is an effective technique for improving bus speeds, reliability, and access to and from downtown, most cities are hesitant to implement such a solution; perhaps it bothers them to see buses coming the "wrong" way on a one-way street. While counterflow lanes are among the cheaper ways to speed buses along their own pathways, they are by no means the only ones. In Philadelphia and Portland exclusive busways have been built which, while more costly, are well landscaped and provide an overall environmental improvement.[11]

Trolleybuses, which run with overhead wires but no rails, are used principally in Europe and South America but have been the subject of a recent revival of interest. Nancy in France has recently completed a new installation, and Bradford in England is proposing to install a twenty-five mile system over a hilly route which is projected to reduce exhaust emissions by over seventy tons per year. A few of the new trolleybuses are even dual mode, with diesel engines for use at special junctions and maintenance depots. The operating costs of these new trolleybuses are significantly lower than diesels, and even though initial costs are higher, they have a life expectancy of ten to twenty years beyond that of a diesel bus. Their noise levels are between 10 db and 30 db lower than that of conventional buses, and their speed around 14% higher.[12]

Another, and more modern, system of special busways is a track which uses guided buses. Essen in Germany and Adelaide

195

in South Australia have recently installed such tracks, about twelve miles in length. The buses used are conventional vehicles but have been equipped with three pairs of solid rubber-tired guide rollers on each side. Operating normally over the suburban street system, these special buses then approach the guideway, whose ends are splayed, at a speed of 25 miles per hour. Once on the track, the driver releases the steering wheel and the bus can roll along at speeds up to 60 miles per hour. Because these busways can handle a great number of fast-moving buses, passenger capacity on such a system has been estimated at as many as 18,000 per hour. In Adelaide a dozen bus routes from different suburban lines converge on the guideway. The capital costs of the guideway are estimated as being one-third lower than light rail, and only 10% higher than conventional bus systems.[13]

Still another special busway is Ottawa-Carleton's Transitway, a 12.5-mile-long system of specially built roads designed to serve up to 360 buses per hour and carry 20,000 riders daily. Unlike a fixed rapid transit system which is tied to rails from point of origin to final destination, it is more flexible and far less costly and allows passengers to travel from their local bus stop to the city center.

One reason why riders appear to have confidence in vehicles running on tracks is that the tracks themselves inspire trust. They tell the rider where the transport will come from and where it will go, and they are some sort of guarantee of its eventual arrival. Many people don't take buses because they can't figure out where the bus stops are, where their buses are headed, or when (and even if) they will arrive. This kind of confusion can be solved by clearly marked busways, and sheltered and architecturally integrated bus stops with clearly posted information about bus numbers, directions, and running intervals. Electronic display boards can tell the riders when their buses are expected to arrive. In a further refinement in Halmstad, Sweden, bus stops have platforms which allow riders to enter the bus without stepping up. An automatic guidance system positions the vehicle doors directly in front of the platform.

A truly innovative bus system would combine all the following elements:

- Reserved lanes, counterflow where possible
- Full priority at traffic signals
- Level loading to enter buses
- Stops architecturally integrated, convenient, and protected
- Good information displays
- Frequent and punctual service

By giving buses special treatment and separating them from the rest of the traffic, the cities of the world have nothing to lose but their private cars.

SOLUTION 20
Separate busways in cities to stimulate public transport.

✧

The young man feels his pockets
And wonders what's to pay.
A. E. Housman, *Last Poems*

The Orange, the Green, and the Black

Even if a city is fortunate enough to possess an efficient public transport system, it must still provide the magic key which makes access to such a system so simple that public transport becomes more attractive than taking a car. Unfortunately at present, that key is in the hands of very few city transport users. The young man feeling in his pocket and wondering what to pay when confronted by a complicated and cumbersome fare structure like that of the Washington Metro, would do a lot better in cities like Bremen, Freiburg, Basel, and Paris. He wouldn't have to calculate what to pay or puzzle out the electronic device which

197

does so but could jump on any train, tram, or bus, go any distance, at any time, with just a fare card in his possession.

The same young man, finding himself in New York City, wouldn't be wondering *what* to pay but *whether* to pay, and would witness there an almost perfect demonstration of what not to do about fare collection. The powers that be in that city decided in 1989 to raise the fare on buses and subways from a flat dollar to $1.15. The good people who sat around the board table to make this decision may have sincerely believed that the extra fifteen cents would bring more money into the transport coffers. Was there, however, even one among them who had ever travelled on a bus or a subway?

New York bus drivers are not allowed to accept a dollar bill because their fare collecting boxes don't handle paper money. They are not allowed to make or carry change because of fears for their safety. This meant that in the past people had to find four quarters or small change adding up to a dollar to take a bus, a thing quite difficult to do on a daily basis. And few people are well enough organized to keep not only four quarters but three additional nickels in their pockets, with double that amount in change if they want to make the return journey. So it was not surprising that ridership, already low, dropped even lower after the new fare was introduced, probably as much for nuisance reasons as for the increased fare.

On the subways the effect was even more disastrous. Long lines started to form in front of change booths to buy the tokens necessary to enter, leading otherwise solid citizens to jump over or crawl under the turnstiles, provided their flesh, as well as their citizenship, was not too, too solid to prevent them from doing so. New York City has now proudly announced the arrest of "artists, grandmothers, and clergymen" for turnstile jumping, bringing down the jump rates by a paltry 1.5%.[14] And as if that weren't enough, extortioners and touts now began making their appearance, selling tokens at scalper's rates or taking money from passengers in return for letting them pass through gates which the extortioners forced open; many turnstiles are, in any case, jammed or broken.

Another transport system that offers a fine example of what

not to do is the one in London where people stand out in the rain, lining up sheepishly in front of the narrow doors on a bus in which the driver is also the one selling the tickets. Since these tickets are often sold on the basis of route traveled or zone traversed, each passenger's price must be calculated while the other passengers get wet. London does have some travel card systems, but they work less well than the continental ones. London public transport is now the most expensive in Europe, and it is often actually cheaper to take a car in London than a bus or the underground, especially if more than one person is traveling. Part of the reason for the high fares is the fare zone system which results in anomalies, high fares for short distances, and cumbersome and time-consuming fare calculations. It is not surprising (though disheartening) that fewer than 20% of British drivers use buses and trains more than once a month. The main reasons given by drivers are high fares and infrequent, unreliable, and unpunctual service.[15]

Abolishing fare zones and instituting a proper fare card which accesses the entire London system might tempt British drivers to leave their vehicles at home. The exasperating point abut the present design of fare structures in places like London and New York is that fare chaos and loss of ridership could have been predicted, and prevented, by the well-paid ladies and gentlemen who devise such systems, had they taken the trouble to study the systems in Basel, Bremen, or Paris. Those cities offer transit riders a fare card, sold on a weekly and monthly basis, avoiding all these problems and accomplishing several purposes at once.

The fare card's first and most important function is to stimulate the use of public transport and give local people the idea that they have a unified, easy-to-use, and low-cost way of getting around their city. According to the Paris Rapid Transit Authority (RATP), the famous *carte orange*, introduced in that city in 1975, has given people the impression that Paris has a comprehensive network of transit systems and has been responsible for attracting them to that system. After the introduction of the carte orange the number of bus users in the city rose by over a third, with about half of the new riders (37,000 people) transferring from automobiles. If we assume that an average of one and a half of these transferees had formerly arrived in Paris by private car, this would have produced a drop of about 25,000 vehicles per day. Use of the carte orange rose from about 900,000 per day in 1976 to over 1,700,000 in 1987, thus almost doubling in its first decade.

On buses, cardholders flash their passes at the driver, but possessing such a card the passenger can also enter by the rear doors, thus making loading efficient. The rear entry is self-policing since riders are watched by their fellow passengers, and there are also occasional spotchecks. On metros riders use their yellow magnetic ticket accompanying the card, which opens the turnstile electronically and is then returned to the user. Yellow tickets for single use can also be bought in groups of ten for people who travel only occasionally.

In Basel, they have invented a fare card which is an example of what the German-speaking countries call *Umweltschutz Abonnement* (awkwardly rendered into English as "environmental protection subscription"). The Basel green card was created in 1984 in direct response to increasing fears about dying forests in central Europe. The price was set at a low SFr 35 (about $25) per month and allows the user not only unlimited travel in Basel, but on the whole suburban system.

This one simple card replaced almost four hundred potential combinations of subscriptions, the mastery of which required the brain of an Einstein. In spite of the orthodox transport doctrine in wealthy Switzerland that tariff changes would not have a great effect on ridership, the new card had a magic effect.[16] By massively reducing the yearly subscription and, above all, by making it simple, the city of Basel ended up with more money and fewer cars. In addition, public transport users got tax breaks for commuting trips which were not given to car users.

A similar green ticket introduced in Bremen was equally successful. In spite of considerable cost reductions over previous fares, the new card still produced a substantial net gain. The same was true for the fare card in Freiburg, which attracted enough riders to compensate the city amply for the lower fares.

A number of German cities use no card at all but an honor

system where passengers buy daily or monthly cards at automatic dispensers. There are no barriers or checkpoints, and the only surveillance is by the very occasional controller who asks passengers for their ticket. This system has given rise to what is called *Schwarzfahren* (traveling black), i.e., taking a chance of not being controlled. There are German businessmen whose only thrill in their otherwise rigidly humdrum daily existence is to ride black. These people have the penalty money ready in their pocket and hand it silently to the approaching conductor, having had their thrill for that day. Others, less well off, go black to save money. The moral quandary of whether to go black or not spoils this kind of system, which does not instill pride in the local populace for their public transport.

A fare card, on the other hand, instills such pride. Citizens know that their money is used efficiently to pay the people who work for them and who keep their city literally in running order. A fare card is self-policing in the sense that travelers "check in" in front of their fellows. And a fare card makes it administratively simple to give reductions to children, students, unemployed, retired, handicapped, and social hardship cases.

With a fare card, a city could also put into practice the idea of using such cards as a simple form of road pricing, where all drivers entering the city are obliged to show the fare card in their windshield. This requires no government outlays and would benefit public transport while restricting cars at the same time.

While this particular combination of transit support and auto deterrence hasn't yet been tried in practice, many cities have found citywide low-cost fare cards to be enormously successful, both in economic and environmental terms. Here is a case where economy and ecology go hand in hand! City fathers and mothers everywhere might well contemplate blessing their city with a fare card.

SOLUTION 21
The use of citywide fare cards to boost public transport.

11

TIGHTENING THE PURSE STRINGS: SOLUTIONS 22–24

We have now looked at ways to close the floodgates and ways to choose alternative transport. Now we go a bit further and see if we can't dissuade people from using their cars by economic means.

As we shall see, that does not mean punishing drivers by making them pay excessive sums to use their cars; it means simply charging them the fair market value of such use.

For Whom the Road Tolls

In trying to bring the car problem under control, we need not limit ourselves to restraining cars physically. We can also discourage car use by making drivers think twice before taking them. The practice of letting cars pay for the privilege of road use is nothing but the ancient custom permitting road builders to sell rather than give away free the road space they have created. Toll roads were known in ancient times and were popular in the Middle Ages.

The bridge of Avignon charged four deniers (pennies) for a wagon, two for a horse and rider, and half a penny for a man with a donkey. Perhaps the people in the famous song *"Sur le pont d'Avignon on y danse on y danse"* did their dancing because they—undoubtedly pedestrians—were able to pass the toll booth without paying. Early British and American turnpikes were built entirely by private companies who had the right to collect tolls. Tolls passed out of fashion in the late 19th century but were revived in the United States by the Pennsylvania Turnpike in the 1930s.

Since the late 1940s, economists have looked into and written about the theory of road pricing, but their recommendations have languished in technical journals or been ignored. Toll roads and road pricing are making a comeback today partly because local governments are beginning to realize that the taxes they collect to build and maintain roads for automobile use do not nearly cover the expense of doing so. Moreover, taxes force the cost of roads on citizens who may not have cars.

Tolls have the double purpose of recompensing the state for the construction and maintenance of the road and of keeping that road open by discouraging excessive use. Modern road pricing is primarily concerned with the second of these functions. Road pricing might be said to be a way of rationing road space and of obliging drivers to pay for the congestion they cause public transport users, cyclists, pedestrians, and freight and emergency vehicles.

In Singapore the world's first example of area road pricing, (as opposed to road tolls) was launched in 1975. Known as Area Licensing Scheme (ALS), it was one of the few World Bank–assisted projects not concerned with costly construction. This scheme required cars passing twenty-eight points of entry into the city to display a prepurchased license. The license cost about $2.50 per day or $50 per month. Company cars were charged double that rate (unlike in Britain where they are tax-assisted) and taxis one-half, while freight and high occupancy vehicles (three or more passengers) went free. Area licensing is estimated to have cut down the cars entering Singapore by about 50% of what it could have been, yet the actual number of vehicles has grown nonetheless because people are either willing to pay, or enter the town before 7:30 A.M. when the system goes into effect. In the evening, when no controls exist, traffic increases by 100%.

The Singapore experiment shows what we are up against even in a successful car restraint measure. In spite of the licensing scheme (which is still in effect), in spite of a metro system, and in spite of new shade trees and seating along sidewalks to stimulate walking, the car in Singapore still "remains the central means of transport."[1]

Perhaps the most celebrated and controversial attempt to institute road pricing, one cited continually by all the experts, was begun in Hong Kong in 1983, when cable loops were laid out in the roadbed at eighteen sites, and electronic number plates were fitted to 2600 cars on a test basis. Roadside stations besides the loops transmitted a coded message to a central computer which identified the vehicle, the time, and the amount for which the owner would be billed for at the end of the month.

While the Singapore system relied on manual checks, the Hong Kong scheme, known as Electronic Road Pricing (ERP), was technically highly sophisticated. But although the electronics proved 99% reliable, local political factors forced abandonment of the system. As expected, drivers revolted against the additional expense, as vehicle taxes had just been raised, and there were also objections to an invasion of privacy because a vehicle's movement could be pinpointed at any time. Drivers seized upon that objection, because both the terms ERP and Automatic Vehicle Identification (AVI) suggest a computerized Big Brother type of surveillance. In fact, both terms are inaccurate. ERP would more accurately have been described by a term like "automatic road-use charging." As for AVI, that designation is likely to give public relation experts heartburn. In point of fact, only the law-breaking vehicle is being identified; the vast majority won't appear in the electronic records.[2]

Objections are often made that road pricing, like a fuel tax increase, is unfair to the poor. But theoretically at least, some of that increased revenue, as well as the increased mobility, benefits public transport and the poor who depend on it; and keeping cars out of a city benefits rich and poor alike. In any case, objections that higher car costs fall upon the poor are often made by people who care little about the welfare of the poor but who use this argument in an attempt to lower their own costs. More serious objections to road pricing are made by John Whitelegg, who worries that letting people pay for the use of roads gives them a kind of license to pollute. He also fears that traffic misery will just spread into adjacent nonpriced areas and that local authorities will be encouraged to think of the revenue as more money for roads, tunnels, and bridges.[3]

ERP was to be introduced by the Dutch Ministry of Transport for the Randstad area (Amsterdam, Rotterdam, and Shiphol airport), an area which is currently being suffocated by traffic, congestion, and pollution. However, the ministry's scheme has for the moment been defeated by a combination of factors ranging from oil interests to the complexity of the electronics involved. When a road pricing scheme is simple, political opposition to it can perhaps be overcome. But when it becomes technically complex and difficult to administer—and thus expensive, like the Dutch system—it has little chance of surviving.

A simpler electronic system than that attempted by the Dutch is operating in Oslo and Ålesund, Norway. (In Oslo, the scheme is unfortunately not used as a car control measure but to make money for more road building.) In that system, called Premid, the driver purchases an ID plate the size of a large matchbox at the local bank. This plate is then placed in the vehicle's side window and read by antennae units mounted on the side of the road, which turn a traffic light green if the plate is up to date, and red if the driver has to proceed to a toll booth. Up to 1500 vehicles per hour can be processed, and the equipment costs about $30,000 for two lanes.[4]

The easiest form of road pricing requires no electronics and few administrative costs and has the advantage of benefiting public transport directly, without government interference. One such proposal, made recently for Stockholm, would require all drivers entering a city to display the local public transport fare card in their windshield. This has the enormous advantage of simplicity and of inducing motorists to try the public transport for which they have already paid. But in spite of its simplicity, the Swedish government postponed introducing this fare card display scheme because it had no faith in a system based on manual control of stickers by traffic wardens.

Psychologically, the soundest approach is making drivers pay each time, which is the most effective way to restrain them and bring home to them the true costs of their trip. In the Hong Kong system, motorists were billed at the end of the month, a bill they would pay along with all their other bills without giving it special notice.

Such payments don't hurt like digging into your pocket for change. In the ideal road-pricing system, drivers would be aware that they are paying for road space the way taxi passengers are aware of the clicking meter. Perhaps the ultimate road-pricing system would use a car that can only be started by inserting a "smart" card that ticks off a number of units for each kilometer driven.

SOLUTION 22
The use of easily administered road pricing to control the number of cars on the road.

✧

> *... and filled their lamps*
> *With everlasting oil, to give due light*
> *To the misled and lonely traveller.*
> Milton, *Comus*

Sextupling the Essence

The French word for fuel (gasoline in America and petrol in England) is *essence,* and this word sums up most people's attachment to motor vehicles and the golden liquid which propels them. Those who realize that the oil we use for our cars causes many problems for the environment look to alternate fuels as a solution to those problems. If we could find a nonpolluting, energy-efficient, and cheap substitute for oil, all would be well, they think. But would it?

In the first place, few of the alternate fuels are at present technically or economically feasible without further research. And then some of these are almost as unfriendly to the environment

WORLD OIL PRODUCTION

Millions of Barrels per Day

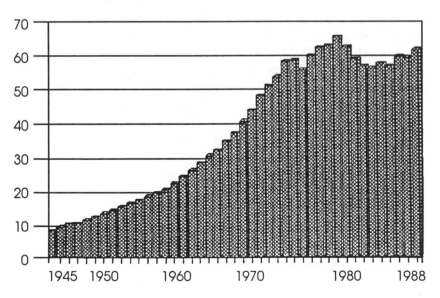

as gasoline/petrol (a few even more so), and most would not help us get cars off the road.

One of the few promising alternate fuels is natural gas, which is plentiful, safe, and costs marginally less for an equivalent gallon. Natural gas was tried in British Columbia after the 1979 oil shocks, where service stations were given inducements to add this fuel to their pumping bays. But because it costs about $1500 per vehicle to convert to such use, only commercial fleets of trucks and cabs took advantage of this option. Private motorists are often doubtful about trying a new fuel, fearing safety and uncertain prices. New fuels also suffer from what is called the chicken-and-the-egg syndrome. Drivers won't use alternate fuels until they are widely distributed, and they won't be widely distributed until drivers use them.

The chicken-and-the-egg syndrome can be bypassed if a government subsidizes and pushes the alternate fuel energetically. This happened in New Zealand where the government launched a major compressed natural gas program in 1979. With the help of grants and loans, some 11% of all cars and light trucks had been converted by 1986, and 400 fuel stations were established. A new government then reduced the incentives in 1985, and the conversion rates fell sharply.

As a result of the oil shocks, the Brazilian government decided to push alcohol, produced from Brazil's plentiful sugar, to replace other fuels. The results of the Brazilian effort (which is still continuing) are very mixed, both in economic and environmental terms. There is not space here to go into the complicated history of the Brazil alcohol experiment, but the lesson appears to be that it is better not to respond to transient economic incentives such as the oil price rises with long-range economic policies if this involves long-range and irreversible restructuring. An alternate fuel policy must look in advance at all its possible effects: economic, environmental, and car restraint—something the Brazilians did not do.[5]

In the United States methanol has been considered because it is a cheap nonpetroleum-based fuel which offers the possibility of reduced dependence on imported oil, improved air quality, and easy vehicle conversion. It can be manufactured from coal,

208

but the process is complex, polluting, and inefficient. It can also be made from natural gas, but 30% to 40% is lost in the conversion, so that natural gas itself appears the preferred option.[6]

Besides alternate fuels, there are also alternatives to the internal combustion engine. Prominent among these are external combustion engines such as Stirling and Rankine (using air and steam) and electric power. Electric vehicles are often thought of as being clean, but it is just as often forgotten that the power they use comes from generators. If the originating power stations burn coal, such vehicles will produce even more carbon dioxide than conventional cars. Still, if electric cars were recharged from an average mix of fossil-, nuclear-, and hydro-generated electricity, greenhouse emissions would fall by about 25%.[7] That 25% gain in environmental terms does not even include the electric car's ability to avoid the pollution caused by starting, idling, and stopping and going.

When those factors are added in, electric vehicles compare very favorably with conventional cars. Electric vehicles are, however, at present limited by the inadequate state of battery technology. We have not yet devised a storage system which is small and light and holds enough power for an extended cruising range. Fuel cells, which convert the chemical energy in hydrogen and other gases directly into electrical energy without mechanical losses may in time make the electric car feasible. The state of California has now passed legislation requiring 2% of all motor vehicles sold in the state in 1998 to be Zero Emission Vehicles (ZEVs), rising to 10% by the year 2003. Barring some unforeseen development in hydrogen or solar power, ZEVs can only mean electric vehicles, which will give that technology a much-needed boost.

We may one day end up with a less polluting and more energy-efficient fuel and motor than we have at present. But that would not solve all our problems. The simplest way to solve those problems and break people's attachment to their vehicles is to raise the price of the fuel that makes those vehicles move, whatever that fuel may be. The only dip in the ever-mounting curve of fuel consumption and car use occurred during the so-called oil shocks of the 1970s. That was also the time that carmakers decided to develop more efficient engines.

♦

209

Electric vehicle of 1903.

During the oil crises there was much talk about the depletion of our resources, and the enormous oil consumption was considered an ecological evil only because we were wasting a nonrenewable resource. So there was much concern about making cars which use that precious oil more efficiently. However, since total oil reserves have grown from 464 billion barrels in 1968 to almost double—917 billion barrels in 1988—oil depletion is today not an issue of great importance.[8] When the oil shocks receded, automakers and general public alike went back to their bad old habits as if nothing had happened. The public stopped demanding energy-efficient vehicles, and the industry stopped concentrating on their research.

We must be clear about our goal here. Is it to save oil, or is it to get the cars off the road and put a stop to the damage associated with their unchecked growth? As with many other car-related issues, attempts to make things better can turn out to be counterproductive. Preserving oil may mean making *more* available for additional millions of cars. And making engines more energy-efficient may mean that motorists pay less to drive a given distance. Though efficient engines certainly pollute less, their higher energy conversion ratios mean that each gallon gives more miles per dollar, and this may encourage yet more auto use, canceling out the environmental advantage.

Time magazine, which cannot be accused of being a radical rag, has proposed sextupling the price of American fuel,[9] thus doubling European prices which are already about three times as high as those in the United States. This would go a way toward reducing subsidies and discouraging drivers. And it would certainly spur the development of fuel-efficient engines and alternate energy sources which may be less polluting. But we have to remember that increasing fuel prices is only a partial solution. A price shock is only effective if it confronts a driver with a sudden rise. If the price creeps up little by little, drivers and industry grumble but adapt to the new level, nullifying the effect of the rise.

What Europeans pay for fuel would cause rioting in the streets of America, yet Europeans calmly pay triple the American price. It is only a sudden jump in the level drivers have grown used to—low or high as it may be—that produces a shock effect. After the initial shock, drivers would normally return to their old habits. And with fuel-efficient cars they could weather such shocks even more easily. Nonetheless, a new and higher pump price would at least enable governments to reduce their car subsidies, and continuous price rises would eventually make people less eager to use their cars.

At present price levels, fuel represents only 15% of a car's operating cost, down from 26% in 1975.[10] Because fuel costs are the most visible of all car-related expenses, this low percentage means that fuel would have to go up substantially to act as a car restraint measure. Fuel-efficient cars already exist, like the Volvo LCP2000, which gets more than 100 miles to the gallon, or Peugeot's ECO 2000, which gets between 70 and 100. But the makers refer to such cars as "crisis" cars to be released when the public clamors for them. The public has no incentive to clamor for them until price shocks are continuous and bring the fuel cost to a much higher percentage than 15%.

GASOLINE/PETROL PRICES AND TAXES			
NATION	PRICE (including tax)	TAX	EQUIVALENT CARBON TAX*
United States	1.32	.3	121
Japan	3.44	1.44	575
Germany	3.52	1.97	787
United Kingdom	3.71	2.08	833
France	4.32	2.95	1181
Italy	5.19	3.56	1423

*Current gasoline taxes translated into a levy on the carbon content of fuel.

Nor does the public now clamor for small cars, switching instead to heavier cars and light-duty trucks which are less efficient than cars and now account for fully one-third of all automobiles sold in the United States.[11] The appeal of these pickup trucks, which now consume half of all the fuel used in the United States, is almost entirely a function of Marlboro-type advertising which associates trucks with freedom and adventure.[12] And finally the carmakers themselves can't be expected to have much interest in small cars because, as Henry Ford II said in 1971, "mini cars mean mini profits."[13]

To change the attitudes of the public and carmakers alike, there is therefore a strong case to be made for raising fuel prices. We need not even raise prices to a punitive level—all we need to do is to charge for fuel what it really costs. As is the case with most other car-related items, drivers do not pay the full cost of the energy they use.

What they pay for, aside from the taxes governments charge, is exploration, production, refining, transport, and delivery of the oil. What they don't pay for are the high costs of defending a secure supply of that oil and the high costs of repairing the damage that this oil does to human and plant health through vehicle

212

emissions and to the environment through routine oil spills, tanker flushings, and fuel station leakage. We spill the equivalent of the *Exxon Valdez* every three weeks, and one-third of all U.S. fuel stations are leaking. Nor do drivers begin to pay for the anticipated and enormous costs of dealing with manifestations of the greenhouse effect.

To bring energy prices to their correct level, a concept called Polluter Pays Principle (PPP) would have to be applied to them. Because this application would bring fuel prices to such a high level that few governments would have the political will to implement them, governments could get around such enormous oil shocks by raising energy prices a certain percentage annually, or penalizing dirty fuels and rewarding clean ones. This would stimulate the search for cleaner alternate fuels, bring energy prices in line with their true costs, and discourage car use.

The German government recently quite cleverly took advantage of the Gulf crisis and the need for East German modernization to announce a fuel tax rise. By waiting for an emergency before announcing a fuel increase, they forestalled political opposition.[14] A 20% annual fuel price rise over a ten year period would be both high enough to discourage car use and low enough to allow essential users to adapt. Some of this tax money would be spent on roads as has traditionally been the case and on other car-related items to reduce government subsidy to automobiles. Much of it would go into a fund for environmental cleanup.

But a portion should be spent on public transport. This would not only help the environment but would be a form of social justice, as the better-off owner-drivers would thus contribute to the costs of providing transport for children, the poor, and the elderly. And this would set up a cycle whereby motorists would have to pay more to drive and at the same time be offered more efficient and cheaper alternate transport.

SOLUTION 23
Higher fuel taxes to discourage car use.

All animals are equal, but some animals are more equal than others.

George Orwell, *Animal Farm*

More Equal Than Others

A devoted motorist, who has come this far in a recital which he must consider very one-sided, is bound to have lost all patience by now. If he were reading all this in a newspaper, he would no doubt rush to his personal computer and fire off an indignant letter to the editor. This is how his letter might be worded:

> Dear Editor,
> What is this all about? A bicyclist pays a couple of hundred for his machine and that's the end of it. He pays no taxes, no registration fees, he doesn't support the economy, and he gets a free ride on the roads.
> We motorists, by contrast, are taxed to the hilt, after having invested thousands in our cars and their maintenance, thereby stimulating the economy and creating jobs for other people. And on top of that we pay ever more for the fuel to keep our cars running. But that's the system we live in: you pays your money and you takes your choice. My choice is cars and freedom.
>
> Yours,
> An Outraged Driver

Well, one might respond, you takes your choice all right, but do you pays your money? Or is it possible that the great car economy, the very symbol and star of our capitalist, free market, private enterprise system, is the subject of hidden state subsidies which are suspiciously akin to the subsidies found in communist economies?

In such economies, we must remember, governments used to hand to their people essential items like food and rent at substantially lower than market costs; and much of the present turbulence in Eastern Bloc countries comes down to the question of how these subsidies can be withdrawn and the free market economy restored in the most painless fashion. Governments and em-

214

pires are tottering in the effort to resolve this question. In many Western and Third World countries a similar subsidy is given to the motorcar, surely a less essential item than food or rent, yet no governments are tottering. The reason for this is simple: The subsidy is so well hidden that governments and their people rarely think of it in those terms.

There have been various attempts to estimate the cost of subsidies to the motor industry. One such study assessed municipal costs of automobile use in Pasadena, California. The study tabulated the cost of such items as car-related city administration, police and traffic court time, public works and debt service, and car-related capital improvements, over and above car-related receipts.

On the basis of that study, using Pasadena as a typical American community with typical amounts spent on car-related items, the total U.S. subsidy was calculated to be in the region of $60 billion—about the present level of welfare payments to people who have low or no incomes.[15] This figure, however, referred only to *municipal* costs over receipts and therefore would not have taken account of highway construction and maintenance costs at state and federal levels.

When those costs are included, the bill for the United States becomes much higher. An estimate given by the Worldwatch Institute of the total car subsidy in the United States comes closer to $300 billion.[16] It is a curious coincidence that this is exactly the amount estimated by the Environmental Protection Agency in 1990 for a total cleanup of hazardous waste sites, acid rain, radioactive waste, and air in the United States.

The California Department of Transportation gives the flat sum of $2500 per vehicle as the difference between what is collected from and what is spent on motor vehicles. Multiplying that figure by the 132 million cars in the American fleet gives us the sum of $330 billion, an estimate even higher than that given by Worldwatch.

German researchers put the full cost of a car-based society in their country between DM 109 billion and DM 117 billion for the year 1986. This estimate included road construction and maintenance, air pollution costs, traffic noise costs, accident and injury costs, and cost of land for parking use. It did not include administration of justice or police court time, the costs of human health arising from exhaust emissions, or the billions in very expensive production time lost by congestion. The revenues collected by the German government from cars and the automobile industry amounted to approximately DM 30 billion in that year.[17] We can conclude, therefore, that the (roughly) DM 80-billion difference between outlay and income amounted to a state subsidy for that year. Dividing that figure by the 32 million vehicles in the German car fleet and putting it into dollar terms, we come out with $2200 of German subsidy per vehicle, a figure quite similar to the American one.

TRUCK COSTS IN GERMANY
Total costs and taxation income for lorries in West Germany in 1987. Mean estimates. All figures in million DM per year.

INCOME (all taxes)	6724
COSTS	
Road expenditure	8730
Accident costs	5030
Distress-related accidents	2600
Air pollution	6350
Noise costs (private dwellings)	9850
Other noise costs	2500
Congestion	2000
Water pollution (from dangerous goods)	3800
Water pollution (from road salting)	2800
Health damage to lorry drivers	1100
Other	1200
TOTAL COSTS	46,000
TOTAL COSTS NOT COVERED BY TAX INCOME	39,300

Even these estimates do not include further and more hidden costs of an automobile-based society. In the United Kingdom well over £2 billion would become available to the state if tax breaks to company-assisted motoring were removed, something the government is now at long last at least considering. At present, 40% of central London drivers use cars subsidized by companies, and thus indirectly by the state, and four out of five British drivers get some form of motoring "perks" from their employers.[18] In Holland, a recent study of a carless community of 5000 dwellings estimated a net saving to the government of 16 million G (about $10 million) in just this one community because the government would save itself the usual car-related costs.

One need not be a cynic to add to the list of motorcar subsidies the high cost of defending Middle East oil. The rationale for that defense is to ensure access to a supply of cheap oil. But is that oil really cheap? The barrel price of oil, not even counting the cost of war, has been estimated to be close to $80, about three times today's actual price if the cost of maintaining troops, foreign aid to Middle East countries, and interest payments to borrow these funds are factored in. That is certainly well above prices of American domestic oil and more attractive alternate fuels.[19]

The real tragedy of this subsidy is not the enormous waste of government money, but the millions of vehicles which are on the road every morning. They are there because drivers consider motoring a bargain, and no wonder—the government picks up the tab for most of it. Automobiles, to put it another way, don't take their proper place in a level playing field, to use current jargon. They have an unfair head start.

Public transport—unlike private personal transport usually essential—is, on the other hand, expected to pay its own way. When it cannot do so, politicians grumble and cut unprofitable lines. Even France, a country with excellent public transport, spends fourteen times less on what the French call *transport en commun* than it does on the private car.[20] In the United Kingdom, British Rail is expected to get along without any subsidies, whereas cars receive not only subsidies but tax breaks. The result is plainly visible every morning on all motorways leading into

London. With the best will in the world, even the most environment-conscious commuters can't afford to take expensive and unreliable trains.

Sometimes even the money spent on public transport is really a hidden car subsidy. Expensive metro construction may conceivably fall into that category since a much cheaper ground level tramway could perhaps have been built at enormous savings. But the tracks at ground level could have impeded a speeding automobile, so under the street they go, which means the masses must descend into the netherworld. Still the subways at least move those masses efficiently and in large numbers, so metros, even when considered a hidden car subsidy, give value for the sums spent on them.

The same cannot be said for highways on which cars roll in the sunshine, often bearing only a single individual. Cost of metro construction, high as it is, pales into insignificance when set alongside the money needed to construct urban expressways. Such costs are now calculated by French engineers to be in the region of Fr 1000 per millimeter (or $5000 an inch.)[21] The projected central artery project in Boston is expected to cost nearly $5 billion. If this cost were passed on to motorists, it would work out to an estimated $14 per trip. If automobiles were charged the real cost of highway construction, a trip from New York to Boston, for example, would cost the motorist the same or more as trainfare for that distance without counting fuel, insurance, and running costs. The train would be then seen as a bargain.

One can quibble with the size of the figures given by various researchers on automobile subsidies, but the fact that such subsidies exist and run into billions is established beyond a doubt. What has not been established is calling a spade a spade: acknowledging that most government handling of the car economy and infrastructure amounts to a well-disguised subsidy.

There are signs, though, that people are beginning to recognize a spade when they see one. In California, where future trends often make their first appearance, a group of conservative San Francisco corporate and political leaders endorsed drastic proposals to discourage single occupancy vehicles in an attempt to eliminate that subsidy. The smaller the number of low occupancy vehicles, the smaller such a subsidy becomes. Their recommendations, some of the most dramatic public policy proposals in California history, include such measures as tripling bridge fees, conversion of key highways into toll roads, mass transit allowances for employees, institution of high-occupancy vehicle privileges, and elimination of free parking.[22]

In California, the chief economist of Pacific Gas and Electric said that "The supply side approach doesn't work. More roads only bring more people."[23] And in New York, the director of bridges and tunnels said, "We won't build more vehicle tunnels into Manhattan because there is no more room for vehicles in Manhattan."[24] Such ideas were until recently considered radical, especially in the United States, but are now gaining support in many communities. Nothing can be done about the hidden subsidies to the automobile until they are widely recognized as such, not only by individuals and local authorities, but by national governments.

National governments, like the partners of unfaithful spouses, often know the facts only after everyone else knows them. So our first task must be to inform ourselves about these subsidies and then make others aware of them so that pressure can be put on governments to take steps toward eliminating them.

SOLUTION 24
Informing the public about government subsidies of automobiles to create political pressure for their removal.

219

12

REARRANGING THE WAY WE LIVE: SOLUTIONS 25–29

So far we have dealt more or less directly with cars and other means of transport that might replace them.

In this next group of solutions we look at more fundamental ways of attacking the problem. We suggest ways of rearranging the way we live to lessen our dependence on cars. This can be done by planning our cities and suburbs so that residences and workplaces are intermingled; by using telecommunications to avoid the daily trip to work; and finally by individuals choosing consciously to make their personal lives less car-dependent.

> *Things fall apart; the center cannot hold;*
> *Mere anarchy is loosed upon the world . . .*
> W. B. Yeats, "The Second Coming"

Making a House a Home

The lines by Yeats lines describe what happens to human settlements arranged haphazardly, without center or plan, or worse yet, with the wrong kind of plan. The American journalist and observer Russell Baker puts it this way:

> When you stood on Main Street (in small town U.S.A.) you could tell yourself "this is the center, the point on which all things converge" and feel the inexplicable but nonetheless vital comfort that results from knowing where you stand in the world and what the score is. On the shopping mall, people know they are standing not at the center but somewhere vaguely off toward the edge of a center that has failed to hold.[1]

The shoppers in this segregated imitation city lack a central focus toward which they will be drawn. They drift from shop to shop like ghostly images in an oppressive dream, without energy or central purpose. Just beyond their imitation city lies another one with exactly the same shops, the same names, the same items for sale, and the same prices. According to social scientist E. V. Walter, people are, "for the first time in human history, systematically building meaningless places."[2] The myriad of these ironically named centers and the "anarchy loosed upon the world" by the road and service infrastructure which goes to support them are among the many accomplishments for which our dear car can claim full credit. Although we should distinguish the chaotic sprawl made up of assorted structures set down willy-nilly from the suburban areas that house and supply the sprawl's customers, they are two sides of the same predicament.

In the sprawls people do their living and working, in the suburbs their sleeping. The two are absolutely dependent on each other, and both rely entirely on personal mechanical transport between them. To do away with sprawls, we have to rearrange our suburbs in the fashion already suggested earlier for cities: make

221

people live closer together, with clearly defined boundaries and greenbelts around them, and site their amenities among them, close enough to be reached by walking or cycling.

To do this we have to resist the continuous pressure from developers for shopping centers to be sited outside cities and towns, on green fields and along motorways or large roads where land is (or was) cheap. Such pressure exists even in Europe where town centers are much more clearly defined than in North America and where greenbelt laws often forbid developments outside a specified line drawn around each community.

In America, where these developments have grown to monstrous proportions, they often serve half a million people within twenty minutes' driving time. Though many of these developments are quite well designed, with offices and shopping, sports, and leisure facilities, they contain an air of unreality about them: "They lack a live-in population and are often unrelated to the surrounding areas and not served by public transport. Access is solely by private cars, forming a sea of parking surrounding each center. These developments simply avoid the problem of building in cities, and use up valuable rural land."[3]

These sprawls continue their unchecked growth in the same alarming fashion as the number of cars on the road, and indeed the two growth rates feed parasitically upon each other. The North Parkway area outside Dallas, for instance, quadrupled in size in the last six years and is expected to rival downtown Dallas —itself already almost totally car-dependent—in office space soon.

Surveys in the United States indicate that three out of five suburban office workers also use their commuting cars to make intermediate stops on the way to and from work, and four out of five use their cars at lunchtime. They do so not because they are particularly addicted to cars but because there are no amenities in the sterile office developments where they work.[4] If they want to drop off their children, get their prescriptions filled, develop their films, shop for dinner, and eat a good lunch, they are forced to take the cars they might formerly have left at home when many of them were still working downtown. But since two-thirds of all jobs created in the United States between 1960–1980 were located in the suburbs, we are not likely to return to those downtown days.[5]

The number one cause of car dependence in America is therefore the kind of land-use planning which leaves people no choice but to depend on their vehicles. The obvious answer to the problems posed by these totally car-dependent developments is to arrange them differently: increase density; mix business, residential, commercial, and industrial uses; and group them in such a way that most destinations can be reached by foot, bicycle, or public transport. In other words, we are back to a vision of towns and cities. Needless to say, all this is easier said than done. Our heritage from the earlier part of this century has been untold acres of dreary suburbs, and more untold acres of even drearier urban sprawl. What are we going to do about them?

They say that it takes a lot of living to make a house a home. A house is just a collection of rooms. When we begin to live in a house, we create centers of activity, a kitchen, a living room, a workroom, among which members of a household circulate. Our present suburbs are bedrooms only and therefore do not constitute a true home. To do something about our existing suburbs we need to make them into living places; we have to "retrofit," as they call it in technical language, repairing, remodeling, and rearranging rather than tearing down and starting all over, to achieve satisfactory results.

Suburban communities are described in the collection of essays *Public Streets for Public Use* as having developed "inward and private worlds" where to be a pedestrian, a bicyclist, or a street vendor is to be a "fish out of water." People in such communities wear "environmental blinders" where each household develops a favorite "mini-environment" for playing, shopping, and living. People travel between these privileged places and put on their environmental blinders because the streetscape is too unsightly to warrant any kind of inspection.[6]

Suburbs are thus the direct opposite of Goethe's ideal because he considered the goal of a journey much less important than what one encountered along the way. What motorists, who are normally goal-oriented, encounter along the way is what they consider mostly obstruction, danger, and distraction. Drivers

New Housing Starts in the United States

Thousands of Units

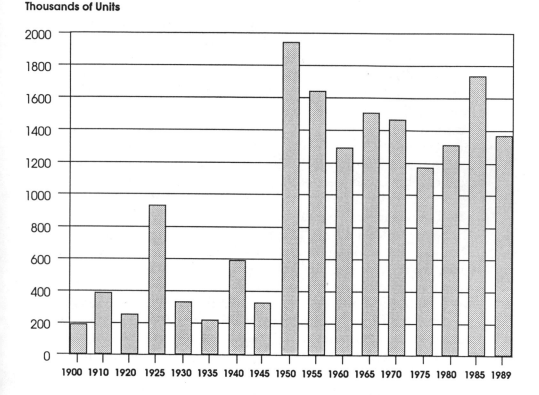

need simple surroundings because too much visual stimulation creates confusion and can lead to accidents. In other words, to design a world safe for drivers, we are obliged to make that world boring.

People on foot require the opposite kind of environment. Jane Jacobs often talks of making blocks short or of offering pedestrians interesting alleyways, passages, or shortcuts.[7] If pedestrians can cut a corner, they will do so even if they save only three yards. Walkers want interesting things to look at and almost always prefer what appears to them as a short distance. They will count the distance up to, say, a passageway, then start counting anew as they turn the corner into the passage, and finally begin again on the third part of the journey on emerging from the passage. The very same three parts when united into a long block become daunting.

The car, on the other hand, requires that one long block, the longer the better since side streets just add danger and confusion. Because suburbs depend on cars, and cars depend on those long blocks, people who live in such communities and travel only by car may not be aware of what their suburb really looks like. Aerial photos of many a suburban community reveal the close relationship that actually exists between residential developments and community services, a proximity perhaps never realized by the people who live there because roads do not make the shortest connections between them. A surprisingly high percentage of suburban homes turn out to be within easy (up to three miles) cycle distance of shopping, schools, parks, offices, bus stops, and even some workplaces. Many are even within walking distance (up to one mile).

What is lacking are the interconnections. Many suburban roads have no sidewalks, and almost none have bicycle paths. Many apartment complexes have parking lots around them which block pedestrians or cyclists from using them as shortcuts or moving from one complex to another. In fact, people on foot are often suspect and are sometimes even questioned by the police.

Ironically, the reason apartment complexes block pedestrians and bicycles from traversing their territory is security; but since such linkages would stimulate a community spirit, they would make these sometimes fenced and guarded properties more secure than before by introducing life and movement and "eyes on the street" as Jane Jacobs called them. One would not have to alter the basic layout of many suburbs very radically to make living urban centers out of them. What they need principally is a cleverly designed pedestrian and bicycle infrastructure, together with strictly enforced speed limits for cars (15 miles per hour) that would tempt pedestrians and cyclists onto suburban streets and would then "self-police" cars towards lower speeds. Making roadbeds narrower and giving the extra width to cyclists and walkers would accomplish the dual purpose of giving them space and making cars slow down and drive more carefully, encouraging thereby even more walkers.

A further step is breaking up some shopping centers and placing individual stores where they do the most good, that is, within people's walking and cycling range. Positioned like that, they serve to draw activity into the street. Jane Jacobs uses the metaphor of chess to compare amenities to important chess pieces controling the movement of the pawns. To save a suburb we must knit it together with many interconnecting pathways, shortcuts, and hidden passages that lead to stores, cafés, and social centers so that people begin to circulate amongst them. The suburb may then cease to be a bedroom community and assume an identity and personality of its own, no longer a "sub" urb or second-class city, but a town.

To encourage such a sense of identity it helps to have physical borders. Medieval towns felt secure within their walls not so much because they were invasion-proof, but because the limits told every resident and every stranger where the city began and ended. Suburbs could have simple arches, for example, in some cases made from trees or hedges, to demarcate the town's en-

Saint Denis, now a Paris suburb, in the sixteenth century.

trances and exits on all roads leading to and from the town. When cars pass under such arches, they are more apt to slow down and behave like invited guests.

The town's name could be prominently displayed at entrances and again at exits, this time with a line barring the name as is done on the continent. There could be signs pointing out anything worth visiting, any notable historical fact, or even the name of the town's ball team or high school.

Even insignificant French towns routinely announce their attractions by displaying them on a large sign at the settlement's entrance: Beauville, its churches, its parks, its hotels, its tennis courts. These signs should be well designed and set apart from the forest of meaningless signs and billboards assaulting visitors to the usual suburb. Beauville may be no prettier than any other suburb, but its people are proud of it. Anything that makes this suburb different from the next one and puts the visiting car on notice that it has entered not a "dreary street gorge" but a town with living human beings is to be welcomed.

The task of making living towns out of lifeless suburbs is not beyond the capacity of a group of interested citizens who take the trouble to study the layout of their town, from aerial photos, if possible. They could then meet with town planning boards to institute traffic-calming techniques on their streets, push for shortcuts, and plan walk and bike paths. They could invite shops, open-air markets, social centers, and cultural activities into their streets, and form committees whose job it is to dress up entrances and exits to emphasize physical borders and the town's identity.

SOLUTION 25
Rethink the concept of suburbs to make sterile bedroom communities into living towns.

✧

> *They spend their time mostly looking forward to the past.*
> John Osborne, *Look Back in Anger*

The Brave Old World

When we move from retrofitting existing suburbs to planning and building new communities, we find a growing number of American designers and developers rejecting the dominant modern methods of creating new residential areas. They are coming to view the community development practices of the past few decades as a terrible blunder and returning to the town planning traditions of the early twentieth century and before. The newest American suburbs look a lot like some of the oldest small towns—a mix of big and little dwellings close enough together that neighbors, schools, and shopping are within walking distance. Enclosed shopping malls are giving way to an open Main Street look, with street corners, soda fountains, and people on the sidewalks.[8]

Andres Duany, a Miami architect, says that the postwar suburb, with its miles of similar houses on huge lots needing constant mowing and weeding, never really worked. Social isolation came as planners, often eschewing sidewalks and squares, tailored suburbs to cars rather than to people. Schools and suburbs were minutes away by car but too far to walk to. These suburbs, continues Duany, did not anticipate that two-thirds of American mothers would have outside jobs. "The suburb is profoundly sexist," Mr. Duany contends. "It assumes that the women will always be there to play chauffeur."[9]

Some sociologists go even further in maintaining that the modern suburb, with its spread-out character and isolation and its obligatory long travel commutes, would not have been possible if women were not performing unpaid their labor of reproduction, thereby freeing their husbands for the luxury of the added travel time.[10] Once installed in such a suburb, women have no choice but to bear the isolation after they bear their children.

For those reasons the word "suburb," having acquired a bad name, is avoided by the new planners who prefer terms like "walk community." One of the most famous of such communities is a development called Seaside, built along a sandy beachfront in the Florida panhandle in the early 1980s. At first glance, what seems to make Seaside special is the old-fashioned style of its houses:

> You won't see picture windows, sliding glass doors, or vinyl siding. Those and other emblems of modern homebuilding are largely prohibited. Seaside is by regulation a place of wood-shingled, clapboard, and board-and-batten houses with deep front porches and shiny tin roofs like those on old houses in rural America. Cupolas and towers rise from some roofs, giving the skyline a picturesque, almost whimsical air.[11]

But Seaside's planners (with Duany among them) have a vision which goes much beyond traditional house design. They puzzle over such questions as how we can create a place where people can enjoy living. How can a new community foster a friendly, social atmosphere? How can its streets and public areas be made inviting enough so people will want to spend time in them? How can a pleasing visual order be achieved while also supplying the inhabitants with their daily needs? To understand what we are up against in creating such communities, we might look at Seaside's immediate neighbors—thirty miles of asphalt, bordered by economy motels, concrete block convenience stores, mansard-roofed refreshment stands, airbrushed T-shirt shops, and fake Tudor townhouses—the sprawl in all its glory.

And even Seaside itself is not an unqualified success. One visitor found that the hopes of reestablishing a front-porch society had largely failed because people were indoors with their TVs and air conditioners. Still, residents can walk the short streets, which are paved with brick, and exchange greetings. And they can conveniently walk to stores, restaurants, and each others' homes.

The most remarkable thing about these walk communities is that houses there sell for much more than a fake Tudor house just a few miles away. The fact that 19th century town planning (as Duany calls it) is financially successful means that planners and developers will finally be attracted to such schemes even if they look with suspicion upon people who use their feet instead of their wheels.

A California developer, who also in the early 1980s had started an old-style, car-based community called Laguna Creek near Sacramento, had second thoughts about continuing in the same fashion on an adjacent 800 acres, even though he had already received county planning approval. "I've been getting the feeling that we just aren't doing well enough in the communities we build," he reflected.[12]

Local environmentalists acquainted him with the work of San Francisco architect Peter Calthorpe who had written what he called *The Pedestrian Pocket Book*. Calthorpe's idea was that of creating pedestrian "pockets" where all development is concentrated within easy walking distance of a transit stop. "We are still building World War II suburbs," Calthorpe said, "as if families were large and had only one breadwinner, as if jobs were all downtown, as if land and energy were endless, and as if another lane on the freeway would end congestion."[13] Calthorpe wanted to connect these pedestrian pockets by light rail lines, but when he was asked to rework the new Laguna Community plans, he found that neither light rail nor bus service existed in the Sacramento suburbs, and that furthermore with six units to the acre for single family houses the density was considered too low to support such services.

We have already mentioned Anglo-Saxon attitudes to high density—the very word makes some people shudder. But it may be said that the human effects of density are up to us; we can let higher density produce negative effects if we design and organize it that way, but we can also make higher density into something beneficial. High density in a suburban context simply means that people live close enough together so they can walk around their communities, and in great enough numbers to make a public transport connection economically feasible.

The arguments for higher density are not only social, but also economic and environmental. A study comparing the costs of installing and servicing amenities for single-family (3 units per acre) suburban dwellings with those of moderate density suburban condominiums (33 units per acre) gives the following examples: For streets and roads, $3000 per single unit versus $800 per condominium unit; for utilities, $5000 per single unit versus $950 for condominium units; 400 gallons of water consumed per day by single units compared to 200 gallons for condos; 150 therms of natural gas per month for singles as against 60 therms for condos; and 10,000 kw hours per year of electricity for singles against 6000 kw hours per year for condominiums.[14]

A comparison of individual houses in Davis, California, with city apartments in San Francisco shows even more drastic differences. Individual houses use 15 times as much roadway, 40 times as much arable land, 50 times as much lumber, 70 times as much landscaping water, and 300 times as much postal delivery route as city apartments. The environmental implications of these figures, when multiplied by millions, are quite staggering.

Coming back now to Peter Calthorpe's pedestrian pockets, the density necessary to support a transit system would have to be calculated in advance, not after the community is built and the damage is done. Calthorpe's choice of light rail, being more expensive than buses, would require yet higher densities unless public transport were subsidized. A correct land use policy would require plans for adequate public transport before giving planning permission.

But calculations of this sort have not, until now, played a very important role in suburban planning. A higher density would not only support transit lines but would add life, movement, and security to the area. The higher noise level of a denser community, where the sounds of crying children, arguing neighbors, or barking dogs may intrude on the isolation of family units, would be compensated for by much less mechanical noise from cruising cars, grinding pickup trucks, lawn mowers, and hedge trimmers.

Unfortunately, planning authorities often do not give permission for the higher densities necessary to make a sprawl into a town, in the mistaken belief that they are protecting the land and property values. In a demonstration of such misguided attitudes, plans for a recent walk community of 3000 dwellings in Ventura County, California, were refused permission by a strict no-growth planning board, even though the plans proposed to leave 70% of the 5500-acre ranch open as a nature reserve and concentrate the rest in a true small-town configuration.[15]

In an ironic twist, the no-growth and environment-friendly planning board turns out, in fact, to be no great improvement over its growth-obsessed predecessor. Neither the growth nor the no-growth planning boards had understood that requiring one (and sometimes as many as ten) acres around each private dwelling makes the community totally car-dependent and spoils the open land, whereas the same high- (or low-) growth can be achieved by higher density centers with open land around them.

There can be little doubt that the tax system has been arranged to aid and abet car-based planning. One could go so far as to say that suburbanization in the United States has been fueled to a large extent by the subsidy of single-family homes through property tax and mortgage interest deductions from federal taxes. Canadians and West Europeans, who get no such benefits, tend to live in denser communities.[16]

This issue probably goes to the heart of a country's political philosophy. Planning as practiced in the United States practically obliges individuals to be separated from their neighbors at the expense of the community at large, since the land assigned to individuals would, in the aggregate, make a very effective greenbelt around a community.

In a public opinion poll of New Jersey residents, 75% of the respondents said development controls should be "strict" to "very strict." By this they undoubtedly meant to give their approval to restrictions on unlimited urban sprawls. But strict controls are a double-edged sword and may as easily be used to cause such a sprawl as to control it.[17] Chaotic sprawl, according to Andres Duany, is not the result of laissez-faire—it is coded and zoned with absolute precision. The codes specify that suburbs must be laid out for complete separation of uses—houses separate from work, work separate from shopping. And instead of being connected to each other, the different areas lead back into one main road, obliging everybody to get on that road to go anywhere.[18]

The Laguna Creek project referred to earlier had to get past the county's traffic engineers and subdivision reviewers. The top planner in that county listed twenty-five ways in which the project didn't comply with county standards, including houses too close to the property line, streets too narrow, too much retail store–related traffic through neighborhood streets, and too many trees![19] Their objection to too many trees was based on the belief that trees cut down the visibility of people in cars. But that argument can be stood on its head: because cars have less visibility they must proceed more slowly and cautiously.

One might say that land-use planning in general has an Alice-in-Wonderland quality about it; it has little to do with real life, and everything to do with what takes place in the planner's head. Even the most advanced of our planners and architects often don't grasp the basic concepts on which a new community should be based. Looking at their drawings one sees acres of single family houses, laid out in "romantic" grid streets. Missing are provisions for higher density apartment units catering to single people, who may just want to rent and who make an interesting addition to the otherwise homogenous group of families. Missing also very often are corner stores, little hidden squares, play space for children near their homes, and interesting promenades. Many of these new communities are just the old subdivision in a modern dress. How did planners arrive at the point of absurdity where one must walk forty minutes to buy a newspaper through residential streets much too wide for the local traffic, but often bereft of even an elementary path for the walker who wants to brave this alien landscape?

Historically, there were two approaches to street layout and city building; one was what might be called the organic or *a posteriori* method and the other the functional or *a priori* approach. Organic streets, which can generally be found in Europe, Asia, and the older cities of North and South America, were laid out incrementally, often on a lot by lot basis; they were as wide or as narrow as they needed to be for a given purpose and took account of land elevations or bodies of water or the amount of traffic they would have to bear.

In the a priori approach, the street grids were laid out in relatively large chunks if not directly on the land, then at least in the developer's head. This idea of laying out American streets in grids goes back to the Land Ordinance of 1785 which established the national grid. That ordinance, along with the commissioner's plan for New York City in 1811, was responsible for spawning the rectangular street system of almost all American towns.

Grid streets were often equally wide whether they were one block connecting links or major arteries; they were stretched indiscriminately across hills or bodies of water even if connecting bridges did not exist or were too narrow. Many grid streets were "paper" streets, remaining unimproved because in real life there was no need for them, even though they had to satisfy the planner's penchant for geometry. They had this in common with Joseph Heller's general in *Catch-22* who liked his bombs to explode in a pattern that would produce a neat aerial photograph.

After Ebenezer Howard's ideas of the Garden City (so much deplored by Jane Jacobs) became fashionable, these a priori planners changed the character of suburban street layouts. They now went in for the more romantic idea of curved streets, respecting hills, and segregating traffic by road width and speed. Although this corrected some of the utter ruthlessness of the rectangular grid system, the geometry of curved streets remained, in the hands of speculators, as arbitrary as the grids themselves.

It is amusing to contrast the work of these planners and speculators, whose plans were conceived, like the mythical Gargantua, full-sprung from their mother's ear, with the 19th century planners and speculators who built most of Victorian London. These latter had no preconceived notions but gave the customers what they wanted, often with splendid results.[20]

Admittedly, the a priori planners had a more difficult job to perform than those in older town centers where a village, like Topsy in *Uncle Tom's Cabin*, "just growed." Planners in a new community must look ahead far enough to decide how an area may change in the future and to allow unforeseen factors to be incorporated.

Often, however, the planners' ideas become self-fulfilling prophecies. If you make very wide streets thinking that at some future date you will have to accommodate a lot of traffic, you invite that traffic to come. If it then arrives you can say "I told you so." If it doesn't, you are stuck with deserted streets which are social barriers inviting danger. In either case the planner has failed to create a viable living environment.

In any case, a viable living environment is probably the last thing a planner thinks about. The logic for making streets in an American subdivision with single-family houses sixty feet wide goes as follows: two lanes, 12 feet each for moving cars; two lanes 8 feet each for parked cars; 5 feet each side for trees, and another 5 feet each side for sidewalks.

But often neither the trees nor the sidewalks make their appearance. Such a street will then be considerably wider than the roadway of the Boulevard Saint Michel in Paris. The two parking lanes are not used since every house not only has one or two garages but a driveway which can accommodate more cars. The whole thing is done to allow a fire engine to pass in the highly unlikely event that cars are parked each side and traffic is moving in one lane. Moreover, single-family houses rarely burn, but the planners favorite argument is that a child may come to harm in a fire. Against this once-in-a-lifetime possibility most of suburbia in the United States eats up space and forces people into their cars.

Even when there aren't strict guidelines, planners sometimes choose unworkable options. Often land-use patterns resulted in wide lot fronts and narrow depths, with houses set back from the road. But just the opposite is needed to encourage walkers; houses should have narrow fronts and deep depths, so that longitudinal blocks are shorter. Seen from a pedestrian point of view, putting a usually useless strip of garden around the sides of houses makes blocks much longer than they need to be. For walking and circulating on the street (and perhaps for the home owner as well) the best and most effective place for a garden is in the rear of a house where it gives the inhabitants privacy and doesn't needlessly lengthen walking trips.

How can we convince planners, themselves as often as not people frozen into an automotive way of life, to consider the needs of people who would like to become more car-independent? How can we overcome the syndrome of planners needing to be convinced by demonstration projects like Seaside, yet not giving permission for such projects until they are convinced?

SOLUTION 26
Planning new towns as integrated and car-independent communities.

✧

> *I teach you the superman.*
> *Man is something that is to be surpassed.*
> Nietzsche, *Also Sprach Zarathustra*

Mart and Supermart

Just as planners fall into the traps of creating inordinately long blocks and sterile service centers that make walking a bore, so too they have a terrible fear of putting retail stores in such blocks. It is as if they fear that the presence of a store would lower the real estate value of a neighborhood in the same way the presence of a differently colored family used to be thought to lower property values.

We have seen in Sacramento that one of the county's objections to the new pocket community of Laguna Creek was traffic generated by retail stores. These planners were apparently quite unable to imagine that anyone might walk or cycle to the neighborhood store, and that this kind of traffic would be of benefit to the area. Such zoning laws, with their strict exclusion of all commercial establishments—even a little corner store—in the otherwise pure residential districts are again a form of segregation, this time suburban apartheid.

Nietzsche, whose ideas of the *Übermensch* may be quite valid, nevertheless gave an unintentional assist to the whole idea that super is better than nonsuper. Well, thank you, dear, dear Friedrich, but we liked the old nonsuperman, miserable little creature that he was. And we liked the old nonsupermarket, miserable little store that it was. Its fruit and vegetables were not sprayed every ten minutes with a fine mist which keeps them fresh-looking forever and has been known to cause strange diseases. Its shelves did not contain thirteen different brands of spaghetti sauce—perhaps there wasn't even one, and you had to go home and make your own. But you could buy one orange and a penny candy if you wanted to.

You had to pay more in the ol' corner store, but your body was not conditioned by blasts of chilly air upon chilly air, nor your mind by blasts of silly air upon silly air; and you didn't have to worry about what Browning called "life's business being just the terrible choice" between one wash powder and another. In the corner store you did not need the listening machine invented by Russell Baker for use at all self-service locations, to which you could direct your comments about the weather and the latest ball scores.

You could converse with a live human being, the proprietor in a white apron, who might even explain to you the difference between one cheese and another. But that friendly proprietor, looking so solid and secure behind his counter, is on his last legs, victim of one more vicious cycle. The more people drive to faraway supermarkets, the smaller gets the selection of the neighborhood store, the higher its prices, and the rottener its apples. And the rottener its apples and its prices, the more people drive to faraway supermarkets or "convenience" stores some of which are open twenty-four hours a day and generate more unnecessary traffic.

The desire to live where one can find a hot pastrami sandwich at four o'clock in the morning—not that you could find one in a convenience store in any case—has become almost a cliché in America. But people may have to give up their mythical—and usually unrealized—desire for such a small-hour snack in the interest of a saner way of life. Perhaps we should take a step backwards and imitate the Austrians who close their stores on Sundays and evenings, and in that way give neighbors some traffic calm and let store personnel take a rest along with their customers.

There are more and more people who will admit that supermarkets are not joyful places to shop in, and that the time and money spent to go there may well cancel out the higher prices of a local store. And supermarkets would fare even less well when compared to open-air markets in those communities lucky enough to have them. But, you might say, supermarkets at least give the public a wide range of shopping facilities and allow it to benefit from competition among them? Or that out-of-town retail development is necessary to keep up with growing consumer spending? Maybe governments do not, in any case, have the power to control such developments? Perhaps market forces are the most efficient means of allocating space for purposes of retail provision? And wouldn't retailers lose most of their customers if parking or car access were restricted?

All these questions have been investigated in an exhaustive English study called *Trouble in Store*. On the question of shopping range and competition, the study found that many recent trends actually operate against the best interests of the consumer. While it is true that consumers benefit from a wider range of goods within a store, the choice of store has narrowed. A large number of small stores has been replaced by a small number of large stores, operated by only a handful of firms. This means the consumer has a limited choice of shops and is likely to travel further to get to one.[21]

The tendency toward monopoly is well advanced within the British and German retail sectors with which this study dealt. At the turn of the century, four out of five convenience-goods retailers were independent; by the late 1980s the British market had become dominated by just five large firms, with further concentrations predicted. The savings in operating costs resulting from internally efficient superstore operation do not seem to have been passed on to the consumer.

The high profit levels common in the British retail sector have probably been used to further corporate growth, new store openings, and takeovers, rather than to lower prices. Many large British retailers, facing market saturation, have moved into other retail areas or abroad in order to sustain their corporate need to grow. The little ol' corner grocery never felt the overpowering need for corporate growth, and if it weren't so threatened by its giant competitors, might actually be able to concentrate on giving customers what they wanted—perhaps not the same as what the corporate giant *wants* those customers to want.

Regarding the question whether out-of-town developments are necessary, the study compared trends in Britain and Germany and found that similar growth rates have been realized in Germany without mindless out-of-center expansion. The location of German shopping centers in the 1970s has moved away from distant green fields and closer to new housing and suburban areas. Although the Germans have not broken up the shopping centers and distributed them in the suburbs, they have at least located them within reasonable distances of where people live.

Where shopping centers existed in out-of-population centers, the study found that they lured trade away from traditional and existing centers rather than creating their own. The people who shop there have to come from some place, and in spite of advances in genetic engineering, the outlying commercial centers have not yet managed to create the new customers which must people the stores to make them profitable.

Do governments have the power to control out-of-town developments? Evidence from North America and Europe suggests that they do if they wish to exercise it. Britain has an oft-stated, though oft-violated, commitment to greenbelts (green areas surrounding all population centers), and the Germans are exercising increased retail planning control to make out-of-center developments more difficult to achieve.

A clearly formulated policy in Europe and North America could bring the urban sprawl under control, since policing machinery already exists to inhibit such developments. What does not yet exist (except in Germany) is the clear policy and the political will. British retailers complain that the lack of guidance from central government is creating uncertainty and increasing the trend toward out-of-center development.

Current levels of investment and consumer spending cannot support both the growth of out-of-center retailing and simultaneous improvement of center-city floor space. A choice has to be made; which is it to be? What retailers perceive to be in their interest, and what is actually in in their interest are not necessarily identical. As with so many other questions having to do with automobile dependence, the untested assumption is always in favor of the car, and for increasing such dependence. Where we have been able to test such assumptions, the results often prove otherwise.

In another study of ten German cities, little relationship was shown to exist between the quantity of car parking and retail activity. In some cases, too much parking actually acted as a detriment, as it obliged pedestrians to traverse large, dangerous, and uninteresting open spaces to go to the shops.[22] Of course, if a shopping center is in the middle of nowhere and cannot be reached by any means other than the private car, then parking and retail turnover are synonymous, and they become self-fulfilling prophecies.

The sad experience of the United States must form the final argument against out-of-center retail facilities and the accommodation of cars at any cost. Downtowns in that country were modified to cater to massive increases in car ownership during the 1950s and 1960s. New roads and parking lots were provided to serve downtowns and relieve road congestion. These new roads quickly filled with newly generated traffic, which eventually made these centers less attractive to shoppers and thus to retailers. At the same time, the new road system had drawn many of the former city-center shoppers to new homes in the suburbs. Many retail firms consequently abandoned downtowns to develop new stores on the periphery of urban areas where motorists could easily reach them using the freeway system. In many cases, offices followed suit, and some suburban downtowns developed around freeway intersections. Road congestion then followed retail decentralization, making the situation ripe for yet another wave of retail decentralization to escape congestion, until the new decentralization became congested in its turn, and so on ad infinitum.

The case for the neighborhood store and the walk community is difficult to prove in isolation from an overall reevaluation of planning policies. Such policies, which take automobile dependence for granted set off cycles which tend to snuff out neighbor-

240

hood stores and the socially attractive environment which we have been discussing. What is needed, therefore, is a change of attitude in the entire range of land-use planning. Planners should begin to question the untested assumption that people like being isolated, and that they like the consequent dependence on the mechanical conveyances necessary for their daily errands.

The general store is one of the best places to test that assumption. Is a store to which people can walk, a place in which they can pick up their mail and exchange gossip a good idea? Would they prefer to live in small communities with a general store and a weekly market where they could shop and meet their friends and neighbors rather than drive miles on congested highways?

To be competitive with supermarkets, the general stores would, of course, have to be well-run and well-stocked and offer their customers a bit of genuine (not fake!) village charm. They would have to be like the place in still another walk community, this one called Harbor Town, near Memphis, Tennessee, where "people walk to the village grocery store along narrow, tree-lined streets, and when they get there the grocer greets them by name."[23]

SOLUTION 27
Bring back corner, village, and general stores as well as open-air markets to stimulate suburban walking and prevent long car trips to distant superstores.

✧

241

The road and the printed word he dismissed as our older
media. Personal movement through territory he considered a
dying form of communication.

Grady Clay on Marshall McLuhan

Let Your Fingers Do the Driving

Well, here we are, using the outmoded print medium to say that
physical movement through territory is far from dead. Au revoir,
Marshall, and bonjour the superstore and the interstate highway
system. Like Marx's dictatorships, McLuhan's roads never with-
ered away, though admittedly they got full of potholes. So we are
now in the peculiar position of possessing both the global village
and the urban sprawl.

McLuhan got carried away by the idea that the electronic revolution would sweep all before it and change our lives, mostly
for the better. Shakespeare, however, reminds us that "the web of
life is of a mingled yarn, good and ill together." The same technology which can do away with roads by substituting electronic
communication can also put traffic on those roads. And then it
can compound the problem by helping to move such traffic right
along, and thus invite yet more.

In an effort to do just that, Los Angeles, for example, has decided to install an electronic control and surveillance system on
the Santa Monica Freeway in order to lessen congestion. In this
system, sensors are built into the roadway which flash signals to
electronic message boards, in-vehicle receivers, and transport
radio stations. Such information indicates to drivers where congestion is heaviest so that they can avoid it; it automatically ad-
justs traffic signals and ramp meters to control congested roads;
and it allows repair trucks to be dispatched to assist incapacitated
vehicles which block traffic.

Such systems, however, suffer from one basic flaw: if they
don't work, then the cost of installing them ($30 million in the
case of the L.A. system) is wasted; and if they do, they will have
the effect of enticing those who switched to pools or public transport right back into their cars, or worse yet, encourage "rat runs"
on less congested back roads to avoid the advertised congestion.
In the end, the extra vehicles lured onto the electronically cleared

242

roads will eventually bring those roads back to their original congested state. Let's face it, a little congestion (unlike a little learning) is not a dangerous thing. Some traffic specialists have even recommended what they call "planned congestion," using congestion as a self-policing and cost-free (though not pollution-free) tool to discourage some motorists and thus avoid total gridlock.

Today's congestion, planned or not, is ample proof that physical movement through territory is far from a dying form of communication. But we can certainly help to minimize such congestion and its accompanying miseries by picking up on McLuhan's ideas of telecommunication to avoid personal movement through space. It would be more useful to concentrate our money and effort on spreading electronic commuting through the global village than on speeding personal commuting through the global urban sprawl.

In the early 1980s many articles in electronic magazines led us to believe that every programmer or systems engineer would soon be working at home in pajamas. When the freeways didn't empty by 1986, many people were tempted to write off telecommuting. But telecommuting didn't go away. It just hasn't grown as fast as some of its futurist proponents had hoped.

Today there are a number of reasons why telecommuting is positioned for steady and significant growth in the 1990s.[24] Among these are the difficulty employers have of finding and keeping good people who may not live near their work; the changing demographics, employee preferences, and need for more flexible work arrangements; and finally the increasing gridlock. Added to this is the gradual removal of technological barriers, as computer prices continue to drop, telecommunications-service offerings expand, and networking becomes well understood and widely used. The pioneering days of telecommunication are over; we now understand success factors as well as risks.

Telecommunication actually benefits from one of our many car-related vicious cycles: the more that employers are anxious to hire in local labor markets, the higher house prices in that market rise, and the further prospective employees have to move to find affordable housing. Once they are far away, they face long commutes on congested roads, thus driving up house prices in

243

nearby labor markets further and feeding the commute/congestion cycle, thereby making telecommuting more attractive.

Of course, some companies just don't have the kind of business in which telecommuting is a viable option, and moreover some organizational cultures don't think kindly of it. Those are the organizations where three to five people are supervised by two managers who don't want to feel superfluous. The fact is that employees do so well working by themselves at home, that this may actually constitute a liability of telecommuting. The better such a system is run, the more some managers will feel themselves to be superfluous.

But the trend of the times is, in any case, against close supervision. Today's employees will no longer put up with it and consider it a misuse of management time. In many offices today only one manager is needed to supervise six to ten employees, and telecommuting is accelerating that trend further. Some managers actually allow their employees with personal computers to telecommute from time to time without the boss's knowledge because they realize that the returns in higher productivity and employee satisfaction outweigh the risks of going against company policy. According to some surveys, telecommuters are as much as 30% more productive working at home than in their conventional work environments. Telecommuters also have a higher morale, experience fewer distractions, and have lower absenteeism rates than their counterparts in the office. And there are additional benefits, such as saving office and parking space and being able to employ handicapped workers.

The telecommunications literature has not yet addressed the natural desire of some employees to get away from their houses (possibly away from their spouses?) and be with their colleagues. If that became a factor, big companies could establish local telecommuting centers, in our new walk communities for example, where people could walk to work, telecommute with their distant offices, and joke with fellow workers.

Even if such local "telework" centers do not yet exist, there are an ever-increasing number of giant corporations who now have telecommuting programs. In the United States, three government agencies—the Southern California Association of Governments (SCAG), the California Department of Transportation (Caltrans), and the city of Fort Collins, Colorado have conducted major telecommuting studies or have initiated pilot projects.

Private corporations have been even quicker to pick up the trend than government agencies. Between 450 and 500 U.S. corporations are to some extent involved in telecommuting and at least thirty—including Mountain Bell, Pacific Bell, New York Telephone, J.C. Penney, and Blue Cross/Blue Shield—have instituted formal programs. If that process continues, Marshall McLuhan, whose name is now barely recognized by the younger generation, may turn out not to have been a false prophet, after all.

SOLUTION 28
The use of telecommuting to cut down the number of vehicles on the road.

✧

> *O born in days when wits were fresh and clear*
> *And life ran gaily as the sparkling Thames;*
> *Before this strange disease of modern life*
> *With its sick hurry, its divided aims,*
> *Its heads o'ertaxed, its palsied hearts, was rife.*
> Matthew Arnold, "The Scholar Gypsy"

This Strange Disease

If it were possible to enter a time machine and go back a hundred years to communicate with Matthew Arnold, the temptation would be great to say to him, "Listen, Matt baby, you ain't seen nothin' yet!"

Transporting him back to our own time, we would place him on a hill overlooking one of the ring roads encircling our major cities and let him observe the scene. What he would see there would be several lanes full of traffic going without cease, twenty-four hours a day, seven days a week, from point A to point B. And next to these lanes several more lanes going in the opposite direction, from point B to point A. What, Mr. Arnold might have wondered, was the purpose of all that movement since, judging by the respective traffic flows, both A and B are equally worth going to? So why did the A's decide to go to B when they undoubtedly could have found all they needed at A, and the B's at B?

Ah, but here we touch one of the mysteries of modern life. We all accept that ceaseless movement unquestioningly as a kind of ritual dance whose meaning and origin are lost in time. Perhaps we are doomed to go round and round that endless circle—often making the tour of the entire city without even entering it—till the end of time.

But there are those who have made a concerted effort to buck the tide of that mighty river. A Philadelphia housewife and free-lance writer describes how she gets along without a car:

> I turned 40 this fall. Although I drive, I've never wanted to own a car. Needless to say, our Philadelphia neighbors are baffled by our car-free existence. When are you going to buy a car has become Why don't you own a car? The simple response Because we don't feel like it cuts no ice with my neighbors. But it makes

246

no sense. You need a car to get around. How can you survive without one? It is useless to explain that we like to walk and that taking the bus or the "el" poses no great hardship.

We haven't ruled out owning a car. It's just that we got by very nicely without one for many years, and continue to do so. Stores, schools, church, library, doctor and dentist are all within walking distance, and a twenty minute el ride takes my husband to his job. When we observe our neighbors returning from a three block drive to an aerobics class we nudge each other and smirk. In return, eyebrows are raised as we trudge in all weather about our errands, and word has been filtered back to us that there have been dark speculations as to whether we possess revoked licenses.

We're not purists or diehards. From time to time we rent cars for family excursions. When I drop off the rental car I have the same feeling as dropping off a friend's child after watching her for a day. It was nice, but it's time to say good-bye.[25]

Another family, this time from Germany, describes their own *Abschied vom Auto* (good-bye to the car):

To say it right off the bat: we are neither Greens nor Luddites sitting at their spinning wheels, even though we have been accused of being touched in the head. We are a large family with five children between the ages of two and nine; mother is primary school teacher, father biologist. Our reasons are simple: the destruction of the environment, the ceaseless construction of new roads, the endless (and useless) talk about catalyzers and Tempo 100 (speed limits) and auto-free Sundays; a government which observes well what happens to the environment but does nothing except talk; a Green party which tells us to take the bus and the train but which often doesn't listen to its own advice; and finally our bad conscience in front of our children.

Like most Germans, we used our car simply for convenience: to get to school, to grandparents, to go shopping, to make excursions. Since we don't have the car, we have become calmer. No more rushing around, no more crying and fighting children in back. Instead I have the weekend bus all to myself. And more's the pity!

My husband's pupils wonder if he hasn't lost his license; but meanwhile I talk to the bus driver instead of shoving my

247

monthly pass at him the way one feeds a dog. Our neighbors' opinions are divided. Some call us crazy, saying cars don't destroy the environment. Some think it's a good idea, but not for them. The youngsters say that one such action can make no difference; they will continue till every one stops.

The car used to cost us DM 450 per month. The buses cost us DM 150. We now shop at the neighborhood store. We now look at cars and the damage they do with an even more critical eye than before. If people would only begin using buses and trains, we would have better service and waste less time making connections. But motorists all say let the others start. We, at any rate, don't regret having started.[26]

The striking thing about these two reports from countries thousands of miles apart is their similarities: both families felt called upon to defend themselves against the charge of being purists or some sort of fanatics; both were suspected of having forfeited their license or even of being crazy.

All right, a suburbanite or country dweller might say, that's all very well for them, they live in cities and walk or take buses. But what about us? How can we even contemplate such a step? We have tried, in these pages, to indicate how—by making the suburb into a village or minicity, and placing schools, churches, libraries, doctors, and stores within walking or busing distance, and making sure there is a bus to cover such distance. Yes, the suburbanites might say, but what about the chicken and the egg syndrome? Without the amenities within walking or busing distance people won't give up their cars, and as long as they have the cars the amenities will stay far away.

Yet families who really want to lead less car-dependent lives can make an attempt to structure their lives around that idea. They can try to buck the trend in which distances between home and workplaces are estimated to increase as much as 80% by the year 2020. They can try to put their homes and their work within easy commuting distance, concentrate their social and cultural life on their local area, renounce faraway activities simply *because* they are faraway, and search out nearby activities simply *because* they are nearby.[27] They can consider getting along with a single car, or rent one like our Philadelphia family, or even try to share one with friends or neighbors.

Ivan Illich has said that motorized vehicles create the remoteness which they alone can shrink. It is up to us to create the proximity which allows us to get along without that particular kind of shrink.

SOLUTION 29
Arranging our lives to be less car-dependent.

13

FINDING THE RIGHT PLACE FOR THE CAR: SOLUTIONS 30–33

After having been rather hard on the car in telling it where it cannot or ought not to go, we now consider how we can find the right place for it. Since cars are not as yet so plentiful in under-developed countries, we look there first to see whether Third-Worlders have found that right place.

Then we turn our attention to the realm of politics and personal education to make sure the right place for the car is recognized by future generations. We look next at what we can do to make cars less destructive, even in their rightful place.

And finally we look at some guidelines on when, and perhaps when not, to take them.

We and World Three

In trying to find the right place for the car, we are going to have a peek at World Three because that world is still less dependent on the car than we are. Since we ourselves have lost sight of a sensible way to use cars, perhaps we can learn something from them.

Well, the peek we are going to take at World Three is likely to make us shudder. Bad as are transport conditions in our part of the world, they are truly appalling in theirs. The real horror of traffic, congestion, and urban chaos at its worst can be seen in its grimmest and most extreme form in places like Mexico City, Sao Paulo, Lagos, Cairo, Manila, Bangkok, New Delhi.

The list goes on and on and includes not only the megacities but also literally thousands of other places in the developing world where the problems are searing, urgent, hugely disruptive, and costly. Under these circumstances, then, is not the right place to start where the needs are greatest? Shall we not go and show them how to make things better?

Well, we had our chance and blew it. If we look back over the last few decades, the period when most of these cities have built up the greater part of their transport and urban road systems, we can see that those responsible for their development have looked for examples and guidance not within their own cultures and traditions but to the West.

They looked at what we were doing in London, Rome, and Los Angeles and decided to do the same things themselves: to build cities based on cars. Former Third-Worlders like Seoul and Taipei have even gone us one better and constructed ten-lane highways, which are now already clogged with traffic!

Many of the poor countries admired us, while we rather followed the sentiment expressed by one of Oscar Wilde's characters: "As for the virtuous poor, one can pity them, of course, but one cannot possibly admire them." We made no attempt to understand their problems or their mode of life as being possibly healthier than ours. Instead, we sent them a steady stream of counsel and encouragement to imitate our superior style and dispatched ambassadors of wisdom from international organizations, specialized consultants, the very nicest banks, bilateral aid agencies, and educational institutions.

They sent their engineers, planners, and policy makers to our universities, learned well what we taught, looked carefully at the examples we provided, and then went back home to apply exactly what they saw and learned. And now they are living with the result. And, like us, they seem unwilling to understand the problem, let alone to do anything about it. It is as if the peoples of the world stand mesmerized before the private automobile. Even in the poorest Third World countries, governments favor cars over other means of transport, perhaps because the officials themselves use them, or perhaps because in our century the automobile is seen as a symbol of power, a way to become strong, rich, and fast-moving, like people in the better-off nations. Hamar women, living in an isolated Ethiopian community which has very little contact with modern life, give their children such names as *Macchina* (car) and *Camione* (truck).

The world thus appears to be divided into those who have been able to acquire the automobiles which quite literally are asphyxiating us, and those who look with envy upon the other half and dream of nothing better than to follow their example. To quote Oscar Wilde one last time, this state of affairs recalls his maxim that "in this world there are only two tragedies. One is not getting what one wants, and the other is getting it."

The fact that people in Third World countries have to live with deadly pollution, congestion, and accident fatalities twenty times higher than in industrial countries when most of them will never own a car doesn't seem to bother anybody, or at least not those who are making the decisions. Car use in Third (or even Second) World countries carries even more hidden dangers than it does in some of the industrially advanced societies.

In the less developed countries, neither the population nor the roads were (or are) ready for the sudden arrival of automobiles in large numbers. One visitor to Yerevan, capital of Soviet Armenia, reports that pedestrians in that city have no rights at all. Drivers don't know the rules of the road or don't care about them. Motorists obey no laws and seem to take pleasure in heading straight for a person on foot. The streets are full of holes, entailing sudden slalom maneuvers on the part of motorists, which can bring a car dangerously close to pedestrians.

In Teheran, the slogan of drivers since 1979 has been "We didn't overthrow the Shah in order to respect traffic lights." Moreover, many underdeveloped societies have strong macho cultures. The car, in those societies, is today the medium which allows the men to express their power and contempt for weaker beings such as women and pedestrians.

In Haiti, only one out of every two hundred people owns a car, yet fully one-third of that country's import budget is devoted to fuel and transportation.[1] Likewise the city of Cairo constructed an elevated highway which costs the state three dollars per vehicle, money which was surely needed elsewhere in this poor city. The building and maintaining of elaborate road systems in these poor countries consumes enormous resources, to the detriment of rail and public transport.

Once the roads are built, there is never enough money to maintain or repair them, so 30% of Third World roads are in poor condition and a further 40% are only fair. Meanwhile public transport is neglected and meets only a fraction of transportation needs—for instance 15% in India and Bangladesh.[2] The World Bank has helped slant transportation projects toward motorized solutions by providing less than one-third of transport funds for public transportation projects.

A Western observer, looking at Third World transport, found the tendency to neglect public transport

> painfully clear all over the world, where the poor wait in the heat, cold, or wet, while the better off drive by in private cars in what should be public space—the streets, alleys, and squares of these cities.[3]

Sometimes even sidewalk space is taken from the teeming masses (as in Caracas, for example) while other cities (like Manila) have imposed constraints on rickshaws and other forms of nonmotorized travel. In Jakarta, officials banned *becaks* (three-wheeled cycle rickshaws) because they supposedly caused traffic congestion (which meant they prevented smooth passage of cars), and authorities in Dakha (Bangladesh) announced plans in

1987 to ban pedicabs, which employed more than a hundred thousand people.[4]

Even the Chinese are beginning to worship the private car and disdain the bicycle which is their transport mainstay. A massive World Bank report on transport in China didn't even mention the word "bicycle." Chinese planners now are calling for cycle traffic to be strictly controlled with the ultimate intention of reducing it to an auxiliary means. A planner called Min Fengkui would prefer the bicycle to be used only for sport and recreation although he knows full well that an ordinary Chinese worker would have to fork over sixteen years of wages for the cheapest Fiat car.[5]

Thus pedestrians and traditional modes of transport are increasingly being marginalized, even in countries where such modes are used by the overwhelming majority. Under these circumstances, what can we expect if some of us show up at their doorstep now and suggest that they should do, not as we have done, but rather as we now say: switch gears and try to develop something along the line of cities without cars or at least cities with a lot fewer cars. What, quite honestly, will be their reaction? Our guess is that they will kindly invite us to pack up our noble sentiments and go back to our comfortable homes, while they wrestle with the problem themselves.

So it now looks as if we can best fulfill our responsibility to these people by learning first how to get it right in our own cities and communities. Then perhaps, once we have some good examples of how it should actually work, we may be in a position to offer help in a more active way.

SOLUTION 30
Stop giving bad advice and dirty cars to Third World countries.

✧

Storm Troops and White Flags

With environmental and energy concerns becoming ever more acute, we can expect many more people in the coming decade to take an interest in the question of what is the right place for the car. Activist groups, for and against, will attempt to make themselves heard by force or political pressure without necessarily understanding the complex issues involved.

Those firmly in favor of unlimited car use have rallied around the battle cry of freedom, without considering the question that ought to follow, namely freedom for whom? For those who turn up their car radio to top decibel levels in a public space? For the would-be silent majority around them? For a single juggernaut lorry? For the hundreds of sleeping villagers? Freedom for cars? Or freedom from cars?

In Germany, the freedom defense, generally made by motorists who argue against any or all restrictions, including speed, seat belts, car restraints, and spot checks, is made under the slogan *Freie Fahrt für freie Bürger* (free passage for free citizens); a slogan dangerously close to the battle cry of the Third Reich—"The storm troops march, so free and clear the streets"—in its implication that street use must be reserved principally for the group in power. We have seen in the past that the indiscriminate use of the word "freedom" can cover a multitude of sins.

Could Milton have had the Association of German Automobile Clubs in mind when he wrote "None can love freedom heartily but good men; the rest love not freedom but license?" Whatever the names of these future activist groups—perhaps the PLO (Pedestrian Liberation Organization) versus the ADL (Auto Defense League)?—the coming battle to limit the number of the world's cars will have its opposing camps. For the moment, the opponents of unlimited car population growth are silent and few, but the same cannot be said for the Auto Defense League, which holds the balance of power almost everywhere.

The adversaries in the coming battle may not always be easily identifiable. In car-conscious California mass transit is now (at least nominally) being supported by the highway lobby, truckers,

255

automobile clubs, and general contractors as a way of alleviating congestion and smog. So conservatives turn out to be for public transport when it used to be thought that the right-leaning establishment is for, and the left-leaning opposition against, unlimited car use.

In any case, when it comes to car-related issues traditional political divisions of right and left are meaningless. In 1979, a demonstration against the effects of lead from auto emissions caused protesters to block traffic coming into Stockholm. The demonstration was severely criticized by two of the leftist parties in Sweden at the time, the Trotskyites and the Maoists, who accused the protesters of not acting in the "interest of the working classes," while the noted Swedish author and social critic Jan Myrdal accused the protesters of being "hostile to technological progress."[6]

As we approach the end of the century and environmental concerns become ever more urgent, we can expect this looming battle to become more vehement, "terrible as an army with banners." A private guerilla war against the car has already begun. In Germany and France, this takes the form of a "ticket and stick-it" campaign where illegal parkers are tagged by the placement of an adhesive label blocking the driver's view. The German label, as yet small and discreet, says *Parke nicht auf unseren Wegen* (don't park on our pathways), while the French take a more humorous approach with *Ben Hur, ton char me gène* (Ben Hur, your chariot annoys me).

Such tactics can easily escalate. A mysterious avenger in the United States gives illegal parkers a warning ticket, and if that is ignored, attacks offenders' tires with a shoemaker's awl. And in Munich, a student in 1989 walked over a car illegally blocking the sidewalk. When he received a 50-mark fine for damaging private property while the offending vehicle went free, the student decided to take things one step further. Some days later he set up a table and calmly proceeded to eat his lunch in the middle of a busy thoroughfare, on the principle that if cars trespass on his territory he can do so on theirs.[7]

And it is even possible that the sacred status of the car which, according to the French magazine *Paris Aujourd'hui*, is now the only object except for Notre Dame Cathedral not to have been decorated with graffiti, may not last forever. Nothing would empty our city streets more quickly of illegally parked cars than a contingent of graffiti guerillas taking their pleasure on the offending vehicles!

Many who are peaceful by nature and loath to get involved in the passions of the day may yet have to take a stand on this issue. If such people don't want to join the clash of ignorant armies, they might make a private decision to shed their personal protective carapace.

And there are other peaceful ways to demonstrate concern for safer and more intelligent car use. Before each holiday weekend in France, the media remind motorists of a campaign known as *Drapeau Blanc* (White Flag). People who wish to show that they are conscious of the threat which hangs over every vehicle on such a weekend display a white flag fluttering from their car's antenna. The white flag signifies that its bearer recognizes the car for what it is: a lethal weapon. The symbol of the white flag is not accidental: it is a peaceful surrender, a willingness to cease engaging in the personal dog fights which take place continuously on our roads. If motorists were to see many drivers with white flags, they might begin to wonder if they, too, shouldn't be more careful. The white flag could act as a kind of reminder to their consciences.

Drivers could further be goaded to proper car use by seeing exemplary behavior on the part of prominent people, our so-called role models, although those role models would have their work cut out if they want to wean people from a wasteful style of life. Jimmy Carter bravely tried to get Americans to follow his example when he walked to his inauguration instead of taking a car and when he lowered the White House thermostat and wore a sweater, but he just made himself unpopular.

The current American president knows which side his bread is buttered on. He set a fine standard in reverse role modeling at the very eve of the Gulf crisis in August 1990. After having committed himself to the dispatch of American troops in defense of oil supplies, he refused to forego even one spin in his fuel-guzzling speedboat, reputed to use twenty-five gallons an hour.

257

That conflict in model behavior between the conservationists and the conspicuous consumers seems to extend from politics to sports and show business. For every star who is publicly concerned about tropical rain forests, we appear to have a world-famous tennis player with a collection of fast cars. For the moment, the majority of our role models fall into this category of conspicuous consumers.

Role modeling is said by psychologists to be important as a device to influence the behavior of children. But since we don't have sufficient numbers of celebrities whose behavior is worth copying, we may have to look closer to home. What more important and natural role models for our children are there than their own parents? To have any effect on the children, a conscious effort to find the correct place for the car ought to start with the family.

After parents come schools, which should examine the entire range of automobile-connected problems we have explored in these pages. The car is a sacred object for most children, who long only to be old enough to drive and own one, and it is never too early for schools and parents to begin raising a child's consciousness about cars. There are many ways in which this can be done. In addition to the traffic safety programs which are at present on some school agendas, there could be child-sponsored and -executed traffic surveys, exhibitions, drawing contests, what cars and safety mean to children, class studies of cars and the environment, and school-stimulated discussions between children and parents.

In one such program in Australia, small children were given the task of asking their parents what life was like when the parents were young. The children returned to school with such responses as:

> When my mum was little she was allowed to go to the park and to the shop by herself. We can't go somewhere by ourselves because there is too much traffic. . . . Mum could stay on the road with her friends because there were not many cars on the road. When mum and dad were young, they could ride on horses and walk on the streets at night. . . . My mum and dad could walk at night and play on the road. I cannot because it is *dangerous*.[8]

A similar thought was expressed by the well-known British author Roald Dahl, writing about his childhood, at age six, in Glamorgan, 1922:

> I can remember clearly the journeys I made to and from school because they were so tremendously exciting. . . . The excitement centered around my new tricycle. I rode to school on it every day with my eldest sister riding on hers. No grown-ups came with us and I can remember, oh so vividly, how the two of us used to go racing at enormous tricycle speeds down the middle of the road. . . . All this, you must realize, was in the good old days when the sight of a motor-car was an event and it was quite safe for tiny children to go tricycling and whooping their way to school in the center of the highway. . . .[9]

The attitude expressed by some road safety specialists is that children are the "guilty" party in traffic accidents. One recently published safety leaflet made the following points: "Children of *all* ages are immature, impulsive, unpredictable, lacking in skill and experience, not doing what they are told. . . ."[10] In other words, they are guilty of being *children*. Our modern car-dominated streets severely restrict and discourage children from going out unsupervised and gaining the independence which is so important for them. As far as children are concerned, the modern world is decidedly "children-unfriendly"—the Germans even have a word for it: *Kinderunfreundlichkeit*.

Unfortunately neither the children themselves nor their parents realize how boxed-in and dependent on adult supervision modern children have become, and how many of their basic rights as children they have lost. In Britain over 900 million hours were spent during 1990 escorting children.[11]

The children's own idea of regaining their freedom is not to free our roads from heavy traffic so that they could circulate in them unsupervised, but to add to that traffic by getting their own cars. To make them understand better what getting your own car may mean, schools could organize trips for children and teenagers to the local car cemetery. Twenty minutes at the wrecker is worth more than three hours of lectures about safety. Nothing brings home more forcefully the power of the lethal

The guilty party in traffic accidents?

weapon which is the car than looking at the crushed and mangled remains of what was once a shiny status symbol. Children will not soon forget such a trip.

But we cannot teach children one thing, and then do another. Children who live in big cities see every day streetsful of chauffeur-driven limousines, often for the use of one single role-model-in-reverse. If anything sends the wrong signal, using a personal transport capsule as big as a house does. The limo's occupant is sending his own signal, to wit, that he is more important than anybody else. And in the world of limos, the less important he really is, the bigger his vehicle must be; because the less important he is, the bigger he wants the world (a world which often equates the size of a vehicle with its occupant) to think he is.

Before we can sort out the proper place for the car in a future more and more affected by ecological concerns, we will have to

go through a phase of political and personal education to understand the issues involved.

SOLUTION 31
Consciousness raising, role modeling, and education
about the worldwide effects of the car.

✦

God Is in the Details

While we wait for the carmakers to give us more user-friendly
vehicles, there is much we can do ourselves, even without driving less, to decrease the negative impact of the motorcar on the
environment. Like Mies van der Rohe, who saw God in the details, we can start paying attention to the small details on our
own vehicles. Little things like care in regulating tire pressure,
properly tuned engines, well-adjusted idling speeds, and use of
the correct fuel can bring about small improvements in car performance which, when multiplied by millions, can save substantial amounts of energy and prevent harmful emissions. Lowering
tire resistance by 10%, for example, can improve fuel efficiency
by 3% to 4%.

Careful driving can make a lot of difference as well, since energy losses due to braking and unnecessary acceleration can
amount to as much as one-third of a vehicle's original kinetic energy.[12] Driving more slowly accomplishes three things: it cuts
down on atmospheric and noise pollution; it reduces energy consumption; and it increases safety. To make drivers aware of their
own excessive speeds, they could choose vehicles equipped with
devices such as speed governors, speed warning devices, cruise
control settings, and "econometers"which tell a driver at what
cruising speed his vehicle performs most economically and with
the least energy loss.

One useful idea to spur greater concern by motorists for environmental damage would be to vary the annual tax vehicles pay according to their environment-friendliness. This is the principle known as "polluter pays." The less polluting the vehicle, the lower the tax, and vice versa. Some sort of environmental barometer (perhaps on a scale from 1 to 10) would need to be established, based on such factors as vehicle size, age, top speed, emission tests, and general condition. There would be annual inspections under this kind of scheme to determine the proper tax rate.

The biggest single step toward curbing global warming, according to the Sierra Club, is to make vehicles more fuel-efficient. According to their figures, a car getting only 18 miles per gallon produces 58 tons of carbon dioxide in its lifetime, whereas a car which can cover 45 miles per gallon produces less than half that amount, or 23 tons.[13] When acquiring a car, we must make sure to choose the most energy-efficient one available, without letting that energy efficiency push us into covering greater distances because of reduced costs. Instructions for better energy conversion and more ecologically oriented car use are now widely available, and bringing a car in line with such recommendations is a must for every conscientious driver.

We would here like to call attention to a detail which is often overlooked in the transport and environment literature. Many motorists *like* the sound of an idling engine. Perhaps the sweet music of their purring motors hath charms to soothe their savage breasts. Every day, in every nook and cranny of the world, unthinking drivers let their motors idle, often for long periods of time.

It may be the driver of a parked refrigerated truck, another one sleeping in the cab of his lorry, a police officer waiting at a speed trap, a farm-tractor driver who is having breakfast, a mail driver sorting his letters, a van driver making a delivery, two motorists engaging in what turns into a half-hour chat—whoever they may be, the idea of shutting off their engines does not occur to them.

For those fascinated by numbers, it can be calculated that if

ARE YOU USING YOUR CAR
IN THE MOST ENERGY-EFFICIENT WAY?
*Answer the following questions with **yes** or **no**.*

1   Do you shut off your engine when your car is standing still three minutes or more (other than in moving traffic)?

2   Do you check your tires at least once a month?

3   Does your car have a speed warning or alerting device?

4   Is your engine tuned at each regular service?

5   Do you have your catalyzer checked at each regular service?

6   Do you make an effort to drive at a steady speed rather than abruptly with sudden braking?

7   Do you stay regularly within posted speed limits?

8   Do you pay attention to the number of miles per gallon when you buy a car?

9   Do you keep a periodic record of how may miles per gallon your car gets?

10   Is your driving record free of moving violations?

SCORES
*Score one for each **yes** answer—the higher the score, the more energy efficient you and your car are.*

0–3   You pay little attention to energy-efficiency in vehicles.

4–6   You pay some attention to energy efficency but could do better.

7–10   You are conscious of energy efficiency and the environment.

only a quarter of the world's car fleet stopped idling for one single minute of one single day, the energy saved thereby would enable a super champion idler to let his engine turn over day and night without stopping for 200 years. That single minute's idling pause on only one day for only a quarter of the world's car fleet would also spare our atmosphere the absorption of something like 25 million pounds of carbon dioxide.[14]

Figures on the damage done to the world by millions of vehicles idling for long periods of time are hard to come by. We have to resort to what the specialists dismiss as anecdotal evidence, but such evidence is in plentiful supply since most people's right to inhabit a quiet and pollution-free world has been trod upon by needlessly idling vehicles. Stopping needless idling and checking all the little details to make cars as energy-efficient and environment-friendly as they can be helps to limit the menace of cars.

SOLUTION 32
Stricter attention to energy efficiency on the part of drivers.

✧

> *But that two-handed engine at the door,*
> *stands ready to smite once, and smite no more.*
>
> Milton, "Lycidas"

Is This Trip Necessary?

In spite of all the bad things we have been saying about it, there is, in fact, a place for the car. To argue otherwise would be to fly in the face of all reality. But where exactly is that place? Probably somewhere in each individual conscience. Even if one could think of ever more draconian guidelines, there is no way of making sure that everyone would follow them. We are all in the position of those two prisoners, A and B, in their prisoner's dilemma. How we use our car has to be the personal choice of each and every one of us.

But here, as a rough guide, are six conditions in which car use may be considered more or less proper:

- Where there is no alternative means of transport. Henry Ford's original idea was to make cars only for the use of farmers in outlying areas, since the countryside usually offers no other transport.

- Where there is an alternative means to go somewhere but no way to get around once there. If the car can be sent by train, so much the better—this is an option drivers exercise all too rarely.

- Where there is a sudden emergency such as a need for a doctor, hospital, or police.

- For business and professional reasons where other options are very inconvenient or impossible.

- Where objects are too heavy for transport on public vehicles.

- Where three or more people can use the car jointly, such as pools, mothers with children, and groups of friends and neighbors.

A private car should certainly not be used where other means of transport exist, as in most cities, or for frivolous reasons, just to

Is This Trip Necessary?

Answer the following questions with a **yes** *or* **no**.

1   Before jumping into the car, do you ask yourself if this trip is necessary?

2   Do you often walk or cycle for distances under one mile?

3   Do you take alternate transport or pools, if available, rather than the car?

4   Has distance between work and residence been a factor in choosing either?

5   Has availability of alternate transport been a factor?

6   Do you make fewer than two major shopping trips per week?

7   Have you attempted to find local amenities (sports, friends, cultural activities, shopping, etc.) for the express purpose of avoiding car use?

8   Are there two or fewer motor vehicles (including motorcycles) in your family?

9   When making travel plans, do you consider ways of getting there without a car?

10   When you consider weekend or leisure activities, does avoiding use of your car play a role in choosing a particular option?

SCORES

Score one point for each **yes** *answer—the higher your score, the more enlightened your attitude toward car dependence.*

0–3   You are not aware of problems connected with car use.

4–6   You have some conscience in regard to proper car use.

7–10   You realize there are problems and are trying to do something about them.

drive somewhere. In light of all the reasons for moderate car use explored here, each proposed journey should be preceded by the question which was used so effectively in the United States during World War II: *Is this trip necessary?*

Could we get to where we want to go by walking or cycling? Could we get there by bus or metro? Could we go on holiday with two suitcases instead of five and take the train? Is the outing in the family car just going to end up with squabbling children and a lunch in a parking lot? Are we jumping into a car just to forget our problems? Are we using the car to hash out those problems—since the two people arguing have a handy excuse for not looking at each other? Are we trying to gain independence or get away from the people we live with? Are we trying to have an adventure, show off, feel secure, calm down, kill time? Could any of these purposes be accomplished in another way, not car-bound?

Such questions should be posed before reaching for the car keys. A small minority may be bothered, somewhere in the depth of their being, every time they do reach for those keys. They may feel there is something wrong, without knowing what or why. It may be a feeling akin to the hesitation some feel before killing a fly. Such a minority, like our two families and many other good souls, manage eventually to arrange a carless style of life for themselves. Are they to remain forever the extravagant exception?

The rest of us, who jump into that two-handed engine at the door should at least recognize that we are using more than two thousand pounds of glass and steel to propel less than two hundred pounds of flesh and blood.

SOLUTION 33
Careful consideration of the necessity for each car trip.

And they sawed the branches upon which they sat,
And called out to each other what they had learned
How one can saw in a better way.
And then fell noisily into the abyss,
And those who watched them shook their heads
And continued sawing with gusto.

Bertold Brecht

CONCLUSION

These lines were quoted by a visiting professor at the 1988 conference on leisure-time traffic in Interlaaken, Switzerland. The professor then answered his own question, "How much traffic does tourism need and how much can it bear?" with a ringing, "Less, much less." The professor, who spoke of the terrible triumph of the motorcar, considered the question of tourist traffic quite literally academic. "We academics will forever continue to formulate theories and proposals to salve our consciences, but we will do nothing." [1]

There are two principal reasons why all of us, whether high school dropouts or Ph.D.'s, continue to do nothing. One of them is ignorance. Virtually all of us are ignorant. Ignorant in not realizing the problem. Or ignorant (perhaps in the Buddhist sense of that word) in not even being able to imagine any other way of life. Even if we spend several hours of each day trapped in our personal bubble on congested roads or buying much more than we need in Muzak-filled supermarkets, we are apt to accept this as the natural state of things.

We may vaguely realize that in some parts of the globe people don't communicate with each other by means of bumper stickers, horn signals, or license plates with names and messages, but face to face in the central market square. We may realize it, and even feel a bit uncomfortable with our present style of life, but then are defeated by the second reason: inertia. It is somehow easier to continue with one, two, three, or even four cars per family and all that goes with it, than to make the effort required to buck the floodtide of automobiles sweeping the world. How could any one of us, alone and powerless, make a meaningful start on such a daunting task?

Well, making such a start, at least in the department of ignorance, has been the subject of this book. With what we now know, you and I together can begin to concentrate on the inertia part. That is the real difficulty. Knowing something is a long way away from doing something about it. The fact that we must immediately cut our emissions by over half just to stay *even* in the race against climatic disaster has not convinced many people to make one less car journey per day.[2] Nor has it convinced many to use boots, bikes, and buses for the short distances which constitute almost half of all car journeys. Must we spend years and years surrounded by the bleak consequences of indiscriminate car use before we can correct this problem?

The reader might well ask which of the measures suggested here promises the quickest and most effective way of correcting the problem. In an ideal world, the answer would be not just one or two but all of them together, and even some not covered here. A whole panoply of sticks and carrots is probably necessary to wean drivers from their vehicles and encourage them to use other ways of getting around. Concentrating on just one or two is equivalent to "rearranging the deck chairs on the *Titanic*."

But we don't live in an ideal world, we live in a more or less intractable world in which we have to fight every inch of the way for even small improvements. That's why we have to make a small beginning in any one of the ways suggested here which happens to suit our own community and then go on from there. A carless Saturday in Lübeck, a partial car ban in Milan, a Keep California Moving Day—these are the building blocks of a virtuous cycle which may lead us, little by little, to a saner way of life.

These pages have running through them a number of underlying themes which we would do well to keep firmly in mind if we want to stimulate that virtuous cycle to a better environment and keep afloat that symbolic *Titanic* we are sailing on. These themes can be summarized as follows:

Shift the Burden from Transport

Much of modern life revolves around transport. Workplaces and residences are moving ever farther from each other, and most leisure-time activities involve transport and travel. Goods inventories have been shifted from storage warehouses to trucks on our roads. There is constant and often needless movement of local products to distant markets and back again. We have made a plea in these pages to reverse that trend and shift the burden of modern life away from transport by living arrangements and land-use planning which obviate the need for so much movement.

Reverse Conventional Traffic Planning

Our traffic planners have for years endeavored to make life easy and obstructionless for automobiles, thus encouraging their use. Their main concern has been to provide the infrastructure needed and to speed along the ever-increasing numbers of cars. (At current growth rates, it must be remembered, there will be 2 billion of them in 2025.) Our idea in these pages has been that an unlimited growth rate for cars is neither desirable, nor necessary, nor inevitable. We don't have to sit helpless and wait for it to happen but can begin to stand traffic engineering wisdom on its head by creating obstructions instead of removing them.

A Penny of Prevention Is Worth a Pound of Cure

A penny spent on arranging streets, on administrative simplicity for transport measures, on preventing problems and abuses before they occur saves many pounds, dollars, and marks otherwise needed to correct them after. Sleeping policemen are better, cheaper, and gentler than the wide-awake kind. Must a city like New York really resort to arresting grandmothers and clergymen for jumping turnstiles when the need for such behavior could have been avoided by a simple fare structure? Must Americans really be forced into using their cars at lunchtime when such use could have been minimized by siting their amenities within easy walking distance? Must London roads really be choked every morning and evening when many cars could have been kept off those roads by government support of rail, by simpler and lower fare structure, and by withdrawal of government subsidies and tax breaks to the car?

Make the Polluter Pay

That principle and its corollary, let the clean user get off lightly, should play an important role in determining a modern tax and pricing policy. Tied to that principle is the idea that prices for most of the goods we consume are too low. They fail to take into account what are sometimes called external costs such as those connected with pollution, noise, congestion, and environmental cleanup which arise from their production and use. In the case of transport the external costs are most certainly high. We have argued here for the removal of the many hidden subsidies to automobiles so that they and the transport they provide can compete on equal terms. But often even a free-market price does not truly reflect all these environmental costs. The price mechanism is one way to restrict the use of damaging products and reward the use of clean ones. In the domain of cars that would mean the dirtier the car the more it should be taxed, while the less it is used, the less its user should pay.

Don't Expect Miracles from Technology

Technology can only solve a very small part of the car crisis. It is, in fact, more apt to make additional problems for us. We have discussed in the prologue and elsewhere the distortion in value that technology has forced on concepts like time and space. Advances in technology which bring about even faster transport and therefore make time and space shrink even further would only exacerbate the conflict between human and mechanical perceptions. Even within the proper domain of technology—the development of a perfectly clean car and matching clean fuel—it would take many years to make an impact on the world car fleet. And it would do very little to solve the problems of congestion, traffic casualties, aesthetic pollution, and destruction of cities and countrysides. Where technology can be useful is in telecommunication to replace cars on the road by computers and fax machines, and in-car gadgets such as speed-warning devices, trip-cost meters, road pricing aids, and other instruments whose purpose is not to speed cars along but to alert drivers to their dangers or costs. To make any real impact on the world car problem, however, there is no miracle shortcut: We have to make do with fewer cars.

Think Globally, Act Locally

This slogan, which was first coined by environmentalist René Dubos, tries to lay the responsibility for the planet at the feet of groups and individuals, challenging them to act in their own community to protect the global environment. Each individual and group action must be tied to the concept of sustainability. Sustainability in its simplest form means not taking more from our earth than we can put back in. The biologist and environmentalist Ernst von Weizsaecker gives it a more radical meaning by defining sustainability as "an economy using only renewable resources (and that at the rate of their replenishment only) and producing only low, nonaccumulating levels of pollution."[3]

We cannot, unfortunately, leave it only to experts to construct such an economy. Since we are the ones using up resources and we are the ones producing pollution, it is up to us to begin moving in that direction. We have a tendency in the modern world to leave anything complicated to specialists or experts in the field. Jane Jacobs reminded us, thirty years ago, that we need not do this:

> The processes that occur in our cities are not arcane, capable of being understood only by experts. They can be understood by almost anybody. By understanding these ordinary arrangements of cause and effect, we can also direct them if we want to.[4]

272

A Report on The Future

Short-Term Actions: Several Months to Two Years
1 Speed limits
2 Fuel taxes
3 Road pricing
4 Parking controls
5 Paratransit
6 Driver education
7 Fare cards
8 Increasing telecommuting

Medium-Term Measures: Two to Five Years
1 Redesign automobiles
2 Alternate fuels
3 "Eco-car" taxes
4 Abandoning car subsidies
5 New vehicle standards
6 More buses and trams
7 Retiring old and dirty cars

Long-Term Approaches: Fifteen to Thirty Years
1 Light and heavy rail
2 New concept vehicles
3 New technologies
4 Major tax overhauls
5 Restructuring of city centers and suburbs
6 Major life style changes

Generational Changes
1 Major changes in urban design
2 Solar energy
3 Hydrogen power
4 New social values
5 Redefinition of work
6 New economics

There is much we can do by using technical and economic means to make the modern world a little more harmonious and bring some order to the frantic way we now move from place to place. But technical and economic measures alone can't do the trick. In the end we must understand the present impasse not only with our minds (as many do already) or our pocketbooks (with fluctuating and often temporary results) but with our entire beings.

The Austrian novelist Robert Musil years ago used the metaphor of a ship's anchor which must tear our living flesh to make us really understand something. Only half of a great awareness takes place in our brain; the other half comes from the dark bottom of our inmost being. To demonstrate what it really means to understand this issue we would have to imagine a city dweller deciding to renounce his car even if such an action caused a fair amount of inconvenience and meant a loss of standing with what used to be called the opposite sex.

Once we really understand, perhaps our senseless search for ever more mobility and ever faster speeds will seem a temporary aberration. And those space-eating boxes with which we surrounded ourselves for our personal transport will seem as strange and distorted as something from the universe of Hieronymus Bosch.

In a historic referendum in June 1988, the people of California voted to approve three transport measures which allow the state to double fuel taxes over the next few years and to issue some $2 billion worth of bonds to improve local rail, commuter, and urban transit. In that state, where there are many more cars than in India, Pakistan, and China combined, the citizens themselves, with little help from governments, experts, or institutions, are apparently beginning to comprehend the problem. Newspaper analysts misinterpreted that result, seeing in the vote for additional taxation the "end of the tax revolt." If these analysts had paid more attention to the mushrooming of car and van pools, traffic management associations, and tripling of bridge tolls, they might have been able to understand that vote for what it was: not the end of the revolt against taxes, but the beginning of the revolt against cars.

Meanwhile most of us (including Californians) continue to climb into our cars, or would if one were available. Most of us do so without even the flicker of a doubt. Humanity is in the position of Goethe's fisherman, in front of whose eyes a mermaid suddenly emerged from the water, beckoning with open arms: "Half drew she him, half sank he down, and was not seen again."

It is therefore an open question whether a society whose members are capable of hiring a limousine to have their dogs picked up and taken to the grooming parlor, or a civilization which goes cheerfully to war to exercise such a right, has the will to change. We may find that we simply do not *want* to change. If so, Musil's anchor has not bitten, or has not bitten deep enough. If that is really the case, if we really persist in our present course knowing full well the prospects which await us, we will deserve all we get.

In that case, we can only shrug our shoulders and mutter as Jaques does in Shakespeare's *As You Like It*, "Sweep on, you fat and greasy citizens! . . ."

EPILOGUE

In these pages I have tried not to be a preacher, a prophet of doom, or an idle dreamer. Instead, I have pointed out the progress that has been made here and there, and the pitfalls and dangers we must be aware of. The task I have set myself has been to observe how people behave in the real world we inhabit, not in the best of all possible worlds.

When you observe people's behavior, it is instructive to start with your own. You become your own private laboratory. And you ask yourself some hard questions. What happens to me when I get into a car? Knowing all the facts which have been presented here, how do I react in my daily life?

Today I live in a small village in the south of France. I like living in the countryside because it tends to isolate one from the worst effects of modern civilization. Perhaps this is just a way of burying one's head in the sand? I work at home when I'm not working elsewhere.

My village has no trains, no buses, no public or paratransit of any kind. It is five miles from a larger town which itself has no trains and only infrequent and little used bus service. There are no stores, no cafés, no weekly markets in my village, and with the exception of daily visits by bread and grocery vans, the fifty or so families here are isolated from the outside world unless they or their visitors possess their own means of transport.

I have tried walking and biking to the nearest town, but there are no shortcuts, walkways, or bike paths. There are no shoulders on the narrow curving roads, and people drive fast and often close to the edges. Moreover the terrain is hilly, it gets hot in the south, and there are no shade trees as there were once upon a time alongside French highways. This means that someone who wants to escape (perhaps quixotically) from the unsightly effects of modern industrial society is forced to rely on the very object at the root of many such effects.

The car I have is an ordinary car—the smallest, most energy-efficient available in a moderate price range. It is not particularly new, or clean, or shiny. It has no signs, no labels, no messages, no stuffed animals, no radio, no cassette player, and no cloth dice hanging from the rearview mirror. If I wanted to arrange a totally carless life, I would probably have to give up the countryside and move to a large city, one served by public transport. Since I am not ready to do this, I try to restrict my car trips to the once-daily round-trip journey to the nearest town five miles away. There are occasions when I must take the car on longer trips, but I never do so when alternate means are available, and I do try to ask myself each time if that trip is necessary.

What happens to me when I get into the car? Do I turn into a tiger, companion to that mythical creature in my tank? Well, I could easily allow myself to if I didn't keep a tight reign on my reactions, which often requires a considerable effort. What is that car in front of me doing, slowing down for no reason at all? Should I honk at him, should I pass him? Or should I perhaps see if I can help him, since he may not be sure where he is going? Should I slow down when I come to a village or town in which no speed limits are posted, and no streets have been calmed? If someone blows his horn or flashes his lights behind me, should I give him the high sign? Should I stop because a mother pushing a baby carriage stands at the crosswalk even though she hasn't started crossing? Will I have time to zip past her and save a minute or two?

What is it about the car which makes me "impatient as the wind" so that slowing down or waiting for thirty seconds becomes a huge problem? And if I did save those seconds, what would I do with them? Should I drive all the way into town and spend ten minutes trying to park in a space which may be illegal, or should I park this side of the bridge and make the foot trip into town with all the other nondrivers? Should I buy more than I can carry on a ten-minute walk, meaning I must find a space close to the shop, but may save another trip into town? Should I take the car when I want a change of scene, or will I instead decide to make a foot circuit of the village? When this car gives out, will I be tempted buy a bigger and better model?

The answers I give to all these questions are not always the "correct" ones. I am struggling with this car problem in the same way you are, and I am by no means mastering it. That shows me what we are up against. But I am trying, and I may end up carless one day, like our two exemplary families and the many other brave souls who have given up the car.

We cannot remake the world overnight. And we are not, in any case, likely to restore to that world the relative calm which existed before the advent of the automobile. But each one of us can contribute to traffic-calming and perhaps people- and economy- and government-calming on a giant scale, so that little by little we again become the masters instead of the slaves of our personal transport means.

Jacques Ellul's observation on all technologies is particularly apt when applied to the automobile: "It makes a good servant but a bad master."

NOTES

PROLOGUE

1. EcoPlan, 10 rue Joseph Bara, 75006 Paris.

Chapter 1   *THE WORLD: BEFORE AND AFTER*

1. Barbara Preston, *The Impact of the Motor Car* (Dyfed: Brefi Press, 1991), 47.

2. Lewis Mumford, *The City in History* (Harmondsworth, Middlesex: Penguin Books Ltd, 1961), 424.

3. H. B. Cresswell, "Seventy Years Back," *Architectural Review* (December 1958).

4. Robert Smith, *A Social History of the Bicycle* (New York: American Heritage Press, 1972), 192–93.

5. Charlotte Brontë, *The Professor* (London: J. M. Dent & Sons, 1974), 10.

6. Benton MacKaye in Tony Hiss, "Encountering the Countryside II," *The New Yorker*, 25 September 1989, 45, 46.

7. Kurt Andersen, "Oldfangled New Towns," *Time*, 20 May 1991.

8. MacKaye in Hiss, "Encountering the Countryside," 46.

9. George Kennan in John Newhouse, "Books: A Deeper Reality," *The New Yorker*, 25 September 1989, 119.

10. Adolf Hitler in Die Grünen im Bundestag, eds., *Welche Freiheit Brauchen Wir?*, trans. W. Zuckermann (Berlin: Elefanten Press, 1989), 18.

11. Jane Kramer, "Letter from Europe," *The New Yorker*, November 1988, 72.

12. Georges Pompidou in F. E. K. Britton, "An End to Urban Motorways," *Built Environment* (October 1974): 504; Ingvar Carlssen, interview in *Dagens Nyheter* 13 September 1990; Peter Bottomley, letter to *Hampstead and Highgate Express*, 14 April 1989.

13. Anthony Crosland, *Transport Policy: A Consultation Document* (London: Department of the Environment, 1976), conclusion.

14 Michael Renner, *Rethinking the Role of the Automobile* (Washington, D.C.: Worldwatch Institute, June 1988), 12.

15. John G. Adams, "Car Ownership Forecasting: Pull the Ladder Up or Climb Back Down?" *Traffic Engineering + Control*, vol. 3, no. 3 (March 1990): 136–41.

16. *Le Monde*, 28 April 1990.

17. *Globe Magazine*, no. 51 (October 1990): 52.

18. Frederic Vester, "The Biocybernetic Approach as a Basis for Planning Our Environment," *Systems Practice*, vol. 1, no. 4 (1988).

Chapter 2   *NATURE: THE OLD GRAY MARE*

1. Helena Smith, *The European,* 29 November 1990, 12.

2. Jean Pierre Gosselin, "Environment: Genuine Solutions," *Mondial de L'Automobile,* Official Magazine (1990): 96–100.

3. Cuddihy et al., in John Whitelegg, ed., "The Future of Urban Transport" (Conference organized by the Public Transport Users Association, Melbourne, 29 November 1989).

4. Michael P. Walsh, "Environmental Challenges Posed by Growing Automobile Use" (Paper presented at International Conference on Tomorrow's Clean and Fuel-Efficient Automobiles, Berlin, March 1991), 3.

5. Al Gore, Jr., "Replies to Skeptics: Questions about Global Warming," *International Herald Tribune,* 23 April 1990.

6. René Dumont, interview with Michael Lecler, *Paris Match,* 17 August 1989, 18, 96, 97, 98, 101.

7. Lester R. Brown, *State of the World 1989* (New York and London: W. W. Norton & Co., 1989).

8. Mitteilungen aus dem Bundesministerium für Forschung und Technologie, "Im stürmischen Meer wird viel Kohlendioxid gebunden," *BMFT Journal* (6 November 1990): 10.

9. Philip Jones and Tom Wigley, "Global Warming Trends," *Scientific American* (August 1990): 66–73.

10. European Conference of Ministers of Transport, *Transport Policy and the Environment* (Paris: ECMT, 1990): 58.

11. Rasmussen in Emin Tengström, "The Automobile and Its Impact on Human Life" (Göteborg: unpublished, 1991), 51.

12. Adams, "Car Ownership Forecasting," 230–35.

13. Peter M. Bode et al., *Alptraum Auto: Eine Hundertjährige Erfindung und ihre Folgen* (München: Raben Verlag, 1986), 93.

14. Robert U. Ayres, "Eco-Restructuring: Managing the Transition to an Ecologically Sustainable Economy" (Draft Prospectus for a Long-Term Multidisciplinary Multi-institution Research Program, Laxenburg, Austria, 3 October 1990), 2.

15. Ernst U. von Weizsaecker, "Sustainability Is a Task for the North," *Journal of International Affairs* (Winter 1991): 4.

16. John Whitelegg, (Remarks to the hearing organized by the European Parliament on Economic and Fiscal Incentives to Promote Environmental Policy Objectives, Brussels, 12 & 22 June 1990).

17. Rachel Carlson, *Silent Spring* (1962; New York: Fawcett, 1967), 13.

Chapter 3   *THE CITY: NECROPOLIS OR ECOPOLIS?*

1. Jane Jacobs, *The Death and Life of Great American Cities* (Harmondsworth, Middlesex: Penguin Books Ltd, 1961), 363.

2. Newman and Kenworthy, *Cities and Automobile Dependence: A Sourcebook* (Aldershot and Brookfield, Vermont: Gower Publishing Company Ltd, 1989), 64.

3. The Swedish Association of Local Authorities, *Reduction of Traffic in City Centers* (Stockholm: SALA, February 1989), 13.

4. John Roberts, *The Big Choke* (London: TEST, for London Weekend Television, 1989), 3.

5. Marshall Berman in David Engwicht, "Human Rights and the Car" (Brisbane: unpublished, 1990), 34.

6. Jacobs, *Death and Life*, 338.

7. Grover Foley, "Mumford on the City," *The Ecologist*, 19 March 1989, 104–110.

8. Ernst U. von Weizsaecker, *Erdpolitik* (Darmstadt: Wissenschaftliche Buchgesellschaft, 1989), 196.

9. Michael J. Bannon et al., eds., *Urbanization and Urban Development* (Dublin: University College, January 1991), iii.

10. Rayner Banham in Harley Sherlock, *Cities are Good for Us* (London: Transport 2000, 1990), 49.

11. R. E. Wycherly in William H. Whyte, *City* (New York: Doubleday, 1988), 339–340.

12. Newman and Kenworthy in Marcia D. Lowe, *Alternatives to the Automobile: Transport in Livable Cities* (Washington: Worldwatch Institute, October 1990), 38.

13. Sherlock, *Cities Are Good for Us*.

14. Jacobs, *Death and Life*, 342.

15. Juri Pill, Toronto Transit Commission, in Marcia D. Lowe, *Alternatives to the Automobile*, 31.

16. Jacobs, *Death and Life*, 345.

Chapter 4   OURSELVES: THE AUTO AND THE EGO

1. *Elle*, trans. W. Zuckermann, 20 March 1991, 95–6.

2. Asplund in Tengström, "The Automobile and Its Impact," 36.

3. Malmberg in Tengström, "The Automobile and Its Impact," 41.

4. "4 My Ego," *In Motion: The Student Guide to Safe Driving*, vol. 4, no. 1 (Fall 1989).

5. Dietlind Preiss in *Welche Freiheit Brauchen Wir?*, 102.

6. Ibid.

7. Mayer Hillman et al., *One False Move . . .* (London: The Policies Studies Institute, 1990).

8. Ibid.

9. Norwegian Study made at the Institute of Transport Economics in Oslo, in Tengström, "The Automobile and Its Impact."

10. Dr. Till Bastian in *Welche Freiheit Brauchen Wir?*, 156–157.

11. T. W. Goldberg in Tengström, "The Automobile and Its Impact."

12. Karin Bruns in *Welche Freiheit Brauchen Wir?*, 79.

13. Falconnet and Lefaucher in *Welche Freiheit Brauchen Wir?*, 64.

14. Dr. Gudrun Axell Knapp in *Welche Freiheit Brauchen Wir?*, 61–68.

15. Dr. Wolfgang Schmidtbauer in *Welche Freiheit Brauchen Wir?*, 144.

16. Knapp, op. cit.

17. Tengström, "The Automobile and Its Impact," 32.

18. Quoted in *Welche Freiheit Brauchen Wir?*, 84.

19. J. M. Cain in D. Laird, "Versions of Eden: The Automobile and the American Novel" in David L. Lewis and Laurence Goldstein, eds., *The Automobile and American Culture* (Ann Arbor: The University of Michigan Press, 1983), 247.

20. Helga Rock, *Welche Freiheit Brauchen Wir?*, 16.

21. Stephen Bayley, "Sex Drive," *The Unesco Courier*, October 1990, 30.

22. Jean Francis Held, "The Automotive Age," *The Unesco Courier*, October 1990, 15.

23. A. Silverleaf and J. Turgel, *Transport Safety and Security* (Oxford: Transport Studies Unit, Oxford University, November 1990), 1.

24. Trinca et al., in Tengström, "The Automobile and Its Impact," 55.

25. John Whitelegg (Speech given to conference organized by Public Transport Users Association of Australia, 29 November 1989).

26. *Auto-Free Press* (January-February 1990): 3.

Chapter 5   THE CHALLENGE: FINDING THE MAGIC WORD

1. Vester, op cit.

2. Roger L. Creighton, *Urban Transportation Planning* (University of Illinois Press, 1970), xv–xvi.

3. Kenneth Orski, "Learning to Live with Traffic Congestion," *Colorado Economic Review* (August 1988): 5.

4. U.S. Department of Transportation, *Planning Guidelines for Suburban Transit* (Washington, D.C.: U. S. Department of Transportation, August 1988), 5.

5. Henry Miller, *Nexus* (New York: Grove Press, 1978), 308.

Chapter 6   LIFTING THE VEIL

1. Jens Priewe, "Fast Cars Die Sooner," *Management Wissen* (February 1988): 1–8.

2. Ayres, "Eco-Restructuring."

3. Unsigned item from "Contraflows," *Transport Report* (UK: July–August 1989).

4. "Chicago to Test Personal Rapid Transit Technology," *Auto-Free Press* (July–August 1990): 2.

5. Stephen Plowden, "The Local Runabout: A Summary" (unpublished, 1987).

6. Hinrich Krey in *Welche Freiheit Brauchen Wir?*, 36.

7. Eberhard von Kuenheim, interview in the *Internation Herald Tribune*, 31 May 1989.

8. Lewis and Goldstein, eds., *The Automobile and American Culture*, 44.

9. Lawrence J. White, *The Automobile Industry Since 1945* (Cambridge: Harvard University Press, 1973).

10. Jesse A. Simon and Joel Woodhull, "Parking Subsidization and Travel Mode Choice," *California Transit*, no. 10 (January–March 1988): 1.

11. Ibid., 1, 3.

12. J. Lindstrom in Tengström, "The Automobile and Its Impact," 28.

13. Sherlock, *Cities are Good for Us*, 65.

14. Ivan Illich, *Energy and Equity* (London: Calder & Boyers, Ltd, 1974), 30–31.

15. Terence Bendixson, "The Costs of Traffic Congestion: Selected Examples" (Information obtained from Terence Bendixson, London, April 1990).

16. Carlo J. Salzano, "Report on the 23rd Annual Joint Conference of Eno Foundation Board of Directors and Board of Consultants," *Transportation Quarterly* (January 1990): 7.

17. In-Car Travel Cost Display has been developed by Professor Steven Cousins, International Ecotechnology Research Centre, Cranfield, Bedfordshire, England.

18. Andy Hamilton (Paper delivered at New England Environmental Conference, March 16–17, 1991).

19. Helmut Holzapfel, "Mobilität, Wahn, Erlebnis, oder Notwendigkeit," in *Welche Feiheit Brauchen Wir?*, trans. W. Zuckermann, 162.

20. John Roberts, *User-Friendly Cities* (London: TEST, 1989), 7.

Chapter 7   CLOSING THE FLOOD GATES

1. Colin Buchanan in Peter Jones, *The Restraint of Road Traffic in Urban Areas* (Oxford: Transport Studies Unit, Oxford University, October 1989), 3.

2. *Environmental Policies for Cities in the 1990s* (Paris: Organization for Economic Cooperation and Development, 1990), 78.

3. Ogunsanya in *Environmental Policies for Cities*, 38.

4. Brian Richards, *Transport in Cities*, (London: Architecture Design and Technology Press, 1990): 78.

5. Jones, *Restraint of Road Traffic*, 42.

6. Rheinischer Merkur, "City Centre Ban on Vehicle in One-Day-A-Month Trial," *The German Tribune*, 10 December 1989.

7. Ibid.

8. Roberts, *User-Friendly Cities*, 17.

9. Kenneth Greenberg, "Toronto: Street Revived," in *Public Streets for Public Use*, Anne Vernez Moudon, ed., (New York: Van Nostrand Reinhold, 1987), 194.

10. CROW Institute, *Van Woonerf Tot Erf* (Ede: C.R.O.W., October 1989), 22..

11. Rolf Monheim, "Reorienting Traffic Planning in German Cities," *Proceedings of the Seventh Annual Pedestrian Conference* (Boulder, Colorado, 1986).

12. *Wiener Kurrier*, 2 February 1991.

13. H. H. Keller, "Traffic Calming Policies in Germany," *Living and Moving in Cities,* Cetur (Paris, 1990): 23–24.

14. Ibid.

15. West Berlin police officer in Tony Paterson, *The European*, October 1990.

16. Keller, op cit.

17. Ibid.

18. Carmen Hass-Klau, *The Pedestrian and City Traffic* (London and New York: Belhaven Press, 1990), 228.

19. Sherlock, *Cities Are Good for Us*, 54–55.

20. Engwicht, "Human Rights and the Car," 81.

21. G. Bebbington, *The Origin of Street Names* (London: Batsford, 1972), 5.

22. Barbara Rosen and Wolfgang Zuckermann, *The Mews of London* (Exeter: Webb & Bower, 1982), 140.

23. Namiki Oka, "Traffic Zone Systems for Both Cars and People," *The Wheel Extended,* Toyota Quarterly, no. 74: 19.

24. From a private communication with the author.

25. Marck Francis, "The Making of Democratic Streets," in *Public Streets for Public Use*, 29.

26. Lawrence O. Houstoun, Jr., "From Street to Mall and Back Again," *Planning* (June 1990): 4.

27. John Roberts, *Quality Streets* (London: TEST, 1989), 12.

28. "Beethoven and Beatles Warn Würzburg's Walkers," *Pedestrian International* (Fall 1990): 4.

29. Bordeaux's policy is the brainchild of right-of-center mayor Chaban-Delmas and his counselor, Mme. Helene Desplats.

30. Jacobs, *Death and Life*, 343.

31. John Roberts, "Car Precincts" (Abstract of paper for the Green Modes Symposium, January 1989).

32. Dr. William Young and John Polak, *Developments in Parking Policy and Management* (Oxford: Transport Studies Unit, Oxford University, November 1990).

33. P. H. Bly and F. V. Webster, "Comparison of Interactive Land Use and Transport Models," *Transportation Research Record*, 1125 (1987): 12.

34. The inventor of that system is Tom Schur, CH 7503 Samedan, Switzerland.

35. John W. Polak et al., "Parking Guidance and Informatin Systems: Performance and Capability," *Traffic Engineering + Control* (October 1990): 19–523.

36. Akos Szoboslay, "Forced Parking Affects Our Lives," *California Transit*, no. 10 (January–March 1988): 3.

37. Ibid.

38. Ibid., 7.

39. Jessica Mathews, "The Transport Situation Is So Bad That It Can Only Get Better," *International Herald Tribune*, 2 April 1991.

40. Stanley Hart, *An Assessment of the Municipal Costs of Automobile Use* (Altadena, California, December 1985).

41. Peter Jones, *Traffic Regulation in Urban Areas, Key Findings from a Research Study* (Oxford Transport Studies Unit, Oxford University, April 1989).

42. Tony Paterson, *The European*, October 1990.

43. Jay A. Winsten, *The Designated Driver Campaign*, The Harvard Alcohol Project, Status Report (Cambridge: Harvard School of Public Health, March 1990).

44. James Cooper, *Freight Needs and Transport Policy* (Oxford and London: Transport Studies Group, Polytechnic of Central London and Oxford University, March 1990), 38.

45. Dispatch in "The Commercial Motor," 15 June 1989, quoted in *Transport Report* (U.K., July-August 1989), 5.

46. Dieter Teufel, "Gesellschaftliche Kosten des Strassengüterverkehrs," *UPI-Bericht*, no. 17, (1989).

47. Insurance Institute for Highway Safety, *Big Trucks* (Washington, D.C.: 1985).

48. Cooper, *Freight Needs and Transport Policy*, 38.

49. Richards, *Transport in Cities*, 83.

Chapter 8   CHOOSING HUMAN POWER

1. Transport 2000, *Feet First, the Case for a Pedestrian Priority* (London: Transport 2000, undated), 2.

2. Illich, *Energy and Equity*, 28.

3. Whitelegg, (Remarks to European Parliament Hearing, 12 & 22 June 1990).

4. Wolfgang Sachs in Tengström, "The Automobile and Its Impact."

5. Rolf Monheim, "Verkehrswissenschaft und Verkehrsplanung im Spannungsfeld von Trends und Zielen," *Der Städtetag* (November 1989).

6. Jack Short, (from the European Conference of Transport Ministers, Address to The European Workshop on Cities and the Global Environment, The Hague, December 1990).

7. Mario Vargas Llosa, *Aunt Julia and the Scriptwriter* (London: Faber and Faber, Ltd, 1983).

8. Mayer Hillman, "The Neglect of Walking in UK Transport and Planning Policy" (Paper for Feet First Symposium, May 1989), 1.

9. Michael A. Replogle in Marcia D. Lowe, *The Bicycle: Vehicle for a Small Planet* (Washington, D.C.: Worldwatch Institute, 1989), 19.

10. Lowe, *The Bicycle*, 6.

11. Ibid., 32.

12. That effort was led by Alex Zuckermann, brother of the author.

13. Metropolitan Transportation Commission, *MTC Regional Bicycle Plan*, (Berkeley: 22 September 1982): 9–17.

14. Ibid., 45.

15. Jacobs, *Death and Life*, 374–376.

16. Rolf Monheim in Engwicht, "Human Rights and the Car," 72.

17. Private communication from Wigan Kahl, Stadtdirector, Munich.

Chapter 9   FIGHTING FIRE WITH ICE

1. Lowe, *The Bicycle*, 6.

2. Francis E. K. Britton, *Taxi Based Paratransit Technology* (Washington: U.S. Department of Transportation, May 1985), 1.

3. Richards, *Transport in Cities*, 87.

4. Association for the Conservation of Energy, *Solving the Greenhouse Dilemma*, World Wide Fund for Nature (UK, undated): 9.

5. The Swedish Association of Local Authorities, *Reduction of Traffic in City Centers* (February 1989): 17.

6. Act Now, "Brentwood Survey Shows Commuters Can Change," *ACT Newsletter*, XIV, 2, (February-March 1990): 3.

7. Ibid., 5.

8. John G. U. Adams, "The Motorist's Dilemma" (Draft of a paper to National Society for Clean Air, Spring Workshop, 27-29 March 1990).

Chapter 10   UNDAMNING THE PUBLIC

1. Jean-Pierre Orfeuil, "Transport, Energy, Environment: A Low Energy Future," (IN-RETS paper given at Berlin Conference Tomorrow's Clean and Fuel-Efficient Automobile, March 1991): 11.

2. Illich, *Energy and Equity*, 42.

3. John Whitelegg, "The Impact of High Speed Trains on Society" (Paper given to Stockholm Conference, High Speed Trains, 12–14 June 1990).

4. Tony Hiss, "Annals of Transportation—Light Rail," *The New Yorker*, 6 March 1989, 72.

5. David Gurin, private communication to author.

6. Renner, *Rethinking the Role of the Automobile*, 50.

7. Alvin L. Spivak, *Fiscal Correction of Road Problems—A Conservative Approach* (California: unpublished, December 1987), 1.

8. Klaus M. Meyer-Abich et al., in Weizsaecker, *Erdpolitik*.

9. Hiss, op. cit., 72.

10. Jacobs, *Death and Life*, 351.

11. Richards, *Transport in Cities*, 94.

12. Ibid.

13. Ibid., 88.

14. Arthur Higbee, "American Topics," *International Herald Tribune*, 25 February 1991.

15. "New Roads and Traffic," *Traffic and Engineering + Control*, February 1991.

16. Tarifverbund Nordwestschweiz, *Rechenschaftsbericht, 1 Jahr TNW Juni 1987-Mai 1988* (Basel: TNW, 1988).

Chapter 11   *TIGHTENING THE PURSE STRINGS*

1. Namiki Oka, "The Automobile's Place in Urban Transport Planning," *The Wheel Extended*, 17.

2. Tony Thompson, "Road Use Charging—the Current State of Technology," *Traffic Engineering + Control*, vol. 31, no. 9 (October 1990), 526.

3. John Whitelegg, private communication with author.

4. Richards, *Transport in Cities*, 74.

5. Albert Hahn, "Brazil: The 'The Alcohol Plan' Reviewed," *International Economics and Financial Markets* (Oxford: Oxford University Press, 1988).

6. Claire Holman et al., *Road Transport and Pollution* (Oxford: Earth Resources Research, Transport Studies Unit, Oxford University, January 1991), 49.

7. James J. MacKenzie, "Reducing U.S. Reliance on Imported Oil: An Assessment of Alternative Transportation Fuels," *World Resources Institute* (Washington, D. C.: October 1990), 7.

8. "BP Statistical Review of World Energy," The British Petroleum Company, 1989.

9. *Time*, January 1990.

10. Renner, *Rethinking the Role of the Automobile*, 33–34.

11. James J. MacKenzie and Michael P. Walsh, *Driving Forces: Motor Vehicle Trends and their Implications for Global Warming, Energy Strategies, and Transportation Planning* (Washington, D.C.: World Resources Institute, December 1990), 24.

12. Andy Hamilton, op cit.

13. Henry Ford II in "Cars, Transport, & Amenity in Urban Places" (Paris: EcoPlan, unpublished, 1990), 123.

14. Agence France Presse dispatch, "Bonn Coalition Agrees on Rise in Gasoline Tax," *International Herald Tribune*, 23 February 1991.

15. Stanley Hart, *An Assessment of the Municpal Costs of Automobile Use* (Altadena, California: December 1985).

16. Renner, *Rethinking the Role of the Automobile*, 48.

17. Teufel et al., (quoted in a speech by John Whitelegg to Public Transport Users Association, Melbourne, Australia, November 1989).

18. Association of London Authorities, *Keep London Moving*(London: ALA, undated), 7.

19. Alan Tonelson and Andrew K. Hurd, "Cheap Oil? Look Closer to Home," *International Herald Tribune*, 5 September 1990.

20. Olivier Postel-Vinay, "Ile de France: un Remede contre l'asphyxie," *Dynasteurs* (May 1990): 66.

21. Ibid., 67.

22. Frank Viviano, "Sweeping Plan to Solve Bay Traffic Mess," *The San Francisco Chronicle*, 15 February 1990.

23. Ibid.

24. Anthony J. Barber, quoted in Andrew L. Yarrow, "New York's Roads Going from Bad to Gridlock," *International Herald Tribune*, September 1990.

Chapter 12   REARRANGING OUR LIVES

1. Quoted in William H. Whyte, *City*, 337–38.

2. E. V. Walter, *Placeways—A Theory of the Human Environment* (Chapel Hill: Unversity of North Carolina Press, 1988), 2

3. Richards, *Transport in Cities*, 5.

4. C. Kenneth Orski, "Can Management of Transportation Demand Help Solve Our Growing Traffic Congestion and Air Pollution Problems?," *Transportation Quarterly* (October 1990): 487, 488.

5. Renner, *Rethinking the Role of the Automobile*, 47.

6. Richard K. Untermann in *Public Streets for Public Use*, 123–124.

7. Jacobs, *Death and Life*, 178ff.

8. Philip Langdon, "A Good Place to Live," *Atlantic Monthly* (March 1988): 39.

9. Andres Duany in Ruth Eckdish Knack, "Repent ye Sinners, Repent," *Planning* (August 1989).

10. Meike Spitzner, quoted in *Welche Freiheit Brauchen Wir?*, 43.

11. Langdon, op cit.

12. Gary Delsohn, "The First Pedestrian Pocket," *Planning* (December 1989): 21.

13. Peter Calthorpe, *The Pedestrian Pocket Book: New Suburban Design Strategy* (Princeton: The Princeton Architectural Press, 1989).

14 . The study "The Cost of Sprawl" was undertaken by the Real Estate Corporation for the Council of Environmental Quality and Housing and Urban Development.

15. "The Ahmanson Ranch," Conceptual Master Plan Summary (Irwindale, California: Home Savings of America F. A., July 1987).

16. Lowe, *Alternatives to the Automobile*, 32.

17. Ibid.

18. Andres Duany, "Shaking Up the Suburbs," interview in *Metropolitan Home* (March 1989): 79.

19. Delsohn, op cit.

20. Rosen and Zuckermann, *The Mews of London*, 19.

21. John Roberts, *Trouble in Store? Retail Locational Policy in Britain and Germany* (London: TEST, 1989).

22. Roberts, *Quality Streets*, 16.

23. Dispatch to *The Commercial Appeal*, Memphis, Tennessee, 7 October 1990.

24. Gil Gordon, "Telecommuting is Here to Stay," *Computerworld*, 4 September 1989.

25. Valerie Hanssens, "Getting Along without a Car—and Nicely, Too," *The Philadelphia Enquirer*, 19 December 1989, section A, 17.

26. Joerg Michael Fey, "Abschied vom Auto" originally in *Die Zeit*, reprinted in Peter M. Bode et al., *Alptraum Auto*, 232–233, trans. W. Zuckermann.

27. Peter Naess, "Concentrating Urban Development to Save Nature," (Research paper for the Norwegian Institute for Urban and Regional Research, March 1991).

Chapter 13   FINDING THE RIGHT PLACE FOR THE CAR

1. Hughes and Replogle in Renner, *Rethinking the Role of the Automobile*, 52.

2. Renner, *Rethinking the Role of the Automobile*, 53.

3. David Gurin, "Planning Transportation in Developing Cities," *Mazingira*, vol. 5 (April 1981).

4. Engwicht, "Human Rights and the Car," 28.

5. Lowe, *Alternatives to the Automobile*, 11.

6. Tengström, "The Automobile and Its Impact," 85.

7. "Wenn ein Fussgänger den Spiess umdreht . . . *Süddeutsche Zeitung*, 29 November 1989.

8. Engwicht, "Human Rights and the Car," 25.

9. Roald Dahl, quoted in Mayer Hillman et al., *One False Move . . .* (London: Policy Studies Institute, 1990), 2.

10. Hillman et al., *One False Move . . .*, 92.

11. Ibid., 87.

12. Renner, *Rethinking the Role of the Automobile*, 31–32.

13. Fact sheet produced by Sierra Club, 100 Bush Street, San Francisco, California 94104.

14. Weizsaecker, "Sustainability is a Task for the North," 2.

CONCLUSION

1. Jost Krippendorf, (Paper presented to the Auswertung Seminar Freizeitverkehr, Interlaaken: 22–23 November 1989), 7.

2. Craig R. Whitney, "UN Warning on Warming: Cut Emissions 60% Now, or Else," *International Herald Tribune*, 27 May 1990.

3. Weizsaecker, "Sustainability is a Task for the North," 3.

4. Jacobs, *Death and Life*, 454.

SELECTED BIBLIOGRAPHY

The research sources for the materials from which this book was assembled are those primarily given in the endnotes. In addition to these, however, a small number of books and articles proved to be particularly influential in expanding the author's knowledge and background in this field. The following is a short list identifying these sources.

Adams, John. "Car Ownership Forecasting." *Traffic Engineering + Control*. March, 1990.

Bellon, Bernard P. *Mercedes in Peace and War*. New York: Columbia University Press, 1990.

Bode, Peter, et al. *Alptraum Auto: Eine Hundertjährige Erfindung und ihre Folgen*. Munich: Raben Verlag, 1986.

Brown, Lester R., ed. *State of the World 1989*. New York: W. W. Norton & Co., 1989.

Brown, Lester R, ed. *State of the World 1990*. New York: W. W. Norton & Co., 1990.

Carson, Rachel. *Silent Spring*. 1962. Reprint. New York: Fawcett, 1967.

European Conference of Ministers of Transport. *Transport Policy and the Environment*. Paris: ECMT, 1990.

EcoPlan. "Cars, Transport, & Amenity in Urban Places." Paris: 1990.

Engwicht, David, "Human Rights and the Car." Brisbane: 1990.

Grünen im Bundestag, eds. *Welche Freiheit Brauchen Wir?* Berlin: Elefanten Press, 1989.

Hillman, Mayer, et al. *One False Move . . .* London: The Policies Studies Institute, 1990.

Hiss, Tony. "Encountering the Countryside." *The New Yorker*. 28 August 1989.

Howard, Ebenzer. *Garden Cities of Tomorrow*. London: Attic Books, 1985.

Illich, Ivan. *Energy and Equity*. London: Calder & Boyers, Ltd, 1974.

Jacobs, Jane. *The Death and Life of Great American Cities*. Harmondsworth: Penguin, 1961.

Jones, Peter. *Restraint of Road Traffic in Urban Areas*. Oxford: Transport Studies Unit, Oxford University, 1989.

Lowe, Marcia D. *The Bicycle: Vehicle for a Small Planet*. Washington, D.C.:Worldwatch Institute, 1989.

Lowe, Marcia D. *Alternatives to the Automobile*. Washington, D.C.: Worldwatch Institute, 1990.

McLuhan, Marshall. *Understanding Media*. London: Routledge & Kegan Paul, Ltd, 1964.

Moudon, Anne Vernez, ed. *Public Streets for Public Use*. New York: Van Nostrand Reinhold, 1987.

Mumford, Lewis. *The City in History*. Harmondsworth: Penguin Books Ltd, 1961.

Newman & Kenworthy. *Cities and Automobile Dependence*. Brookfield, Vermont and Aldershot, Hampshire: Gower Publishing Co, 1989.

Organization for Economic Cooperation and Development. *Transport and the Environment*. Paris: OECD, 1988.

Renner, Michael. *Rethinking the Role of the Automobile*. Washington, D.C.: Worldwatch Institute, 1988.

Richards, Brian. *Transport in Cities*. London: Architecture Design and Technology Press, 1990.

Roberts, John. *Trouble in Store: Retail Locational Policy in Britain and Germany*. London: TEST, 1989.

Roberts, John. *User-Friendly Cities*. London: TEST, 1989.

Sherlock, Harley. *Cities Are Good for Us*. London: Transport 2000, 1990.

Smith, Robert. *A Social History of the Bicycle*. New York: American Heritage Press, 1972.

Tengström, Emin. "The Automobile and its Impact on Human Life." Göteborg: 1991.

Weizsaecker, Ernst. *Erdpolitik*. Darmstadt: Wissentschaftliche Buchgesellschaft, 1989.

Whitelegg, John, ed. "Traffic Congestion." Institute of British Geographers, to be published 1991.

Whyte, William H. *City*. New York: Doubleday, 1988.

INDEX

End of the Road
was designed and typeset in Palton by Kate Mueller/
Chelsea Green Publishing Company. It was printed on
Odyssey Book Blue White by Arcata Graphics Book Group.